Our Fathers, Ourselves

[DAUGHTERS, FATHERS, AND
THE CHANGING AMERICAN FAMILY]

Dr. Peggy Drexler

RODALE.

© 2011 by Peggy Drexler, PhD

Rodale books may be purchased for business or promotional
use or for special sales. For information, please write to:
Special Markets Department, Rodale Inc., 733 Third Avenue, New York, NY 10017.

Printed in the United States of America
Rodale Inc. makes every effort to use acid-free ∞, recycled paper ♲.

Book design by Sara Stemen

Library of Congress Cataloging-in-Publication Data is on file with the publisher.

ISBN-10: 1–60529–360–1 hardcover
ISBN-13: 978–1–60529–360–8 hardcover

Distributed to the trade by Macmillan
2   4   6   8   10   9   7   5   3   hardcover

We inspire and enable people to improve their lives and the world around them.
www.rodalebooks.com

To my husband, the father of my daughter,
who has helped her become the young woman she is.

Contents

[v]

Why I Wrote This Book

C ONVENTIONAL wisdom has it that you should write about what you know. Being a somewhat unconventional person, however, I find myself writing about something I have not personally known but passionately want to understand. Just as a teenager playing Juliet imagines a world where being sealed alive inside a tomb is preferable to marrying the aristocrat next door, or an archaeologist cradles a cracked clay pot and wonders about the ancient hands that shaped it, so I try to conjure that foreign land where girls grow up with two parents, not one, and one of them is forever and always, for better or for worse, her dad.

In the realm of fathers and daughters, I am an outsider. I hold no citizenship there, nor can I converse with its inhabitants in a common language. I have traveled there only on the visas of social science, parenthood, and curiosity. When I am there, I listen closely to what its inhabitants are saying; when I speak, it is usually to ask questions.

My father died of a heart attack when I was three-and-a-half years old, leaving three daughters under the age of ten, my mother a widow at thirty-three, and me a lifetime of wondering what I missed. When I became old enough to miss him, I imagined him living in the massive old elm tree outside my bedroom window, hidden in its lush leaves and watching over me as I slept. Looking back, I realize how young my mother was when he died, and how it must have seemed logical—necessary, even—for her to find someone to fill the void in her heart and our family. She did marry again some years later; I was about ten, my sisters were thirteen and fifteen. I remember the man she married as being tall and very handsome (my mother was unusually attractive as well, and I have a child's impression of them looking beautiful together, especially when they dressed to go out for the evening). He was a quiet, gentle person, and from what I recall, a perfectly decent fellow. Still, I have no vivid memories of doing things with him or being close to him; I cannot recall the color of his eyes, the sound of his voice, or the smell of his aftershave.

If my relationship with my stepfather was short on bliss, it was also short on drama, which I attribute to the benign detachment with which he regarded my sisters and me. It's not that he was never around; like many of my friends' dads, he came home after work, ate dinner with us, and was available to take us places when we were still too young to navigate the Philadelphia suburbs on our own. He did many things that real fathers do: He mowed the lawn, took out the garbage, and did the driving if we were all going someplace together. But when it came to the intensity with which my friends' dads occasionally erupted—usually in response to learning that his daughter was running around with a guy on a motorcycle who had a pack of Lucky Strikes tucked up his T-shirt sleeve—that was not a feature of my teenage years (full disclosure: I had no objections at the time). Although my mother and my stepfather must have had their share of disagreements, I have no memory of him speaking harshly to her, and, looking back from the vantage point of my own long-haul marriage, it seems to me that they conducted their rather shorter one with intimacy and restraint. But when it came to my sisters and me, my stepfather's behavior was governed by a policy of amiable disengagement. He was never nasty, cold, or mean to us. But I don't remember any ecstatic moments of joy, comfort, or contentment in his company, either.

I was fifteen when the marriage ended. Because the relationship was not a tempestuous one, I'm fairly certain the split had less to do with incompatibility than with finances. The bottom line is that when I was in sixth grade, my mother's new husband came to live with us and then, five years later, he moved out. When he left, I must have missed his presence at the dinner table or (true to teenage form) in the driver's seat when I needed to go someplace, but I didn't feel as if an essential part of my life had gone missing. I harbored no feelings that my dad had abandoned the family and left me desolate. The reality was, I had lost my father long ago.

Now, a lifetime later, the girl I was then is still firmly ensconced in the woman I have become. Married to the same man for more than thirty years, I am mother to a grown son long out of the house and a daughter who is about to begin her first year at college. I am immersed in work I love, work that retains its charge and keeps my imagination humming. As a medical school faculty member, I interact with some of the freshest, nimblest minds in the nation; as a research psychologist, I am a trusted listener, privy to the innermost thoughts and ruminations of people in search of themselves and their roles in the world. While working on this book, I was privileged to listen as scores of women contemplated aloud—forcefully, wistfully, and sometimes tearfully—their connections with their fathers. Through it all, I listened for chords that either resonated with or differed from our society's and culture's received wisdom about what fathers and daughters should and actually do mean to each other.

I had some ideas about what to expect.

In my first book, *Raising Boys Without Men*, I tackled the question of what it takes for a boy in our culture to develop into a man. The book grew out of a ten-year research project started in 1996 in which I compared boys growing up in two-parent lesbian families to boys growing up in heterosexual mother-father families. For the book, I expanded my focus and included other types of woman-headed households challenging the traditional view that a woman needs a man around the house and in her bed for her son to develop into a healthy, virile, heterosexual man. I spent years interviewing, spending time with, and getting to know two groups of boys and their parents. One group of boys came from traditional one-man, one-woman families; the other group came from families headed by women, whether they were single mothers by choice, mothers rendered single by divorce or the death of a partner, or two-parent lesbian families. What I found was that boyishness and masculinity seemed as firmly hardwired in the sons of woman-headed families as they were in the sons of woman-and-man-headed families. Nothing I found indicated that women rearing boys without fathers were placing their sons at a disadvantage, or that these boys' transitions from boyhood to manhood would be any more or less fraught with gender conflict, doubt, and struggle than those of the boys living in more traditional homes. I found this profoundly encouraging, as did a host of experts in the fields of gender development and social science. (Some social conservatives saw fit to demur with varying degrees of vigor and civility, but that's another story.) I concluded that the capacity to love, nurture, and coach Little League baseball are human characteristics, unique to neither males nor females and shared by both.

Raising Boys was a satisfying fusion of professional and

personal passion. I had long been fascinated by the dynamics of sexual orientation and gender identity and by observing the forces that influence boys and girls to grow into the kinds of men and women they become. As the mother of a son and a daughter, I had witnessed up close the different ways they responded to me, my husband, and their friends, and had observed the evolution of their personalities, senses of humor, and concepts of self. Moreover, I had had an opportunity to observe and contemplate the relative limits of nature and nurture (as can any parent of more than one child): Here were a boy and a girl reared in the same household by the same parents, yet exhibiting different interests, talents, and tastes. They were similar in some ways, different in others. And while some of their characteristics were clearly dictated by genes, others were less traceable. As I watched my daughter grow, I wondered, where did she get her confidence, her independence, her drive? Was she born that way or did she learn it? And if she did learn it, whom did she learn it from—me, my husband, or both of us?

While my husband and I were awaiting our daughter's birth, I pictured myself feeding and cuddling her and anticipated the protectiveness and love that our son would grow to feel for his little sister. But what I never imagined was the deep and complex bond that would evolve between our daughter and my husband, and the vivid, close-up view it gave me of what I had missed.

As father to a much wanted, eagerly awaited daughter, my husband offered a robust example of all I had imagined as a child, and more. He is a clothing retailer known for his kinetic energy, relentless creativity, and unswerving faith in his gut instincts, which he deploys with a zest and bravado that have served him well. I had long observed and admired these expressions of confident, risk-taking power and enjoyed, when our son was little, imagining that he might naturally absorb and eventually manifest some of his father's qualities, as sons are wont to do. What I had not imagined, however, was how these behaviors would influence our daughter. Although I believe that boldness and decisiveness are inherently human rather than masculine traits, I had not entertained the notion that my husband's vibrant, muscular expressions of self-confidence might shape our baby girl's personality as much as they had her brother's. Watching the way this played out was a revelation.

Unfolding before me in our daughter's nursery, at the dinner table, and in our backyard were intensified versions of the interactions I'd observed between my childhood friends and their dads. From her earliest days, I watched our daughter respond to her dad's physical gestures, facial expressions, and voice. I noticed the gleam in her eyes when he praised her artwork and the way her back straightened when she knew he really grasped the meaning of something she had tried to say. I marveled at how she asked him about his day at work and closely attended to his animated responses. The more he told her, the more interested she became.

I saw how my husband conferred legitimacy on our daughter's interest by creating tangible opportunities for her. When she was in third grade or so, he started taking her to work with him when she didn't have school. First, she learned the filing system and dispatched documents to their proper resting places; later, she ran errands for staff members. As her computer skills and powers of discernment grew, her dad assigned her to scan fashion blogs and Web sites and report on what she found. When she got older, she toiled in the sample closet, tidying and organizing racks of garments and pulling clothes for magazine photo shoots; as she gained confidence in her visual composition skills, she helped style the company's store windows. She was never given busywork, but rather was always assigned tasks that were both commensurate with her ability and which, when successfully completed, would benefit the company in some way, however small.

When my husband took our daughter to work, she was no

longer daddy's little girl; she was a junior employee who had been given real responsibility and was expected to deliver real results. She embraced the challenge with an open, enthusiastic heart, so much so that at the end of the day she wouldn't want to leave. I'll never forget the time my husband came home shaking his head after one of his little girl's workdays. "I cannot believe she did not want to go home with me," he said, caroming around the kitchen, vibrating with disbelief. "She kept insisting she wanted to stay late with the rest of the creative department. When I asked her how she planned on getting home, she said she'd take a cab." (She was nine at the time.)

I was witnessing what I had never experienced: how a father inadvertently fortifies his daughter through the way he inhabits the world in her presence, and how she models herself on him, in whole or in part, to create her best and most effective self. For years, whenever we were driving and got lost, it was our daughter who would grab the map and figure out where we were (now she is mistress of the GPS). When the power went out in the house a few years ago, it was she who lit a candle, exhumed the electrical system plans from a closet, and went off with her father to investigate the problem. At the start of her senior year in high school, she decided where she wanted to go to college and notified us of her plan to apply for early decision admission. We reminded her that there were many other schools she might want to consider and that applying anywhere as an early decision candidate meant that, were she accepted, she'd be obliged to enroll. She told us that that was precisely what she hoped would happen. And you know what? It did.

Some of our daughter's intelligence and moxie were no doubt hers from birth, a happy confluence of nature and good fortune. And I know that her highly developed sense of self and aspirations have benefited from my mother love and investments of time and energy. But there is no doubt that the attention she received from the strong and confident man who is her father catalyzed her own will to succeed and forged within her a self-esteem and independence that she'll have for the rest of her life. It's her father who engages with her and "chills" with her, as she would say; he accompanies her to ice hockey and basketball games, he walks with her, skis with her, and talks with her.

He also lets her know when he thinks she has acted in a way that is, shall we say, not in keeping with her highest self. I remember an episode from when she was in middle school. Her dad was driving her and a couple of her friends to a slumber party; he was in the front seat and the girls were in the back, chattering with unsuspended animation. As he tells it, after a while the chattering tapered off and was replaced by an uncharacteristic silence, punctuated occasionally by giggles and gasps. Peering into the rearview mirror he saw our daughter, sitting in the middle, shielding her mouth with her hand and whispering energetically into the ear of one of the girls while the other sat staring out the window (looking none too cheerful, apparently). After they had arrived, my husband took her aside and, out of earshot of her friends, said, "You know, I saw what you did back there and I think it wasn't right. You had a secret with one of your friends and excluded the other—that hurts people's feelings." As he explains it, it was important that he teach his child good values, which to my husband means eschewing cliques and never making someone feel as if she or he doesn't belong, among other things. I love this story because of what it reveals about his sensibilities, as both a man and a father. Reared largely by his mother and other female relatives, he is what I think of as a "head and heart" kind of guy: a man who relies on his feelings as well as his intellect to inform the way he lives. Some of his contributions to our daughter's upbringing—in this case, admonishing her to be sensitive to other people's feelings—have been in areas typically tended by mothers. Which is what makes the connection between each daughter and father unique: Beyond the stereotypical gender roles in which mothers teach sons how to sew on a button and iron a shirt and fathers teach daughters how to jack up a car and change a flat tire, there is that other terrain inhabited by every father and daughter, mother and son, in which the rareness of each personality exerts its singular force on the other. Whereas I too have taught our children about empathy and caring, when it comes from their father, it's different from when it comes from me. What our kids learn from their father is different from what they learn from me, because he and I work in different worlds and his world confers a different kind of authority on him than mine does on me.

As I write this, my daughter is working six days a week as an intern in her father's company before she departs for college in the fall. She assembles press packets and gift bags; coordinates publicity events and sends celebrity photos to stores three days a week; and works on the sales floor and in the stockroom unpacking cartons and unfolding and, painstakingly and in a highly specific way, refolding clothes for display. The work is seldom glamorous, with the exception of one day when she got to meet Tom Cruise and Katie Holmes at a photo shoot (she was as starstruck as a little kid); that was huge. But for the rest of what so far has been an exceptionally hot summer, she will work long hours for low pay in her father's world, watching what he does and how he does it, discovering and testing her own mettle according to his example. As I watched her grow from winsome little girl into vulnerable adolescent and now into competent adult, it became increasingly clear that if mother love grants you safe harbor and shelter from the storm, perhaps father love provides ballast for the vessel of the self and a sextant to help it navigate the world.

I was hooked.

The more I saw how my daughter was evolving and flourishing under my husband's guidance, the more determined I became to explore the complex dynamics between daughters and fathers. And the more I found out, the more curious I became. Why, as I learned when researching *Raising Boys*, did some child placement agencies set greater store in having a father in the family when placing a boy than when placing a girl? One agency official told me that when foster home placement or adoption of a boy by a single mother was considered, the agency always made sure she had arranged for the child to be exposed to a male role model. Why, then, wasn't the agency concerned about a girl growing up without a male role model? Because, the official told me, there is "probably a bias that it's not as important [for a girl to grow up with a father as it is for a boy], frankly, when it is." [1]

Since then, data have begun to replace the anecdotal conjectures. In 2009, biologist Anna Katharina Braun, PhD, and her colleagues at the Institute of Biology at Otto von Guericke University in Magdeburg, Germany, released preliminary findings from a study they are conducting on infant degus, small, highly social rodents typically raised by two parents. In the experiment, the degu dads are removed from the cage shortly after the litter is born and the pups are left to grow to maturity—which takes about ninety days—with their mothers. So far, the results are astonishing: Not only do the father-deprived pups exhibit more impulsive and aggressive behaviors than the pups with fathers, their brains also develop differently. Neurons in the brains of the father-deprived pups have slower-growing and in some cases shorter dendrites (twiglike extensions that conduct electrical impulses between neurons). Moreover, these dendritic differences were found to occur in the amygdala, the part of the brain responsible for, among other things, modulating emotional responses. Dr. Braun's team has concluded that being deprived of a father delays and may also inhibit the development of brain circuitry. [2]

In another study, this time using mandarin voles (small rodents whose young are usually raised by both parents), Xia

Zhang, MD, PhD, a senior scientist at the University of Ottawa Institute of Mental Health Research, along with colleagues in China, found that father deprivation affected their subjects rather differently: Voles who had been separated from their fathers, whether from birth or a very young age, were less physically active and seemed more anxious and less outgoing than their fully parented counterparts.[3] While it is too soon to draw conclusions about how the physical and psychological development of small fatherless rodents may apply to that of small fatherless human beings, there is ample evidence to anticipate a connection.

The more I thought about it, the more questions I had. Why do we take as gospel the notion that mother love can make or break a child's self-concept, self-esteem, and psychological well-being while glossing over the father's contributions to these basic elements of personal development? And when we do acknowledge the importance of a father to his child, why do we almost always picture the child as a boy? If, as common wisdom has it, a father provides his son with a model of virility, competency, power, and strength, why does he not also do so for his daughter? And if he does provide a model of these qualities for his daughter, how does she, however unwittingly, adapt and assimilate these qualities to her own needs and into her own life as a girl and a woman?

This, then, was the question: If dads are showing their sons how to be strong and effective navigators of their lives, might they not be doing the same for their daughters? I resolved to find out.

I decided to interview a variety of women across the country. I intentionally sought out women who had attained an appreciable degree of personal and/or professional success because I wanted to examine what effect, if any, their fathers had had on their ability to make things work out well for themselves. I ultimately interviewed seventy-five women, most of whom were between the ages of nineteen and forty. There were several exceptions: two single mothers by choice ages forty-five and fifty-four, five CEOs between the ages of forty-one and eighty-five (the outlier, the octogenarian, and an entertaining subject as well), a fifty-eight-year-old mother of a young interviewee who wanted to be interviewed herself, and an exceptionally mature seventeen-year-old whose story warranted expanding the boundaries a bit.

I selected participants with an eye toward achieving as much diversity as possible. Geographically, they were all over the map, from Oregon to Rhode Island, Louisiana to Massachusetts, Washington, DC, to Washington State, Missouri to New York State. Of these, eight had emigrated from places as far-flung as Germany, Switzerland, the Netherlands, England, Canada, and Colombia. One woman emigrated from Russia as a child, and another arrived from Denmark as the eighteen-year-old bride of a young American she met when he was backpacking across her country. Several were first-generation Americans, including two unrelated descendants of Holocaust survivors, several born of Indian parents, and a highly accomplished graduate student whose South Asia–born mother and father were pressuring her to submit to an arranged marriage.

There was racial, religious, ethnic, and cultural diversity as well. I spoke with white, black, Asian, and mixed-race women, Episcopalians and Baptists, Catholics and Jews, a Muslim, several women who said they considered themselves atheists, and a few others who described their religious affiliation as "none."

I spoke with women who had been reared in vastly divergent circumstances, ranging from borderline poverty to rampant luxury. Participants included a first-generation college graduate from the Deep South with an Ivy League master's degree whose father could neither read nor write, and an expatriate member of a European royal family. I interviewed lawyers, medical students, schoolteachers, nurses, a corrections officer, a yoga instructor, a physicist, a landscape architect, a restaurant server, a life coach, the CEO of a family-owned structural steel foundry, and a single mother by choice whose inheritance relieved her of the obligation to work outside the home, to name a few.

To convey these women's lives with candor, I have related each one's age and basic circumstances as she portrayed them at the time of her interview. If you read about a thirty-two-year-old prosecutor, you may infer that her story was inspired by an attorney of roughly the same age. That said, I altered other details to protect their privacy; the prosecutor might actually be a public defender. A Wall Street stockbroker might have been transferred to the Chicago Mercantile Exchange, and the CEO of a family-owned tool and die factory may instead be heading up a construction company. In essence, I tried to paint portraits that reside comfortably within the lines of these women's actual lives and present honest likenesses, if not photographic images, of who they are.

I reached out to as many women as I could, inviting them to speak from the heart about their fathers, their families, and themselves. They enlightened me, intrigued me, and occasionally shocked me. Each of them contributed to my understanding of how today's daughters and fathers are altering the landscape of the traditional American family, and how their mothers are contributing and adjusting to the change. I am grateful for what they taught me, and for the chance to share their stories with you.

[PART I]

Fathers and Daughters:
Searching for Meaning

When the Father came home from work he sat in his chair and opened his newspaper and was not to be bothered, not that anyone would dream of such a thing. He had had a hard day at work: all days at work were by definition hard days. Nobody had any clear idea what fathers did by day; we might have asked and been given a job title like lawyer or superintendent or bureau chief, but we knew nothing about what this entailed except that it was hard, and beyond our comprehension. Fathers never discussed it, any more than the Delphic oracles would have babbled about their mysteries around the house.

—BARBARA HOLLAND, AMERICAN AUTHOR (1933–2010)[1]

CHAPTER I

Fathers and Daughters: What's Changed, and What Hasn't

I EMBARKED on my quest with several hundred hours' worth of conversations careering around in my head, ricocheting off the nuggets of wisdom I had gleaned from decades of working with families. I have spent my career studying men and women, boys and girls—who they are, what they want, how they act, and how they are changing. I'm an ardent student of how children are shaped by their relationships with the men and women in their families, and how these early forces affect their life choices: what work they do, who they love, how they behave, and how they manage their emotional and physical health.

As I reviewed the interview transcripts, my mind was clamoring with questions. Foremost among them were, how are today's fathers serving as models of strength and assertiveness for their daughters? How much of this example are their daughters observing, absorbing, and deploying in their lives? If a father imbues his daughter with faith in her ability to fend for herself, how much of a difference does it make in her life? And, if a daughter does successfully fend for herself, how does that affect her relationship with her dad?

We know all about the cataclysmic transformation the feminist movement hath wrought in the lives of girls and women over the last forty years, and about the ways it has upended traditional (and often oppressive) notions of sex and gender roles in the family, at work, and in society. Today, nearly fifty years after the publication of Betty Friedan's *The Feminine Mystique*, women continue to be the change they wish to see in the world. With dogged persistence, women have gone from infiltrating to in some cases dominating institutions and professions that used to exclude them. During the 2003–2004 academic year, 49.6 percent of first-year medical students were women[1]—an all-time high—compared to 28.7 percent in 1980–1981 and 11 percent in 1970–1971.[2] (In 2009–2010, the percentage of female first-year medical students was 47.9.)[3]

The law profession's gender balance has also shifted wildly. Sarah Weddington, who with Linda Coffey successfully argued *Roe v. Wade* before the US Supreme Court in the early 1970s, graduated from the University of Texas School of Law in 1967; when she started, there were 5 women in her class of 250—a whopping 2 percent.[4] Today, nearly half of all law school applicants are women.[5]

And it isn't just white-collar professionals who have risen in the ranks; their camouflage-clothed sisters are joining them in force. In September 2009, the United States Army Command named Sergeant Major Teresa L. King commandant of its sole drill sergeant school, located at Fort Jackson, South Carolina. She is the first woman ever to run an army drill sergeant school. This is no small thing: Sergeant Major King, along with seventy-eight instructors whom she commands, supervises drill sergeant training for the entire US Army. Her achievement is even more impressive when you consider that even though women comprise 13 percent of army personnel, only 8 percent of the army's sergeants major and command sergeants major—the highest-ranking enlisted soldiers—are women. Sergeant Major King, who was forty-eight at the time of her appointment, said that as a young girl, she declined her mother's offer to teach her how to cook, preferring to play basketball and drive her father's tractor. When one of her brothers or sisters got in hot water with their parents, she presented herself as a substitute spanking object (don't underestimate her fearlessness—she was one of twelve kids). "'When I look in the mirror, I don't see a female. I see a soldier,'" Sergeant Major King said.[6]

Not to be outdone by the army, the US Navy made some history of its own in April 2010 when it reversed its long-standing policy against allowing women to serve on submarines. Only three months later, it toppled another barrier when it appointed as commander of Carrier Strike Group Two Rear Admiral Nora Tyson, the first woman in history to be granted such a command. Rear Admiral Tyson's strike group consists of the USS *George H.W. Bush*, which is the navy's newest aircraft carrier, four guided-missile cruisers, six guided-missile destroyers, two frigates, and eight squadrons of aircraft. In talking with reporters after the change-of-command ceremony, Rear Admiral Tyson said, "'As far as the trailblazing piece, I understand I am the first woman on the job. . . . But I'm a professional just like my fellow officers are, and my fellow strike group commanders.'"[7] It is notable if not surprising that both she and Sergeant Major King downplayed their identification as females, emphasizing instead their identities as professional military personnel.

The ascension of women to military positions formerly restricted to men indicated to me that some daughters had decided that walking in their fathers' shoes felt more fitting, more comfortable, more *right* than walking in their mothers'. Now, with statistics galore, about 120 hours of interviews echoing in my head, and 1,600 pages of transcriptions shuffling through my fingers, I sat down to analyze what I'd heard and learned.

It was exactly as I thought it would be, except when it wasn't.

OMG! DAUGHTERS NEVER STOP NEEDING THEIR DADS AND ALMOST ALWAYS FORGIVE THEM

In keeping with their much-trumpeted advances at work and at home, I thought the women I spoke to would celebrate the vast professional and personal opportunities available to them, and they did. They spoke of six-figure salaries, budding medical careers, happy marriages and harmonious domestic partnerships, worldwide travels, and ambitions to accomplish great and noble goals. But they also expressed something that made me sit up and take notice: No matter how successful they were or how much they had achieved, and no matter how content they were in their own marriages and the families they had formed, they still wanted and in some cases hungered for their fathers' love and approval. Even among women whose fathers had neglected and in some cases abused them, there was a yearning for connection, reconciliation, and the sublime satisfaction of knowing that, in spite of everything, their fathers loved, admired, and approved of them.

I had read copiously about the phenomenon of father hunger, but as I thought about it in the new context of the interviews, I realized that nearly everything I'd read had explored the issue almost exclusively in the context of starving sons, with daughters seldom being thrown a scrap. In a Father's Day newspaper piece about her own father hunger, essayist and literary critic Daphne Merkin cited a book on the subject whose case studies contained very few about daughters and whose author acknowledged the gap to less than Merkin's satisfaction. "'Of course, girls need their fathers too,'" she quoted him as writing. "'It may be, however, that either they need them more when they reach Oedipal age or they can make out better without them before that time.' Or it may be," Merkin drily noted, "that the response of daughters, whether young or older, to paternal abuse or indifference simply didn't capture [the author's] interest."[8]

I hold with Merkin, who invokes notoriously powerful father-daughter pairs such as the seventeenth-century painter Artemisia Gentileschi and her father Orazio, Anna Freud and Sigmund, and Jackie Onassis and "Black Jack" Bouvier as subjects of fascination (Miley Cyrus and Billy Ray?—your call) in lamenting the apparent lack of interest in father-daughter alienation. I was particularly struck by this lack after conducting interview after interview in which women expressed their unwavering wish that their dads would be more forthcoming in expressing their pride in them.

This was especially astonishing coming from women whose fathers had treated them less than gallantly and in some cases even cruelly. Why, I wondered, would you covet the affection and respect of someone who mistreated you? It didn't seem to matter. When it came to their fathers, these women had an inexhaustible capacity for forgiveness that they had for no one else, notably their mothers. This wasn't a complete surprise, as I've endured more than my share of family battles at which my daughter tossed cherry blossoms to my husband while hurling cherry bombs at me. But what did grab my attention was the consistency of the pattern: With few exceptions, most of the women I spoke to were far more lenient with their dads than they were with their moms.

Why should this be?

One reason, and it's a big one, is that a father is the first man a girl gets to know on intimate terms. He's bigger and stronger than Mommy, and in many families, he wields the most power.

The young daughter naturally wants and needs him to be perfect, so she downplays both his flaws and her disappointments, transforming his shortcomings into pluses so she can continue to see him as the ideal dad. Like many girls who grew up without fathers, I invented one, and he was perfect. He was always there when I needed him; he was affectionate, kind, patient, and funny; he always had time for me, was never cross or grumpy, and greeted my every word and gesture with unmitigated delight. He wasn't real, of course, but he was my ideal, and the idealization stage is critical in the development of a girl's view of the mysterious XY side of the universe. It teaches her that men can be loving, caring, strong, and protective, and totally in her camp. No dad is perfect, but for a time, his daughter needs to see him that way so she can develop the capacity to trust men and feel confident in their company. If things go well, she eventually realizes that all fathers are fallible, including hers, a finding that in no way diminishes her love and admiration for the man who is her dad.

But in some cases a daughter never outgrows her need to see her father as perfect. In the next chapter, you'll meet a thirty-two-year-old executive who said in all sincerity, "Dad always knows the answer. I learned long ago that he is always right. It's true. He is always right." To appreciate the lopsidedness of this position, try to imagine a woman of the same age earnestly asserting that her mother always knows the answer and is always right. Can't do it? Neither can I.

But why? Why are daughters so much more accepting of their fathers' flaws and foibles than they are of their mothers'? Author and journalist Victoria Secunda, who has written extensively about women's relationships with their mothers and fathers, suggests that children indulge their fathers' frailties because fathers are around less often, which increases their value. "It makes perfect sense to impart to fathers heroic qualities," she writes. "Surely, [children] think, Daddy would be here if he could;

he must be doing something *very* [Secunda's italics] important out there."⁹ The little girl learns early on to understand her father's absences as evidence of his eminence in the world, whereas, on her evolving map of it, her mother's absences signify a lack of devotion to her. Secunda further suggests that daughters also idealize their fathers because "*it is their training* [Secunda's italics] to read between the silences, to interpret the dark moods, to flesh out the unspoken feelings of men. Being understanding of one's father is a daughter's labor of love. By compensating for Daddy's absence in this way, a girl keeps him close, if only in her head. But what's kept close is the fantastic image, not the real, human father. To see Daddy's flaws is to deidealize him. And to lose an idealized daddy is to jeopardize not only his tenuous, piecemeal love and protection but also one's last court of appeal if the relationship with Mommy falls apart." ¹⁰

This makes sense: If you spend less time with Dad than you do with Mom, your knowledge of him feels shallower and your connection with him flimsier than they do with her. You're not as sure of where his limits lie and how far you can go before he'll blow his stack, so you deploy your emotional intelligence and powers of observation to intuit what's going on with him while keeping a safe distance. But with Mom, there is no distance: You're always in each other's faces because you're talking to each other all the time. Linguist Deborah Tannen, PhD, whose specialty is decoding the nuances that derail our attempts to communicate with one another, asserts that "talk typically plays a larger and more complex role in girls' and women's relationships than it does in boys' and men's," adding that "among girls and women, talk is the glue that holds a relationship together—and also the explosive that can blow it apart." ¹¹

This might explain the Roman candle that flared in a story a woman told me about her daughter, who had recently returned from a junior year abroad. "She'd put on some weight," the mother said, "but I vowed to myself I wouldn't say a word about it, and I didn't. We were in the family room and she sat down on the couch next to my husband, and he made a lame remark about how voluptuous she'd become after living in Italy. And she gives me this withering look and says, 'So, Mom, now you've got Dad doing your dirty work for you, huh?' I was so furious I had to leave the room." Who could blame her? This daughter was so attached to the idea of having a perfect dad that she could neither fathom him hurting her feelings nor tolerate the idea of being angry with him. To rationalize the pain his remark caused her, she fabricated a scenario that cast her mother in the role of Machiavellian manipulator and her father as feckless innocent. Her need to see her dad as perfect was paramount; better to demonize Mom than acknowledge Dad as flawed.

So there it was, and so it is: Despite everything women have achieved and the freedoms they have won, they still have not liberated themselves from the need to forgive their fathers and, in so doing, reassure themselves that they are indeed loved by them.

DIFFERENT ROLES FOR DIFFERENT DADS

Many women said they enjoyed good relationships with their fathers and had concrete memories to call upon. They remembered their dads cheering them on at soccer and tennis matches, helping with homework, and providing an oasis of rationality during stormy interludes with their moms. When I asked them about the notion of masculine strength and assertiveness and what their experience of it had been with their fathers, they described going to work with their dads, helping them in the garden and toolshed, attending and watching sporting events together, and the thrill of being interlopers in the exotic world of men. Some also described dads doing decidedly un-dadlike chores: "My mom didn't know how to brush long hair, so he taught my sister and me how to brush hair; also, he was the first one that bought my tampons for me," a college student said.

Others praised their fathers' wisdom when it came to boyfriend problems, as did this twenty-five-year-old administrator who recalled a time when she was struggling with a relationship. "I was in my bedroom and my dad came in, closed the door, and brought in all these love letters that he'd written to my mom from a period when they were seventeen and had broken up. He read them to me. He said, 'It's okay to be confused. You'll find your way.' I think it was humbling for him to bring out those letters because it had been my mother who had rejected him, but it really made me feel he was willing to share with me his personal experiences and that he understood how I was feeling at that point in my life."

Still others appreciated their fathers' straightforward approaches to dealing with emotional turmoil. "He definitely doesn't try and sugarcoat things," said a twenty-six-year-old graduate student. "When anything has gone bad, it's 'Look, this is life. You have to deal with it. Time will heal it. You have to move on. You can't let other people affect you like that, because you don't have any control over it. All you have control over is yourself.'"

These daughters acknowledged how their fathers' encouragement and affection had imbued them with confidence and a sense of purpose, and they spoke warmly of the men who were the first loves of their lives. The interviews were heartening, if not surprising: The dads were emotionally engaged and involved in their daughters' lives, and the daughters were both aware of and grateful for the gift they had received.

Then there were the others, women who spoke of distance and disappointment, resentment and regret. Some had controlling fathers who quashed their forays into self-expression; others disparaged their fathers for allowing themselves to be dominated by their wives. I heard about fathers who were quick to criticize and slow to praise and fathers who listened too little and drank too much. I heard about a divorced dad who vacationed in Europe every year but never had enough money for child support and a father who brought his parents to live with the family and proceeded to brazenly favor them over his wife and only child. One father informed his daughter that he was leaving his vast estate to be divided among her three brothers—none of whom worked, living instead off their parents' largesse—while leaving nothing to her because she ran her own business and had a husband to provide for her (she has since persuaded him to revise his will).

Another talked his daughter into leaving her job as design director for a Los Angeles luxury hotel firm to rescue the family's foundering industrial machinery plant in the Midwest. She didn't want to do it, but, out of loyalty to her dad, she agreed to go out there and restore the plant's viability so it could be sold. She resigned from her hotel position, relocated her husband and kids to Michigan, and, within three years, won the trust of the workers, rehabilitated the plant, and found a buyer for the business. She went to see her father and triumphantly told him the news, whereupon he informed her that he had no plans to sell. "He thought we'd stay there forever, until I was in my sixties, and then my brother could take over. He told me that in July. In August, we moved back to California. I did not speak to him for a year." Even though the episode had happened more than twenty years earlier, this father's betrayal—manipulating his daughter into upending her life to create a business opportunity for her much younger half-brother—still stung as this woman related the story. And I listened with disbelief as a thirty-one-year-old recovering alcoholic described the beginning of her drinking career. Her age? Eleven. Her mentor and drinking buddy? Her dad.

As striking as some of these stories were, perhaps even more so were the resourcefulness and resiliency of their protagonists. As I noted earlier, to a greater or lesser degree, every woman expressed affection for her father. Daughters who enjoyed harmonious relationships with their dads invariably admitted to some areas of dissonance; these were experienced as either blips on otherwise placid radar screens or well-charted trouble spots that they either avoided or cultivated as arenas of recurrent and sometimes spirited debate. In cases where the relationship was strained, daughters said they wished things would go better with their dads. Even in cases where it seemed to me that cutting off all contact might be warranted and even desirable, none of the daughters had done or expressed a wish to do so. No matter how dissatisfied or wounded some of these women were, not one of them repudiated her father. Which surprised me, as I've already said. Having no memory of my own father, I likewise had no inkling of the need for connection these women were manifesting. But there it was: No matter how selfish, stingy, narcissistic, or downright cruel some of these men sounded to me, their daughters were willing to forgive them, if not forget.

"Sure, I learned about confidence from my dad. But not in the way you think."

Some relationships—six of which you'll read about later—featured a father who intentionally, mindfully, or sometimes unwittingly handed down to his daughter a sense of her own potency that was uniquely attributable to him. Justine's father, a physician, allowed her to watch and sometimes assist him when he treated patients (with their consent, one hopes); Fran's father, to dissuade her from being too trusting of authority, proclaimed the sky green and the grass purple, requiring her to persuade him otherwise (she did, well before the rubber hit the road in kindergarten). Unorthodox? Clearly. Recommended? Not necessarily. Nonetheless, these and some other fathers made deliberate efforts to pass on to their daughters pieces of themselves and their experiences, ostensibly for the good of the girls they were rearing and the women they would become.

But it wasn't only highly engaged, open-minded fathers who imbued their daughters with strength and self-confidence. As it turns out, there was no shortage of traditional-minded, work-obsessed, remote, uninvolved, or my-way-or-the-highway-type dads who taught their daughters a thing or two about asserting their autonomy and getting their needs met. That's another thing that impressed me: So many women seemed to have been able to evaluate their fathers' behaviors and teachings; discard what didn't work for them; and embrace, absorb, and assimilate what did.

Clare, a recent college graduate whose parents divorced when she was seven, said she was still angry with her father for being aloof and flaky when she was a child. "I never wanted to go to my dad's apartment," she said. "I never had a room there. I'd sleep on a dirty couch. He used to forget to put sunscreen on us. I got lost a couple of times. I mean, he'd forget to feed us." It was hard to see any good coming out of the relationship until later in the interview, when I asked her if the guys she dated were at all similar to her dad. She responded with a flat no. "More than any of my friends or peers, I think I demand the most care and respect. A lot of my friends have been in relationships where they get walked on. I am always the first person to say, 'Why do you stand for this?' No matter who I date, no one will treat me badly. I think a lot of this has to do subconsciously with my dad." (You *go*, Clare—and so much for the myth of girls always marrying guys just like their dads.)

Even Ariel, whose father suffered an emotional breakdown that rendered him nonfunctional and verbally abusive for much of her adolescence, extracted something of value from this family tragedy by developing ways of coping with the emotional turmoil that roiled her soul. By learning to maintain her equanimity amid the household chaos, she is now able to deal with the challenges of managing the eighty people who currently report to her at work.

Perhaps most striking was the sense that a father's appreciation of his daughter's potential betokened his (however unconscious) belief that she could, with his mentoring and guidance, assume the exalted position that had heretofore been reserved for sons. Many women said that as children, their fathers treated them no differently than their brothers, and in some cases like the sons they didn't have. Lucia, a third-year medical student and only child, attributed her solid performance in med school to her lack of coddling. "My dad had this philosophy of raising me like a boy; he didn't want me to be girly or to feel like I wasn't as capable as a man. If I would fall and start crying, my parents would brush me off and say, 'Okay, you're all right.' They'd console me and encourage me to go back out there. My dad would say, 'Big girls don't cry.'" When I asked Lucia if she found medical school difficult, she replied, "It's challenging in the way you have to put a lot of time in. You can't just get by on being smart. You have to be dedicated. But when I've put the time in, I've never had problems."

This notion of brains not being enough, that you have to work hard to succeed, is a far cry from the received wisdom that all a girl needs is a pretty face and a sugar daddy to get what she wants in the world. For hundreds of years, a girl's prospects were dictated more or less by her appearance and how much money her father made rather than on what she made of herself. Now, women such as Lucia are not only relying on their own agency to succeed, but acknowledging it as well. "I feel like I'm pretty self-confident in a way that sometimes other women aren't," she said. How does a young woman become so self-assured? I'm willing to bet that her parents' expectations in general, and her father's in particular, had a lot to do with it.

Others think so, too. In the early 1970s, psychologist Lora Heims Tessman, PhD, interviewed the first women to attend the Massachusetts Institute of Technology and found that their fathers were highly involved in their upbringing (these women were born in the early to mid-1950s, when most dads didn't participate much in childrearing). In addition, they also said their fathers' pride in their intelligence, competence, and intellectual vigor helped them succeed.[12]

There is also evidence that a father's nurturing of his daughter's capabilities may impart different benefits than her mother's do. In his book *Fatherneed*, child psychiatrist Kyle Pruett, MD, asserts that dads nurture kids differently than moms do—that, in fact, fathers do not mother: "Fathers tend to encourage the child verbally, or with their physical presence alone, to bear the frustration and stick with the task, thus often enabling the daughter to pass the point at which help would have been offered by the mother."[13] I witnessed this at point-blank range when my daughter was four years old. Having mastered training-wheels technique, she was eager to bicycle down the street on two wheels like a big kid, but balked at removing the training wheels because she was afraid she'd fall. My husband proposed a Saturday excursion to the park and our daughter gleefully accepted, anticipating the weekend with mounting excitement—until she woke up Saturday morning complaining of a stomachache and asking for a reprieve. I told my husband I thought we should let her stay home, but he would have none of it. Reminding her of how eager she'd been to lose the extra wheels, he insisted that she screw up her courage and honor her commitment. Off to the park they went. When they returned, our daughter was trilling with excitement, so proud was she that she'd learned to ride a two-wheeler. Her pride was founded in her sense of having accomplished a daunting task, of having mastered not only the act of balancing on a bicycle, but also of having mastered her own failure of nerve. Had I prevailed and kept her home, my desire to spare her discomfort would have denied her a triumphant day that she and her dad still talk about.

A common area of high expectations for the women I interviewed was education. A large proportion of them said that their parents expected them to excel in school, and they did. This wasn't particularly surprising, especially in light of Tessman's MIT study; what was surprising was that they said they often exceeded their brothers' achievements. Over and over again, I heard about brothers who had slacked off academically and disappointed their parents, who then focused their hopes on their daughters. Several women spoke of adult brothers who were still seeking their purposes in life and whose careers had yet to take off and groused about fathers who were slipping cash to their floundering sons while complaining to their solvent daughters about the situation. "My dad keeps saying, 'I don't know what to do about your brother, he can't seem to get on his feet,'" one woman said. "I told him, 'Stop giving him money all the time—he'll get on his feet soon enough.'" Well, I thought, that's a switch—now the daughters were making money and the sons were taking it. Fathers were finally seeing their daughters as equal (and sometimes superior) to their sons in intelligence, motivation, financial independence, and ability to take care of themselves.

Except when it came to sexuality. There, it seemed, fathers often saw daughters as separate from and not quite equal to sons.

When daughters grow up

The meddling mother who won't let go is a comedic mainstay of literature, theater, and film. What could be more ridiculous than an aging woman's desperate attempts to control the burgeoning autonomy of her growing (or grown) child? To my knowledge, there is no male counterpart to this classic and contemptible female stereotype. Yet, in the course of interviewing women, I found numerous examples of fathers who were reluctant to accommodate their daughters' growing need for and right to independence. Frequently, these fathers granted their sons privileges they withheld from their daughters, much to their daughters' dismay and resentment. The overwhelming majority of these fathers were acting out of concern for their daughters' safety; in their view, girls needed more protection than boys and they were fulfilling their fatherly obligations by restricting their daughters' access to situations that might lead them astray or into harm's way. Their good intentions notwithstanding, I took note of the ambivalence implicit in many of these fathers' actions, especially when they occurred in the context of an otherwise trusting relationship. I heard many daughters extol the intellectual rapport they shared with their dads, only to then bemoan their fathers' hopelessly outdated attitudes toward teenage girls and what they ought and ought not be allowed to do. The meeting of a father's and daughter's minds only went so far, I learned, when notions of female freedom came into play.

Rebecca, the daughter of an Alaskan-born father of Japanese ancestry and a Jewish American mother and reared in a nonreligious home ("We do Christmas and Hanukkah as family activities but not as a religious experience"), was pursuing a doctorate in marine biology and about to leave for Australia when we spoke. She said she was very close to her seventy-three-year-old father, whom she described as a nonconformist and as having had a strong influence on both her personal and intellectual development.

"He's an ornithologist at a small, elite liberal arts college. He always wears the same black jeans that have holes in them that have been duct-taped together, and T-shirts that were free in the late '80s and now have holes in them. Even if we buy him clothes he doesn't want to wear them, because he thinks the ones he has are perfectly good and he shouldn't waste them. His explanation is 'If they have a problem with it, that's their problem, not mine.'

"We think alike," Rebecca continued. "My dad and I send each other articles. That's been the case for about five years or so. He mails me letters a couple of times a week and includes a couple of articles. He cuts them out and writes captions on them. They're nice. I talk on the phone more with my mom. But having my dad send me a couple letters a week, there's a different type of connection there that I appreciate." I understood what Rebecca liked about receiving those letters and clippings, replete with information and the implication that her father enjoyed engaging with her intellect. In fact, receiving news clippings from their fathers was something that quite a few daughters mentioned: Over and over again, I heard about dads who connected with their daughters through the sharing of information. Rebecca's experience was typical of many women's: They connected with their mothers emotionally over the telephone and connected with their fathers intellectually over the exchange of ideas. That this connection with the father was primarily intellectual rather than emotional did not detract from its importance; rather, its value resided in the father presupposing that his daughter was someone who thinks as well as feels. This distinction wasn't lost on the daughters; like Rebecca, they appreciated the unique nature of the connection.

As Rebecca spoke, I envisioned her dad as an elderly hippie, holding fast to his antiestablishment views and challenging traditional standards of propriety. Except, it turned out, when it came to his daughter's adolescence. Rebecca's kid brother was allowed to take the bus by himself and ride his bicycle after dark, but Rebecca was not, which irritated her immensely at the time (when we spoke, she said that in retrospect, she thought her father was probably right). Her father also complained when, as a high school student, Rebecca would drive to meet her boyfriend rather than insist that he pick her up at home, an attitude she described as a relic from when he was a teenager in the early 1950s (an observation with which I agree).

I was cheered by Rebecca's perceptiveness. She had the perspective to understand that his attitude toward her freedom was more a reflection of the era in which he had been born rather than of whether or not he believed she could be trusted. She also seemed to have a robust sense of self, evidenced by her story of declining to apply for admission to the small, highly competitive liberal arts college her father had graduated from and fervently hoped she would attend. Instead, she attended a large, highly competitive university in the same state.

Rebecca's best friend ended up attending her father's alma mater instead. "I think he was excited that someone was going there," she said, "but I got irritated at it, because he should be excited that I'm going to a school that is equally as good, if different." Clearly, her father's nonconformist ways had rubbed off on Rebecca, and to good effect. Still, I found it ironic that someone who was so nontraditional in his professional dress should enforce a double standard in the treatment of his children, especially in light of the intellectual curiosity he shared with his daughter.

Likewise, Pragna, a thirty-year-old dental student whose father was an Indian-born surgeon raised in the Hindu faith and whose Caucasian mother was born in Delaware and raised Catholic, felt that her parents were much stricter with her and her older brother than they were with her younger sister and brother, and that both boys were at a distinct advantage because of their sex. "When I was little, I kept a list of the privileges my older brother was given at whatever ages he was given them, so that I could be sure I had the same as he did," Pragna said. "There was a difference between the way the boys and the girls in our house were treated in the sense that my brother could have a later curfew than I did, and it wasn't just because he was older. It was because he was a guy." She lamented the fact that her father talked to her brothers about girls but never spoke with her and her sister about boys, putting them at a disadvantage when it came to their fledgling social lives, the details of which she felt compelled to hide. "I'd have little boyfriends here and there from sixth grade on, but it was never something I told my parents about; it was something my friends and I talked about. . . . I went to boarding school for high school. I think a lot of the kids there thought it was so strict, and for me it was like, really? I had more freedom, more leeway, at school than at home." (Pragna said her mother didn't provide much information about boys, either, instead avoiding the subject as best she could.)

Despite her parents' admonishments, Pragna managed to separate their views on propriety from her own. When Pragna was away at college, she attended a fraternity mixer that involved dining, dancing, and an overnight stay. When she got back to her dorm the next day, all hell had broken loose. Her parents had phoned and her roommate told them that Pragna had been out all night. "What my parents knew about fraternities was what they saw on television, which was always the bad news about someone dying or getting raped. So they were worried and nervous that something bad had happened because I wasn't back. I had all these missed calls. I called and my dad was like, 'What do you mean you went on an overnight? I don't understand.' I was like, 'Do you trust me, Dad?' He said yes. I said, 'If you trust me, then you have nothing to worry about and we're not even having this conversation.' I felt like he dropped it at that." Later, when Pragna was in her late twenties and moved in with a boyfriend after dating him for seven months, she was still anxious about how her father might react. "I told my mom first and she kind of told him," she said. "I had to say, 'So Mom told you the news.' He made this scowl face. I was like, 'I know you don't like it, but I know you'll come to accept it. You love my boyfriend, so this is all a good thing.' We never talked about it as much as I talked about it with my mom, but I felt like he trusted my decision, even though it wasn't something he approved of."

Pragna's perception that her father trusted her ability to choose well for herself despite his disapproval was heartening. Pressing beyond both the moment and her father's scowl, she had repeatedly called upon something real and meaningful—her father's trust in her judgment and, later, his affection for her boyfriend—asserting the fundamental truth that because she had made decisions that were good for her, they would be good for her father as well.

It would be disingenuous not to acknowledge here the ethnic elements in the last two stories—the religious and cultural backgrounds in which both Pragna and Rebecca's fathers were reared, Indian-Hindu and Alaskan-Japanese-Christian, respectively—not to mention their ages, seventy and seventy-three. These factors no doubt influenced their views on what were fitting rules for daughters and for sons. That said, I do not see these stories as anomalies or relevant to only an exotic sliver of Americana, especially in light of the influx of Asian immigrants to this country. Although the number of Japanese arriving has tapered off in recent years, the number of Indians has swelled. In 2005, the Asian Indian population in the United States was 2,480,000—0.85 percent of the total population[14]—up from 1,900,000, or 0.68 percent, in 2000.[15] It seems to me, then, that with more daughters of Asian American ancestry coming of age than ever before, so will their stories become more common. Thus it is fitting that they should appear here. Nor, I should add, are outdated attitudes toward daughters monopolized by foreign-born fathers of advanced years: Many men, even some young ones, see it as their sacred obligation to protect their little girls from the sordid depredations of womanhood, even when it means depriving them of the right to grow up.

When fathers dominate or get too close: The dark side of being daddy's little girl

The myth of the pampered daughter's lucky lot in life reads more like a grim fairy tale in reality. Adorable and adored as a child, her joy and laughter enthrall her father, who revels in his ability to so easily please this beguiling, feminine creature. Her sheer pleasure in his presence captivates him, her delight in him warms him, her luxuriant love for him reassures him. He loves the way she makes him feel—big and strong, smart and powerful, worthy and wise. To make her happy makes his day.

She changes as she grows, but what doesn't change is the pleasure her father feels in her happiness. As she matures, the thought of her suffering remains as unbearable to him as it was when she was a child. He will do whatever it takes to protect her from harm, from sadness, from pain. Many of these daughters are spoiled by their fathers, who rush in with car keys, money, and indulgent yeses because saying no would create conflict, which they are loath to provoke. Her every whim fulfilled, the daughter is spared the pain of disappointment and the discomfort of compromise. She in turn basks in the knowledge of her power to please her father and learns to respond more to his pleasure than to her own. Her happiness, not her growth, is paramount. Whatever she desires, Daddy will provide; however she wishes to occupy herself, Daddy will see to it that she is entertained, educated, amused, and accoutered to her satisfaction. She may look like a woman, but she's still his little girl, helpless and vulnerable and in perpetual need of his savoir faire and protection.

The trouble is, she *is* a woman; she is *not* a little girl. And what may feel like loving, fatherly closeness to a child may constitute stifling, intrusive force to an adolescent, whether she knows it or not. As a girl's sexuality blossoms, she is besieged by wildly vacillating yearnings that hurl her into ecstasy one moment and onto the rocks of self-loathing the next. She starts to feel attractions for people she may never have noticed before, and throughout it all she is trying to figure out how the girl she has been will morph into the woman she will become. It is a tempestuous time for a girl, as well as for her parents—her father no less than her mother. Many men withdraw from their daughters as they start to mature, feeling awkward about their new womanliness and wanting to be close without knowing how close it's appropriate to be. Some pull away too much; others, not enough. Still others find a way to be close to their daughters that is satisfactory to both of them.

As the mother of a college-age daughter, I've given more than a passing thought to teenage girls and sexuality. I have also written about it in the context of the phenomenon of the purity ball—a formal event involving black tie or suits for fathers and gowns for daughters—at which, in an elaborate and solemn ceremony, the daughter signs a pledge to her father to stay a virgin until she marries. The father in turn pledges to defend her purity until he gives her away to her husband. Many of the girls are in their teens, some in their twenties, some as young as ten.[16]

What troubles me about these events is that they legitimize a ritual in which a father asserts his dominion over his daughter's sexuality, a commodity that he, as its agreed-upon guardian, will eventually convey to the man she marries.

It seems to me that someone is missing from this transaction.

When a girl becomes a passenger on, rather than the navigator of, her own journey of sexual discovery, she abdicates a basic human right in her transition from child to adult and renounces her power to participate in the creation of her most intimate self. Perhaps the aspect of most concern is that she has been asked to renounce her power by her parents, who, in their quest to prevent their daughter from becoming a girl gone wild, may be inhibiting her from venturing into the wild corners of her sexuality by placing a looming image of her father before her.

There is no question that a father's responsibilities have grown both more numerous and more complex over the years. No longer can he acquit himself admirably by merely providing financial support for his daughter, protecting her from harm, and teaching her how to operate a manual transmission. Now he must also serve as her buddy, mentor, emotional anchor, sports coach, companion, confidant, and personal shopper (one father you'll read about drove his daughter all over the New York–New Jersey metropolitan area in search of the perfect prom dress). Still, as a famous Frenchman once wrote, *plus ça change, plus c'est le même chose*— the more it changes, the more it is the same thing.[17] And it's true: Many of the women I interviewed said that no matter how intelligent, strong, competent, and independent they were, their fathers still feared for their safety and saw themselves, on some level and in some way, as their daughters' protectors.

But defender of her virginity?

The purity ball is meant to strengthen the bond between daughters and fathers, providing an opportunity "for fathers to take that special young lady out and create a memorable evening, one that they will treasure forever," as a video clip on one Web site devoted to publicizing these events says. It also features a lovely girl of about fifteen in a white dress who says, smiling, "It was really fun. And I enjoyed going out with my dad, because it was an example of what a real date should be like."[18]

For a girl to dress up and enjoy an elegant evening out with her father is often a good thing. Where I see a potential problem is that a young woman may conflate the feelings she has while foxtrotting with her father with those she might experience in the arms of a boy she likes, all in the service of preserving her virginity. When a daughter's myriad and complex feelings for her father are threaded through the web of her blossoming sexuality, she could end up with a tangled erotic identity. I'm not saying that all daughters who participate with their fathers in purity ball rituals are doomed to thwarted sexual development. But I will say this: When a girl is encouraged to involve her father in the evolution of her sexual identity and invoke his support in drawing and defending its boundaries, she risks becoming daddy's little girl gone lost, unable to distinguish her needs and desires from those of the men in her life.

Apropos of this, I asked the daughters I interviewed if they perceived themselves as having been their fathers' favorite when they were growing up. In numerous cases they acknowledged that yes, now that they thought about it, they probably were daddy's little girl at some point when they were kids. These were women who had amicable relationships with their fathers in adulthood, enjoying their company while still keeping track of where their fathers' visions of them ended and their actual selves began. But there were others whose boundaries were not so well defined and whose stories offered a glimpse into what happens when daddy's little girl never grows out of childhood and into her own womanly skin.

Dianne was such a person. About five foot five and slender with long blonde hair pulled back in a ponytail, she wore black jeans and a crisp white shirt and carried a large, slouchy designer bag that must have cost upwards of a thousand dollars. She seemed upbeat and cheerful and smiled brightly whenever our eyes met over the low table between us.

She said she was thirty-three, worked as a drama therapist, and had been married for just under a year to Daniel, whom she described as an insurance executive who was really good with money (that would explain the bag). They had no children but were looking forward to starting a family within the next few years. She had grown up in Missouri, where her parents and three of her five brothers still lived. When I asked if she had looked for a husband who shared her father's qualities, she nodded. "I'm so fortunate that my parents are still together. My dad always wore the pants in the family relationship, and my husband does, too," she said.

Dianne sounded like a woman from a bygone era. She not only acknowledged that her father dominated her mother in their marriage, but also went out and found someone just like him to dominate her in her own. So much for my alleged myth busting a few pages back; some women still do indeed marry their fathers—intentionally, in this case.

Dianne grew up as the youngest of six children in a religious Catholic family. Her mother had four brothers, all of whom were lawyers, and five sisters, all of whom were teachers, as she was; between them they produced thirty children, all of whom had attended Catholic schools. I was impressed: For Dianne's grandparents to have paid the tuition for ten kids to go to parochial school in the 1940s and 1950s was no small accomplishment. It also seemed progressive that the girls in the family had all made careers for themselves, even though they had chosen them along traditional gender lines. I asked what it was like to grow up in such a large extended family.

"I really feel I had a princess childhood, not because I was spoiled, but because I got to play and my mom was a wonderful cook, and we always made cookies," Dianne said. "The relationship that I have with my father is very close and special. I feel like I lived my whole childhood in a pink tutu and everything was perfect."

Ordinarily my antennae would have pricked up at the mention of a perfect childhood, but they were already at attention. She had me at "tutu."

"But my father is an alcoholic," Dianne continued. "He hasn't drunk since I was in third or fourth grade, but I knew nothing of it. I don't remember anything. Maybe I remember an occasional fight late at night, but he never mistreated me in any way. We didn't see a lot of him when we were little, but he worked a lot, too. When my dad would be in bad moods, I'd always be the one to make him laugh."

Things began to look decidedly less perfect.

Dianne's role in the family had been to cheer up and entertain her father, a chemist who struggled with depression and drink and spent most of his time at the university where he taught. She said that she probably was his favorite child, most likely because she was his only daughter and able to boost his morale. "We had this relationship where [I was] always upbeat and always fun, always coming home with a funny story. 'Guess what the kids did at school? There was a senior prank and this kid got a universal remote control, and every time the teacher pressed play, the kid pressed stop.' My dad would laugh so hard. I think he's dealt with bouts of depression in his life." As she described these scenes, eyes wide and flashing, I glimpsed the little girl she once was, ministering to her father's ailing spirit.

Dianne spoke of her father with empathy at the start of the interview, emphasizing that he had never been abusive to anyone in the family; ten minutes later, however, she allowed that he was sometimes nasty to her mother and had gotten physical with her brothers, all of whom fought back (she said he had never been physical with her). "I can even remember them getting into fights. . . . Now they all get along with my father very well and love him very much, but they all gave him the 'f—you' many times as they got older," she said. Her portrait of her father was etched with compassion and pity; she related how, as a child, he said he would cower under the bed with his siblings as his own drunken father hurled objects across the room, and how helpless he was now, with her mother out of town caring for an ailing sister ("He e-mailed me that he can't figure out how to work the coffee maker and that he's spent fifty dollars over the last two weeks on take-out coffee").

Patterns began to emerge. One consisted of Dianne denigrating her accomplishments and refusing to acknowledge her role in her success. When I commented that she'd gotten her degree from a highly selective school, she said that her SAT scores were lower than the medians at the East Coast colleges she had applied to and that the only reason they had all accepted her was because she came from Missouri. When I asked how she had managed to land a plum position at a television station right out of college, she dismissed this as a stroke of luck. In her eyes, nothing she achieved was due to her own gumption or ability; serendipity, good fortune, or affirmative action for blonde-haired, blue-eyed Midwesterners always saved the day.

Most troubling of all was Dianne's pattern of subjugating her wants and needs, first to those of her father and now to her husband's. Early in the interview she said that, like her mother, she preferred not to argue with her husband. "To avoid a fight, sometimes I'll even say, 'Fine, you're right,' even if I believe differently or think it happened a different way, just because I don't like confrontation," she said. Later, she said she had wanted to move in with Daniel when they were dating but didn't because her parents forbade it. (She did, however, assert herself and move in with him four months after they got engaged.)

And then there was Daniel.

Early on in the interview, Dianne had drawn parallels between her father and her husband. "They both have great senses of humor, are pretty intense in their careers, but just so much fun when they're not. I don't know what Daniel's like when he works, but I've heard that he can be a firecracker. But around me, never. He's fun. It's the same with my dad. I would say they both kind of run the family. . . . Daniel can't wait to have kids. He's all about having kids, being a father, making sure the kids are educated and see the world, so I don't doubt that he's going to be a great parent. We joke, saying that he is definitely going to be the disciplinarian, because I'd probably be like my mom and trim the crusts off the sandwiches." Okay, I thought; maybe Daniel's got some of the father's fervor and exuberance without the drunken vitriol. I took the plunge.

"Does he drink at all?"

"He does, but socially, when we go out."

"Not excessively?"

"No, not excessively." A cloud crossed her face. "Although I am thinking that sometimes he does, when we go out," she continued. "Not at home. He won't drink at home or drink in the day, but on the weekend sometimes, he'll go out and stay out. As I say it, I feel like . . . I don't know. I told him it's all going to change once I start having babies." Well, I thought, maybe it will change, but it probably won't. If a man has been married for less than a year and already needs to go out without his wife and stay out until all hours, adding kids to the mix isn't likely to induce him to stay home. My heart ached for this young woman.

"How does he act when he drinks too much?" I asked.

"He's just fun. He says that when he was going through his bouts of depression that he drank a lot more. He couldn't find a career." Here was another similarity between the men in Dianne's life: depression. Dianne was appearing more and more to be a classic example of the young woman who marries her father. I pressed on.

"Does your husband have a temper like your dad?"

"Well," she said, gazing at the night-darkened window, "he likes things to be a certain way. He's almost OCD. He wants the closets to be arranged a certain way, with the towels all folded in thirds and no edges facing out, and the clothes all organized by color on those skinny, fuzzy hangers. Okay, I'll do it. When we were looking to buy an apartment, it couldn't be on an odd-numbered street or an odd-numbered floor because he likes numbers to be square. He doesn't like any mess. And then there's the whole money thing. He knows this guy, a financial manager, who he says is really good with investments, so he has all my paychecks direct-deposited into these funds and securities and this guy manages them for us. I don't understand where the money is going. I should take the time and learn, but I don't know what any of it means and my paycheck is nothing every month. Now he handles all the money. All the checks we got as wedding presents, he deposited them into his account."

There have been times when, as a research psychologist (and as a former psychotherapist), I've had to struggle to maintain neutral expressions on my face and in my voice. This was one of them. I took a deep, cleansing breath before I spoke.

"You don't share a bank account, then?"

"We used to but we don't now. I don't know . . . he's never told me I can't get something. Today I told him, 'Oh, I came up with a way to save money. I never take the subway—I walk to and from work.' I did the math in my head and it ended up being $960 a year. And he said, 'I'm sure this is a scheme to get some new fall clothes or . . .'" Her voice trailed off. "But he's very loyal and dedicated. I never question what he's doing. I know he wants the best for me."

I never question what he's doing. I know he wants the best for me. Once again, it seemed that someone was missing from this transaction.

There's nothing wrong with trusting your husband's judgment and believing he holds your best interests close to his heart. But based on what Dianne had told me, I was convinced that her words were evidence of her abject refusal to deploy her powers of intelligence, discernment, and basic common sense on her own behalf. And as much as I wanted to hold Dianne's husband responsible for commandeering her life, I knew he couldn't do it without her permission and her help.

Why would a bright, educated, articulate young woman be so willing to relinquish her opinions, her paychecks, her power? What interior logic persuaded her that her husband—seemingly a highly eccentric person, to say the least—was so much better equipped than she to make momentous decisions that affected them both? How could she be such a willing accomplice to the slow, steady erosion of her essential self?

I think it's because she learned early on the pleasure of pleasing her father, an ongoing dynamic that inextricably entangled her emotions with his. He was an alcoholic who grappled with depression and spent most of his time at work; how could a little girl resist a chance to cheer up her daddy when he was at home? Seeing his face crease into a smile and watching him convulse with laughter while listening to her stories became one with Dianne's sense of purpose. Any emotions that did not serve it were shunted aside, for Dianne's mission in life was to bring joy to her beloved, beleaguered father. The fear and anger she felt when he lashed out at her mother and pummeled her brothers were set aside so she could present a smiling, cheerful countenance, the coin of this princess's realm.

Now, in her marriage, she was still playing the role of the obedient and complaisant child, averting the conflicts that would inevitably arise were she to assert herself. Following her mother's example, she preserved the equilibrium of her marriage by adjusting her desires, needs, and expectations to conform to those of her husband. By letting Daniel make all the decisions and routinely deferring to his judgment, she believed she was securing her place in his affections. What she was really doing, of course, was putting herself utterly at the mercy of another person and abdicating her responsibility to herself—a self that was, I believe, well on its way to extinction. A child cannot advocate for herself; her survival is dependent on the kindness and forbearance of loving adults. No one can blame her for doing whatever she has to in order to keep that kindness and forbearance coming her way, even if it entails the abnegation of her still evolving, childlike self. But once she is grown, it is her responsibility—as it is the responsibility of every adult—to advocate for herself in the world. By abdicating this responsibility, Dianne was tacitly enforcing the notion that there was only one adult in the marriage, and it wasn't her.

The thing is, to look at Dianne, you wouldn't sense that

anything was wrong. She was well dressed, well groomed, and well spoken; she maintained eye contact and smiled often and easily—too easily, I feared. To me, Dianne was the quintessential daddy's little girl and a perfect example of why it works well for the daddy but not for the girl. While the father's already formed adult self basks in his daughter's love and attention, the daughter's evolving self becomes deformed, responding more to his delight than to her own. She grows up understanding herself as a giver of happiness and pleasure rather than a receiver of it, and becomes alienated from her own genuine feelings. Without having access to her own feelings, her emotional compass is forever pointed toward the feelings of others, directing her toward their gratification rather than her own.

"I don't know what it's like to be depressed a day of my life," Dianne said toward the end of the interview. "My husband says he's dealt with bouts of depression too, but me, I'm happy every day. Every part of my life has been the best part of my life. I loved middle school. High school was so much fun. College was great. My junior year abroad was the best. I loved working in TV. Now I love doing drama therapy. It's just my personality."

I nodded. It was her personality. But it was not of her own making.

DIANNE is an example of a young woman whose sense of her own powers peaked in childhood, when with nothing more than exuberance and a grin she could transform her father's mood from melancholy to joy. Sadly, the confidence she derived from cheering her father did not serve her well, as it strengthened her resolve to repress her authentic self rather than emboldened her will to express it. She wasn't the only one who had this experience. A thirty-two-year-old single woman said her father taught her that it was her responsibility to always be nice and make people comfortable, with the result that when she dates a guy, she allows him to treat her like a doormat. Another woman was so enmeshed in her parents' acrimonious marriage that she became her father's confidante, internalizing his hostility toward her mother and allowing it to obliterate any empathy she might have felt for her, along with their relationship. In these cases, the daughters' real feelings were either distorted or derailed by their fathers' influence until they were unable to determine where their fathers' feelings ended and their own began. This disengagement from the self renders the daughter unable to advocate for herself, a particular disadvantage when it comes to romance.

When things go well between a father and daughter, the girl observes the man's masculine force, a generous sense not of masculine entitlement but of natural male possibility. The daughter then has opportunities to absorb it into her system, and she creates her own ways of manifesting it in her life. Like Lucia, the confident medical student, many of the women I spoke to had achieved this elusive alchemy and spoke of its fortifying effects, crediting it with enhancing their self-assurance in their dealings with men. Others spoke of dads who provided well, protected well, or meant well, but whose capacity to fortify their daughters was a hit-or-miss affair. But even the daughters who felt they didn't get everything they needed from their dads had one thing in common: They all wished they had. Because when they did get what they needed, it felt so good.

When dad is too distant: The loneliness of the long-distance daughter

At the other end of the spectrum is the father who doesn't get close enough to his daughter to give her the affection, guidance, and self-assurance she needs. Often, these dads don't realize that they are disconnected; they are merely repeating the patterns they witnessed in their own homes, when their own fathers left for work early in the morning, came home exhausted, repaired to the couch or their favorite chair, and distracted themselves with the newspaper, the television, or, more recently, the computer. As Iris, a twenty-five-year-old graduate student said, "My mom knew everything that was going on with homework, friends, picking us up from school. She was very involved. My dad's role was more to come home tired, be given dinner, watch TV, and sort of zone out. He'd be watching TV and I'd try to chime in with something about the basketball game or something—I didn't know that much about sports because I wasn't that interested, but I was trying to find points to reach him." To dads like this, home is a safe place to relax and decompress from the strictures of work. They are content to be home with their wives and children; they're just not necessarily aware of where in the house their loved ones are or what they are doing.

"He was loving and kind and a very nice man, but he never engaged fully in our upbringing," said Greta, a thirty-six-year-old advertising executive, of her father. "While he worked from our home the majority of the time, there wasn't a lot of family time that included him. There was one point in junior high school where I wasn't getting a homework assignment done and I wasn't willing to work on it, so I called up my girlfriend and asked her if I could use her work. My mom was gone, so I knew the timing was right to make that phone call. I knew that my dad was in the house, but he was so apathetic and not involved. I had no qualms about making this phone call to a girlfriend to ask her to help me cheat while my dad was within earshot. I think it's a good example of me thinking he was so passive and so indifferent that quite frankly, I didn't think he'd hear or give a shit." Daughters were remarkably savvy about the perks of having disengaged dads. "One time I took frequent flyer miles from my dad's account and flew to

London with my boyfriend," said Melissa, a thirty-year-old radio producer. "The only reason I got caught was because my mother was talking to me on the phone and I said I was going to dinner, but it was noon back at home. She said, 'Where the hell are you?'"

High jinks and zany antics aside, a father's lack of connection with a daughter can have lifelong repercussions. And the lack of connection may be selective: An otherwise simpatico father-daughter relationship may fall prey to a blind spot in the father's emotional side mirror. Ellen, a fifty-eight-year-old college mental health counselor and the mother of an interviewee, described a painful childhood in which, when Ellen was ten months old, her adoptive mother contracted polio, rendering her severely disabled and confined to a medical facility for the remaining years of her life. Ellen described her father as loving and attentive during this time, but said that he had what she called a blind spot when it came to the son he and his wife had adopted, who was several years older than Ellen and, to hear her describe it, extremely troubled. "He was a scary guy, my brother. Sociopathic, sadistic. He'd light matches and throw them at me. He'd kick me and trip me and hit me in the blink of an eye." He also abused her sexually until she was in her early teens, but Ellen said she never told her father because she felt he had enough to deal with and she didn't want to burden him further. Then, when she was fifteen, she went for a medical checkup and the physician, a friend of the family, asked Ellen if she had been sexually active. She burst into tears and told him what had been going on, at which point the doctor said he was required to tell Ellen's father despite her objections. By the time she got home, the doctor had called. Ellen said she and her father talked briefly about the situation but it was never mentioned again, nor were there any repercussions for her brother.

Ellen went on to describe an extraordinary scene that occurred ten years later, after her mother had died and Ellen had come out as a lesbian. She was on vacation in the Bahamas with her father and stepmother at the time. "My stepmother was really getting on me for being a man-hater, that type of thing. I was in a lesbian relationship, a raving feminist, a socialist. So she was being critical of me. We were out to dinner. I was getting pissed and I said something about my brother raping me. She looked shocked. My father looked shocked. I looked at him, I looked at her. I said, 'I always wondered if my father told you about this.' Then we both looked at my father, and he looked at me and said, 'Well, I forgot.'"

Which he probably had. But you don't forget about something like that unless you want to forget, which he clearly had. Even though he loved Ellen and enjoyed a good relationship with her, the constellation of hardships that had befallen him—caring for a disabled wife for more than fifteen years, being a single father to a daughter and a troubled son—were so daunting that he was unable to do right by his daughter. Now, forty years later, she was still dealing with the fallout.

Other women said their relationships with their fathers had never been close. Martha, a never-married business executive in her early thirties, grew up the youngest of seven children. Her mother was a homemaker; her father worked as a television repairman in the mornings and owned his own power-washing business, which he worked at in the afternoons. He was also an alcoholic and had died several months before the interview. Martha was still grieving when she came to see me.

Martha said she had felt disconnected from her father throughout her childhood. There was never enough money, and she grew up feeling she had to hustle and help out; sometimes she accompanied her father on power-washing jobs, helping him tote the compressor and move the hose. She described how, when she was in college, she made extra money by hiring herself out, "shoveling snow and helping with hard, physical work, things I felt comfortable with because I had helped my dad with his business."

After graduation, she went to work for a startup technology firm, where she enjoyed several years of hefty commissions during the dot-com boom. Business was so good that, only five years out of college, Martha made nearly half a million dollars in one year, something she was obviously and understandably proud of.

Martha wore no makeup that I could discern and seemed both self-possessed and sincere. Her hair was short and spiky and her eyes connected frequently with mine. She paused occasionally to think before speaking, and her answers were informed by a high degree of thoughtfulness and insight. Two of her reflections were especially memorable.

"There wasn't an encouragement factor growing up," she said. "He never said, 'You look nice.' I had no idea I was clawing for 'You're doing a good job,' no idea. . . . As much as I don't drag up resentment, I do have life envy when I see daughters whose fathers are still alive or just involved in their lives. It could just be that I hear a girl in the office on the phone with her dad and she's asking his advice, or being at a wedding and seeing my high school friend with her dad, and knowing how much he was involved in every phase of her decision making. What I do is I say to myself, which makes me feel better, 'Well, you have character because of not having that influence, and you've figured out how to navigate your way, and that matters. That's okay.' But I do have life envy. It still comes up."

What also came up was that for three years, Martha had been involved in a relationship that she said was a great example of trying to date her dad. Pete was twelve years older, worked as a carpenter for stage sets, and was "quiet, didn't care about material things but would be a caretaker. The shortcomings that Pete had resembled very well those that my father had. I think my natural instinct was to want someone like my dad because it feels comfortable; it feels nice to have someone watching over me and taking care of me. At the same time, I can see that that doesn't make for the perfect scenario. I felt very guilty getting out of [that relationship]. I couldn't cut if off; I kept going back into it. I think leaving him resembles my growing in confidence about my sense of who I am and what I want."

I agree. I also think it was hard for Martha to separate from Pete because the relationship was her attempt to create the intimacy she never had with her father. Like Dianne, Martha was drawn to a man who resembled her father in ways that felt good to her; unlike Dianne, she came to understand that she was re-creating confining aspects of her childhood relationship with her dad along with the familiar feelings of comfort and safety. Whereas Dianne needed a mate who would dominate the marriage as her father had his, Martha learned that she wanted a mate who could provide the warmth and protection that her father had while improving on rather than duplicating the original.

Her insights aside, Martha continued to yearn for, and blossom under, the glow of her father's approval, as was revealed in the intense satisfaction she derived from his reaction to learning the full extent of her financial success.

"I was able to get my mom a car, because she had a clunker that was always breaking down. And I bought my little apartment here. So, my income was showing. But my memory of feeling happy about it was that we went to a boat show; my brothers and my father came. As we were walking around, I shared with my dad the number. I don't think he'd put it together before then. He knew I was doing well and taking care of myself, but when I told him, he stopped dead in his tracks. I have a vivid memory of it, and I felt so proud to be able to share that with him, because he was overwhelmed. He was laughing. He couldn't believe it. So yeah—those are definitely the rewards."

As she said this, Martha's face was suffused with light: eyes glittering, mouth stretched wide in a grin, and eyebrows arched as if to say, Pretty cool, huh? I not only saw her pleasure in the memory, I felt it. And I felt something else: The certainty that however much pleasure Martha took in her success, it was dwarfed by the visceral delight she felt in her father's exultation. Sure, making half a million dollars five years out of college was pretty cool, and I've no doubt it made her happy to be able to buy a car for her mother and an apartment for herself. But I also know that seeing her father stop dead in his tracks, the better to take in the enormity of her accomplishment, was, as those ubiquitous credit card commercials would describe it, priceless.

Martha's happiness moved me; it also reinforced what I'd learned about daughters yearning for their fathers' approval, which seemed rooted in their childhoods. Over and over, women told me that as girls, they dreaded the possibility that they might disappoint their fathers: Getting a D on a report card, quitting the soccer team after their dads had urged them to take up the sport, lying about studying with a friend when they were out with a boyfriend and seeing the look on their dads' faces when they found out—these anecdotes were related with liberal doses of rue and regret. And, whereas they were poignant, they were not surprising: It made sense that a girl whose father valued education would be pained to bring home a D, and eminently logical that a girl would be loath to disappoint her dad by quitting a sport he loved or being caught in a lie. All of these stories made sense in the context of a daughter doing less than her best or achieving less than she'd hoped, and the obvious conclusion was that the dread of disappointing her dad would dissipate in direct proportion to her capacity to do better or achieve more. All well and good.

But here again was the obverse of that scenario, a grown woman reveling in her father's pride in her accomplishments. It confirmed beyond question that a woman's need to please her father is usually not vanquished by her success. When she hits the jackpot, there's something in her that wants him to see it, acknowledge it, and admire it. It may not matter that she has attained wealth or fame, been honored in her field, or been showered with kudos by colleagues and friends. What may matter most, I now knew, is that a daughter know that her father is proud of her. And I realized something else: that daughters of distant dads often had a heightened need for their fathers' approval. What they hadn't gotten in childhood, they still sought as adults.

I thought back to the universal desire of interviewees—even those who had suffered mightily at their fathers' hands—to maintain, nurture, or repair their relationships with their fathers. There was a pervasive yearning among these daughters to keep the connection healthy and humming, and where it was wounded, to heal it and make it whole. Which explained why the daughters I spoke to were so willing to forgive their fathers. With forgiveness comes the possibility of connection, healing, and redemption.

And what of the daughter who outgrows her father? If she has come into her own as an adult, she can certainly adjust and thrive. But, as I learned from one young woman, she may grieve for her loss.

Amanda, a twenty-five-year-old kindergarten teacher, expressed her frustration with a father who had become increasingly detached. At constant odds with her mother during her childhood, she had turned to him for comfort, treasuring his gentleness, his warmth, and his intellectual vigor.

"He sparked an interest for me in politics, in social change; we have that in common," she said. "With men, I think my dad set me up for disappointment in certain ways. He's pretty great. He's pretty gentle and understanding." Then, when she became a teenager, he was unable to make the adjustment. "My dad still operates like I am a little girl sometimes," she said, "so his techniques for comforting me are dated. I don't want him to bring me a cup of hot chocolate; that's not what helps me today." What would help her, Amanda said, would be if her dad would listen to her when she talks about things she is passionate about. Instead, he glazes over and stops listening. "I work in early childhood education. That's not something he is interested in. I think he thinks it is glorified babysitting. I wish he'd step outside of his comfort zone and learn about some things that he doesn't know about, particularly the things that I am interested in.

"I used to think, like lots of people probably do, that my dad was the greatest ever. He knew everything. Then I grew out of that. I still think he's great, but I don't think he is omniscient. I feel bad saying I feel like a lot of what was really valuable about our relationship has passed, and he doesn't stimulate me a lot these days. I mean, he's there. I know he will love me and take care of me if I really need it. That's not a small thing, you know? I can always go to his house. But I don't feel like it's him anymore who is really pushing me to explore myself or climb a new mountain."

I heard what Amanda was saying. And I was happy that she was pushing herself to climb new mountains, even if her father wasn't. But I heard the sadness in her voice, and I knew what she had lost.

CHAPTER 2

Father Knows Best, Least, and Everything In Between: Themes and Variations

W H E N I began listening to the stories that the women in this book shared with me, each of their relationships with their fathers seemed unique, fraught with its own particular glories, debacles, and dynamics. But as the number of interviews grew, some patterns and themes began to emerge. One of the most compelling was that the women who had enjoyed strong relationships with their fathers as children seemed for the most part to have grown into adults possessed of maturity, self-confidence, and a sense of purpose. Other recurring themes—such as daughters favoring their dads over their moms—were as obvious in the stories related to me as they are in my household. Here is an, alas, typical exchange I had with my daughter not long ago.

DAUGHTER: You know, Dad never gets mad.
MOM: What about at me, last night?
DAUGHTER: You deserved it.

Needless to say, I had a different perspective on the previous evening's contretemps. But the point was that whether I deserved it or not, my daughter took the side of her father—the one who never gets mad—when he got mad at me. This was not an isolated incident; some years earlier, there was another time when I could not win for losing. It was a summer evening, and the next morning my husband and I were to make the sixty-mile drive from our weekend cottage in Bodega Bay, California, to my daughter's camp for visiting day. I'd prepared several packages of goodies for her and her bunkmates, and we got into bed anticipating a sun-dappled afternoon applauding her athletic prowess and extolling the peerless aesthetics of her arts and crafts creations.

I dozed off, but awoke some time later to a groan issuing from the other side of the bed. My better half said something was wrong with his stomach, but I should try and get some sleep; he'd let me know if things got worse. They did, and soon we were both lying awake, he in increasing pain and I in take-charge mode. It was not quite five in the morning but I decided, over the objections of my husband ("It's too early to call! No one will be there!"), to phone his internist back home in San Francisco (I informed the patient that that's what answering services are for). As extraordinary luck would have it, the doctor had just flown home from Europe, was awake, and took the call. Hearing the symptoms (low belly pain, getting worse), he suggested we come to the office just to be safe. We hobbled out to the car and drove the seventy miles back to San Francisco, where the good doctor ushered my husband into his exam room and turned to me. "I'll run some tests and will call you when we know something. In the meantime, you may as well head up to the camp. Your husband can follow later. He'll be fine."

I traipsed back to the car, phoned the camp, told my daughter what was happening, turned around, and got back on the freeway heading north. Two hours later, I pulled into the camp parking lot and my cell phone rang (you know what's coming, don't you?): It was my husband, who, in a pinched voice, told me he had appendicitis, was scheduled for emergency surgery, and wanted me there when they wheeled him in. Resisting an impulse to rend my garments and tear out my hair, I weighed my options, made a decision, turned the car around, headed back to the freeway, and phoned my daughter, who listened for about seven seconds before erupting in sobs. Furious sobs. Furious, extravagant, strident sobs reproaching me, her harried, anxious mother, who had been barreling up and down the California coast for the last five hours like a demented NASCAR driver.

"I can't believe you're doing this!" she wailed. "How can you leave me? How can you go back to the hospital when you know how upset I am about Dad?" It took me all the way to Geyserville (a forty-five minute drive) to get her to calm down. Even when she did, she still begrudged me the decision to be with her father rather than with her, and took her sweet time about acknowledging the dilemma I was in. Thus I learned that my daughter could be a lot more understanding of her father's needs (not to mention her own) than of her mother's. Now, after researching this book, I've also learned that she's not the only daughter who feels this way.

Another pattern I observed is that daughters who felt closer to their fathers were also more competitive with and critical of their mothers. Justine, a physician, and Nina, an executive, both of whom joined their fathers' professions, openly acknowledged that they admired their fathers' accomplishments and intellects more than their mothers' contributions. Justine was relatively oblique in her comments, saying that whereas she and her siblings wanted both parents' approval, her father's held more import because he'd been in a career and out in the world. Nina was more direct, saying that her mother was a good wife but unable to make decisions or function well under pressure and praising her father's competence. Both women expressed affection and empathy for their mothers, but also disparaged their ability to operate effectively in the outside world and, in Nina's case, at home. It's hard to know whether these daughters allied themselves with their dads because of an innate kinship with them, because they felt alienated from and by their mothers, or both. Whatever the reasons, there was a distinct tendency by women who identified closely with their dads to regard their dads' achievements with more respect and awe than they did those of their mothers.

Those are some notable themes I found. Here are some others.

Daughters yearned for fathers to listen more, fix less

It was a common refrain: A daughter would be struggling with a problem—dealing with an impossible supervisor at work, perhaps, or trying to decipher the bewildering behaviors of a man she was dating—and decide to share her problem with her dad. She'd call him on the phone or show up at the house and tell him all about the situation she was wrestling with, relating its nuances and complexities in detail.

So what does the old man do? He tells her how to solve the problem, that's what. And the daughter throws her arms around his neck and hugs him, grateful for his love and wisdom and thankful to have a solution to her conundrum, right?

Not exactly.

"Sometimes I get frustrated when I want to talk about something that I am upset about, because he is always trying to fix it," said Rebecca, the marine biologist I mentioned in Chapter 1 whose iconoclastic older dad wears holey clothes to work. "My brother does the same thing. Sometimes I just want to explain why I am upset without anyone telling me how to fix it."

If you're a woman reading this, you're probably nodding

your head in recognition. If you're a man, you may be shaking yours in perplexity. And you'd be right in either case.

It's not exactly news that women like to talk about their feelings; as it turns out, they also like to talk about their thinkings. Women thrive on connection, and one of the ways we connect is by talking. And talking is one of the ways we solve problems: We untangle a problem by sensing the feelings it inspires in us, putting the feelings into words (lots of them, sometimes) and launching the words into space, often in the presence of another person. Sometimes we're looking for a response, but not always. Sometimes we're merely looking for an opportunity to coalesce into language the chaos of feelings the problem has engendered and, in so doing, accord shape and meaning to the feelings, the better to know how to respond to them. Makes perfect sense to me.

But not necessarily to men, as it turns out. In *You Just Don't Understand*, Deborah Tannen's seminal work on the distinctly different ways that men and women communicate, she shares a cunning observation: The act of listening means something different to men than to women. "Some men really *don't* [Tannen's italics] want to listen at length because they feel it frames them as subordinate," she writes.[1] She suggests that when men converse, they jockey for position by interrupting one another—posing questions, interjecting comments, and proffering information; by doing this, they assert that they are actively evaluating and responding to what they're hearing. Listening for long, uninterrupted stretches could suggest (to a man, at least) a passive acceptance of what is being said, making the listener feel, however inaptly, subordinate to the speaker. In the case of a father listening to a daughter as she recounts her troubles, it's easy to imagine him aching for his little girl and wanting to rescue her: What's the good of listening if he doesn't *do* something? So he does what he thinks his daughter wants him to do, which is advise her on how to fix the problem and make her pain go away. And all too often, she feels as if her dad hasn't been listening when in fact he has; it's just that to him, listening without doing something feels as though he isn't helping his daughter. (For suggestions on how to approach this situation, see "What If Your Dad Doesn't Listen?" on page 206.)

Daughters wished their fathers had fostered their independence and expected more of them

Quite a few women either implied or said outright that they would have preferred it if their fathers had encouraged them to be bolder and more assertive, especially in their professional lives. The curious thing is, the women who felt this way varied widely in their levels of success. Whereas many thought they might be able to achieve more if their fathers had encouraged them more, others were among the boldest, most assertive, most successful women I spoke to. A nuanced picture emerged: Among this group, no matter how much a woman had achieved, she still expressed regret that her father had not pushed her more. Theresa, a thirty-two-year-old creative director for a cable television station who was making more than $100,000 a year, said, "When I was a senior in college I was offered two jobs at the same time. One was close to my parents' house, where I was living, and started at $32,000 a year, which wasn't very much; the other one started at $22,000 a year, which was even less, and was farther away from home. Still, I could see right away, based on the people I'd be working with and what they did, that there was more potential and growth opportunity for me in the lower-paying job. So while my dad thought I was absolutely crazy, I took the job for $10,000 less despite what he wanted me to do. My dad can build anything, he can fix anything. But for business decisions, I don't rely on him. That's where I feel like maybe I'm smarter than him, to be honest." Theresa said this with reluctance, as if she felt she were betraying her father by saying she believed her intelligence and business savvy exceeded his. Still, she did not allow filial loyalty to override her own better judgment. "At the end of the day," she said, "the one thing about me is that I have always done what I want to do."

It was when a daughter didn't know what it was that she wanted to do that she felt most hindered by her father's reticence to push her harder. Early in my interview with Maureen, a thirty-one-year-old high school math teacher, she described her father as very controlling and her mother as bearing the brunt of this in their marriage. When I asked Maureen if her father had treated her any differently from her brother, she said no, her father was fair-minded and had always treated her and her brother very much the same. But a few minutes later she said that when she was growing up, her father had frequently touted teaching as a great career for women who also wanted to have a family (Maureen's mother was a schoolteacher), comments that may have influenced her unduly to pursue a career as a teacher. "I became a teacher after I did a year of volunteer service on the West Coast after college," she said. "He did encourage me to go to education school, and I decided to go. . . . I ended up staying on where I did my student teaching. I loved it. But at times I don't love it, and I wish I had done something else. He probably wouldn't have encouraged my brother to be a teacher because it's hard to live off a teacher's salary. I do wonder: If my father had pushed me to go to law school, would I have done it?"

I found it curious that Maureen, who had the wherewithal to marry an emotionally expressive Italian (born in Milan, no less) with whom she said she had no trouble asserting herself, felt her father had essentially dictated her choice of career. (Also that she didn't seem to see that, at thirty-one, she was still plenty young enough to go to law school if that's what she truly wanted.) Unlike Theresa, Maureen felt like she hadn't always done what she wanted to do, perhaps because she hadn't yet figured out what that was.

And maybe that was because she had never felt compelled to do so: If your mother teaches school and your father extols the virtues of the profession, why look any further? Because, of course, the obvious choice may not be the right one. But it tends to be the easy one, which is how Maureen ended up in a career that she felt ambivalent about. In trying to fulfill her father's vision of who she was, she hadn't taken the time to figure out her own vision. Although she lacked Theresa's sense of self, she shared Theresa's conviction that her father's expectations of her had affected the way she perceived her own potential and shaped her ambition.

The bottom line? Regardless of how much they had achieved, many daughters wished their fathers had pushed them harder and urged them to take more risks. That is, except when . . .

Daughters wished their fathers had been more protective of them

There's a riveting moment toward the end of *An Education*, a 2009 film about a scholarly, college-bound sixteen-year-old girl in England who is seduced by a charming, mysterious thirtysomething fellow. With her help, he insinuates himself into her family, flattering her parents until they are as besotted with him as she is. They aid and abet the questionable romance, turning a blind eye to the older man's obvious motives and supporting their daughter's decision to give up her college plans in favor of becoming a young wife. When things end badly, the girl's outraged father tells her that he's going to confront the cad and take him to task.

"We have to have this out," he says. "If you won't do it, I will. I'm still your father."

"Oh, you're my father again, are you?" the daughter cries. "What were you when you encouraged me to throw my life away? Silly schoolgirls are always getting seduced by glamorous older men, but what about you two?" [2]

In this moment, a rebellious teenager was reminding her father that he had neglected his sacred obligation to protect her—protection she had connived with her lover to evade just a few days earlier, but which she now realized she needed and wanted.

Yes, I know, this seems to contradict the wishes of the preceding group of women, who wished their dads had been less protective. But just as the seduced movie teenager evaded her parents' protection only to reproach them for failing to provide it, so do real teenagers fight like crazy to escape restrictions only to wish later that their parents—especially their dads—had provided the protection they so energetically fought to escape. Valerie, a recent college graduate, spoke of how hurt she was that her parents had seldom phoned her when she was away at college and never offered to make the fifty-mile drive to take her out to dinner. In her senior year she finally blew up at them, excoriating them with accusations that they were unloving and cold. Her mother became defensive, but her father, the calmer of the two, apologized for their trespasses. "We didn't know you wanted to see us," he said. "Let's go visit you more." So her parents started calling and they started inviting her out, and what do you think happened? She never had time for them, that's what. "My weekends really were booked," Valerie said. "I probably could have made room, but we never had dinner. All I really wanted was for them to just attempt to call me and ask to have dinner." Ah, yes: This daughter didn't actually want to see her parents, she just wanted to know that they wanted to see *her*. We had a similar episode with our own daughter a few months ago when, after a cavalcade of mind-numbing arguments about extending her curfew, my husband relented and told her it wasn't necessary for her to come into our bedroom as she always did to tell us she was home. "You know, I won't be living here much longer," she said, affronted. "Why don't you want me to come into your room to say good night and let you know I'm home?" Oh, brother.

I heard more stories like this than I could have imagined.

Blair, a thirty-six-year-old freelance cinematographer living in New England, said her father made her feel as if she could do anything, which included the brave act of coming out as a lesbian when she was thirty. "He was a little surprised, but then cool with it," she says. "My partner now, we got married two years ago. He was excited about that. We were going to go off and get married, but no, he wanted a big wedding"—which her parents gave her and to which they invited all their friends. Blair's father was a baseball fan, and when she was a kid growing up in Cleveland, they would ride their bikes to Jacobs Field to watch the Indians play. "He taught me how to score a baseball game," she said. "He taught me how to tip the ushers so you could get a better seat." This struck me as uniquely guy-type secret information. How many women—let alone young girls—know that they can launch themselves out of the nosebleed seats by tipping a stadium employee? I sure didn't.

Blair described how, after a sojourn in Europe after college, she ended up living back at home with her parents, languishing in a waitressing job. One day, her father gently asked her what her plans were. When she said she'd really like to move out west, he encouraged her to join AmeriCorps VISTA. "He was like, 'That will get you out there and then you can figure out what you want to do.' At the time I had a friend who wanted to move out west but whose parents were encouraging her to stay close to home. She said, 'You're so lucky that you can do that.' I realized that my real luck was that I had parents telling me, 'You can do anything' whereas this girl's parents were bribing her with a car to stay home. I realized I wasn't lucky that I could move out west, I was lucky that I never saw barriers. My parents, especially my dad, never saw barriers. He said, 'Move out there! Why are you sticking around here?'"

Bravo, Dad! And brava to Blair for recognizing her good

fortune at having a father who urged her to take risks and follow her heart. I was heartened to hear this story about a dad encouraging his daughter to leave the safety of his home to pursue her dreams. I was also intrigued to hear that he sought Blair's counsel when it came to dealing with her brother, who was living "off the grid," as Blair called it, doing good works in the Third World.

"My brother's living in Africa and he's got one big project after another. At the end of the day, my dad ends up having to pay his bills, giving him a credit card extension. So my dad will come to me and say, 'I don't know what to do about your brother.' I get very hard-line: 'Just tell him you're not going to give him any more money and he will figure it out. Stop giving him money. You're enabling him.'" Blair had the savvy to see that her father's cash infusions weren't doing her brother any favors, and she clearly disapproved of them. I asked her if her father subsidized her, and the answer was an emphatic no. Then this story came out.

"I had a very bad breakup with my ex. We had bought property in New York and I was left with an apartment that I couldn't afford. Even though my parents don't have a lot of money, I wanted to hear from them, 'Don't worry, we're here for you.' But they didn't say that. They were like, 'Oh, that's a lot of money!' I was in the middle of so much trauma; I just needed to hear, 'We'll help you out for three months; don't worry.' They help my brother out all the time. Once in a while I will make a comment to my dad and say, 'You always act like I'm going to be okay,' and my dad will say, 'Because you are. You're always okay.' They're more protective of my brother because he's the baby. In that moment, I just wanted to hear that they were there for me financially as well, and they weren't. At the same time, when I was younger and traveled abroad and ran out of money, my dad would put money in my account. He'd throw an extra whatever in there and didn't make me feel bad that I ran out of money."

Contradictions abounded. Blair objected to her father giving money to her brother, objected to her father not giving money
to her, and then described how her father had given money to
her. I wondered if the father's rationale for supporting his son in
Africa was the same one he'd used for supporting Blair when she
was in Europe: Both kids were overseas, exploring the worlds
outside and inside themselves, and not yet established in their
careers. Perhaps Blair's dad had advised her against buying the
New York apartment with her ex-partner and hadn't felt obligated
to bail her out when the relationship went south. There was a lot
of background I wasn't privy to, after all, and I could easily
understand how Blair's father might have felt it was her responsibility, not his, to haul herself out of the real-estate quagmire she'd
gotten herself into.

I also understood Blair's frustration: Children, however
advanced in years, never seem to outgrow the need to know that
their parents are as devoted to them as they are to their siblings.
Still, the irony didn't escape me: The paternal attitude to which
Blair objected had likely been responsible for making her as self-
sufficient as she was—a self-sufficiency of which she was justly
proud. It was telling that despite her father's certainty and pride
that she could take care of herself, Blair still wished he had acted
as if he weren't quite so sure.

"Both [of my parents] were very laissez-faire in their parenting," she said. "Sometimes I wanted to feel more protected. At different times in my life where I felt like I was wronged by a school
official or somebody else, [my dad] wasn't going to go in there and
fight. He was like, 'This is a lesson on how life's unfair and people
suck sometimes.' But he wasn't going to go in there and protect
me." Maybe not. But had he gone in there and protected her, I bet
Blair wouldn't have been so competent at protecting herself.

Helle, a thirty-one-year-old costume designer from Denmark who left her homeland when she married a young American

tourist, lamented her parents' similarly hands-off parenting style. "I know I got into trouble in my younger years because of the lack of boundaries. I met my ex when I was seventeen. I was barely eighteen when I moved to the US. I was very adamant about going, but I wasn't sure how my parents felt about it, because they were so 'Whatever you think, you know what's best for you.' . . . I definitely felt a little lonely and directionless in the way that they raised us, because I felt like, 'I need you guys here to help guide me through my life. Where is my guidance?'"

As the mother of a teenage girl, I can imagine how Helle would likely have reacted had her parents put their collective foot down and told her that no daughter of theirs was going to get married, let alone go gallivanting off to America, at eighteen; she'd probably have pitched a fit and might have done it in any case. But now, nearly fourteen years later, mother to a young son and legally separated from the man she'd followed across the ocean, Helle regretted having been given the freedom to live her life when she may have been too young to know what she was getting herself into.

Some daughters found protection and were grateful for it

Then there were the daughters whose fathers made them feel safe and sheltered when they were growing up, a feeling that persisted into adulthood. Lest you think they were all reared in the golden glow of idyllic childhoods, however, think again: More than a few of these nurturing fathers were operating under considerable duress.

Consider sisters and college students Shannon and Erin, ages twenty-one and nineteen, respectively, who grew up in rural Kentucky and whose father, a former university administrator, stayed home with the children while his wife supported the family. There were five children, all born two years apart, the eldest a twenty-three-year-old wheelchair-bound son who suffered from cerebral palsy and lived at home with his younger sister and brother, ages seventeen and fifteen. Further complicating the atypical scenario was the fact that the mother, an ophthalmologist, suffered from a psychiatric disorder and was less than vigilant about taking her medication, rendering her vulnerable to unpredictable, volatile moods. Shannon and Erin, both of whom spoke to me over the phone from their dorm rooms, said their relationship with their mother (whom Shannon described as impatient and sometimes irrational) had been difficult but was improving now that they were older. Both cited their father as the stabilizing force in their childhoods.

"He was the one who held us all together," Erin said. "He kept my siblings and me from fighting too much. He made sure our mom didn't get too upset with us and that we didn't get too upset with her. He helped us stay close to each other. He was the one who made us a family." Shannon said he took temporary jobs as a soccer coach, library clerk, and substitute teacher here and there, "but almost any day of the week, we'd come home from school and my dad would be there. He'd cook our dinners. He'd stay in the living room until we went to sleep. He'd wake us up the next morning and he'd drive us to school. . . . When I was little, all three of us girls were in one room and we were like, 'Dad! You're going to walk us down the aisle when we get married, right?' And he said, 'Yup, I'm going to walk all of you down the aisle to a man who doesn't deserve any of you.'"

The security, comfort, and humor this father provided cast a mantle of normalcy over his children's shoulders, which in turn made them want to please him. "A big motivating factor throughout most of my life has been wanting to make my dad proud of me," Shannon said. Erin echoed her sister: "He always had high expectations for me. After a while, my desire to do well for him turned into my desire to do well for myself."

Seventeen-year-old Charlotte's story provides another glimpse of a father prevailing in unusually stressful circumstances. Charlotte's mother had died of cancer many years earlier and her father had not remarried, she told me over the phone from her home in Seattle. "He's been both parents since I was three and a half. He's the most generous, kind person I know. He's not a professor, but he always seems like one to me," she said. Charlotte's father traveled a great deal for work when she was little, but, she said, "I've been lucky because I've had a woman named Opal who has been my caretaker since I was eleven months old. That said, my dad is in many ways more present than some of my friends' parents who work here [in town]. When he's here, he really is here. We always eat dinner together. I basically tell him everything." A seventeen-year-old girl who tells her father everything? As with Erin and Shannon, the reliable presence of an emotionally stable and available father fostered an atmosphere of safety and trust in the family.

During the interview, I was struck by Charlotte's preternatural maturity, which manifested in her capacity to see her father as well as herself with more lucidity than the typical teenager can. A clue to its origin emerged when she told me that her father had always treated her like an adult, even when she was quite young. She described how, when his friends would come for dinner, she would sit on a chair topped with a phone book and eat with the adults. "He gave me a respect that seemed beyond my years. It taught me to think of myself not as a child that couldn't understand the things that were going on, so I never felt limited by my age as to what I could be a part of," she said.

I was reminded of the bracing and heartrending trust that informed the relationship between Scout and her father in Harper Lee's 1960 masterpiece *To Kill a Mockingbird*. Scout's father is the redoubtable Atticus Finch, played in the 1962 film by Gregory Peck and modeled by Lee on her own father, a small-town lawyer respected for his decency and commitment to justice. (Alice Finch Lee, Harper Lee's older sister, was born in 1911 and, as of this writing, is still practicing law—yes, you read that right—in Monroeville, Alabama. In a recent interview, she said that their father had died in 1962, but was around long enough to witness the honor accorded his daughter's book: "He was here when it came out and when she won the Pulitzer. He knew about that. He was a very proud father, a very proud father.")[3] In the book, Atticus, a white Alabama lawyer, defends a black man accused of rape during the Great Depression, which hurls him and his children into a cauldron of public censure and ridicule. He is also a father rearing a young daughter and son alone after the death of his wife. When someone asks Atticus why he is taking up the cause of such a despised individual, his response is that if he didn't, he would not be able to hold his head up in front of his children.[4] This notion that children are sentient beings possessing powers of discernment as keen as adults'—and in some cases keener— conveys the same nobility of spirit that I believe prompted Charlotte's father to indulge her presence at his dinner parties. By including her, he implied that even if she didn't have something to bring to the table, she might take something away from it—a tacit affirmation of his faith in her intelligence and judgment that was not lost on Charlotte.

"Even though he was respectful and treated me as an adult, there was stuff that he had to do for me," Charlotte said at the close of the interview. "He made dinner. He signed me up for everything. He came to all of the events. He still does some of those, but sometimes I make dinner. He makes sure I am able to make my own appointments and I make sure I keep them. It's transitioning me into being a fully functioning adult who can take care of my own business."

Listening to Charlotte speak, it was easy to imagine that I had stumbled upon the perfect father-daughter relationship. Despite a cataclysmic loss, this man had managed to rear an intelligent, articulate, secure child who, it should be noted, fulsomely acknowledged her father's role in making her who she was. Was the relationship loving, honest, and ennobled by mutual respect? It certainly sounded that way. Was it perfect? No, it couldn't be perfect, because there's no such thing. If I've learned anything from doing these interviews, it's that there are no perfect relationships and no perfect families. Even the happiest, most well-adjusted kids have some struggles growing up, and even those daughters who lavishly praised their dads' parenting philosophies and techniques admitted to some thorny episodes here and there. It was no different with Charlotte, who alluded to an occasional small disagreement with her father but said she had never been grounded. The most distressing consequence she'd ever suffered for a transgression? "The worst thing for me is if my dad ever said, 'I'm disappointed in you.' That's worse than grounding for me."

Some daughters attributed their unease, awkwardness, or unfulfilling interactions with men to their flawed relationships with their fathers

This theme did not come as a complete surprise; traditional psychoanalytic and conventional theories of psychological development hold that a girl's relationship with her father in large part shapes her concept of herself as a woman and, in turn, the way she presents herself to men and what she expects of them. This occurs naturally as father and daughter relate to each other first within the context of the family and later out in the world, and it provides the growing girl with a sort of GPS—gender positioning system, if you will—that helps her locate herself on the rocky, uncharted moonscape of male-female interactions. But what was noteworthy was that even in the midst of new findings on the fluidity of sexual identity, the expanding dimensions of social roles, and society's growing acceptance of unconventional families, daughters still seemed to feel that having a good relationship with their fathers was fundamental to women's confidence and ease in dealing with men.

A graduate student reared by a lesbian couple told me she felt that growing up without a father had inhibited her ability to connect fully with men. "I've had a number of sexual experiences with men, and I've had emotional experiences with men, but I've never had both together," she said. And several professional women said they felt their awkward relationships with their fathers made it hard for them to banter naturally with male coworkers and assert themselves with male supervisors.

Mallory, a thirty-four-year-old chiropractor, said she often got attention from men, but was unsure of how to handle it. Her parents, both in their sixties, had divorced several years earlier after more than thirty years of marriage, a break that Mallory said had devastated her. She said she harbored a great deal of anger toward her father, whom she accused of being unloving and insufficiently interested in her, traits she blamed for her awkwardness with men.

"If I see someone out in public who I might be interested in, my tendency is to look away and try to hide from them instead of trying to be more out there," she said. "I don't feel I know how to flirt very well or engage with men very well. I sometimes have a hard time recognizing the appropriate dynamics between myself and men that I'm working with and with whom I'm interacting in my life. I think that's because of my problematic relationship with my father. I think I didn't learn how to engage and navigate those kinds of dynamics because we didn't have a close relationship, especially after puberty and then adulthood."

Mallory said that her father had been in a combined MD–PhD program when she was little and, although he was busy much of the time, her interactions with him were good because he tended to get along well with children. (Her mother worked part-time but mostly stayed at home with Mallory and her younger brother.) After graduation, Mallory's father took a tenure-track position at a university. She said she did not have many memories from that time, but described one that had stuck.

"After he started teaching, he would talk to me about medical cases—that's something I have a pretty strong memory of. He would tell me the case, describe the symptoms, and I would try to decide what had happened, what would happen, or what the diagnosis would be. I must have been in fourth or fifth grade. I enjoyed it because I think I've always had an analytical mind and I like to think about things. It was time that we spent together, I think it was usually at bedtime, so I definitely enjoyed talking about that kind of stuff and spending that time with him."

Here was an instance of a father engaging his young daughter's intellect, and it mattered—twenty-five years later, it was one of Mallory's most vivid childhood memories. During the interview, she alluded several times to her penchant for critical thinking and said that these early forays into medical detective work had led her toward her chiropractic career, which she believed made use of both her analytical and emotional skills.

So what happened between Mallory and her father? Several things. First, there was adolescence with its fabled mother-daughter maelstroms that, in Mallory's case, altered the dynamic with her dad.

"My mom is a critical person, and she tends to want everyone to succeed and [is] a little bit pushy about it, and I think my dad always tried to counteract that by being less pushy," she said. "I definitely fought with my mom a lot more. We would argue a lot, and I don't really remember any arguments with my dad. He would try to play the opposite things to my mom, so I think he really made an effort to try to be less overbearing, be uninvolved.

What happened, though, is it turned out to be more like he was detached and withdrawn. So there was a counteraction against my mom, but it wasn't like he was engaged. That was a problem; I don't think that was very healthy for me." This was instructive: Mallory argued frequently with her mother, yet she was much more forgiving of her than of her father, whose attempts to be less pushy were experienced by Mallory as detachment and lack of caring. This was different from what I'd been hearing thus far. This daughter was more forgiving of her mother than of her father.

Then Mallory left for boarding school in tenth grade, a decision she says she made herself. Her mother phoned several times a week and they chatted about personal things, mostly at her mother's urging, but when her mother passed the phone to her dad, their exchanges were perfunctory. By the time Mallory went to college, she experienced her father's laid-back approach to their relationship as a willful withdrawal from everything but the most superficial aspects of her life.

"I think that if I had had a better sense of myself and how I related to men, I would have gained that from him. If you're with your father you could be flirtatious with him, learn how to be that way without taking things too far or giving people the wrong idea, because in a relationship between a father and daughter there's always going to be a really hard boundary, but you can learn how to play with it. That's what I feel I have a hard time with."

This interview impressed me on several levels, the deepest perhaps being the extent of Mallory's psychological astuteness, which enabled her to diagnose, to her own satisfaction, the source of her awkwardness with men. It also granted her insight into how the dynamics of her parents' marriage had curbed her ability to conduct a fulfilling romance of her own.

"Looking back, I started to notice things that I maybe didn't notice when I was a kid," Mallory said. "But the thing that sticks out to me a lot, that I do remember from that time, is that my parents never got into any types of arguments. On the surface, their relationship didn't seem to have a lot of difficulty or strife. I see that as a problem. My mom was able to express more negative feelings, but my dad was always trying be laid back, and underneath I think he was actually unhappy about a lot of things."

Many couples hide their differences from their children, and I agree that if you feel a knock-down, drag-out fight coming on, you should curb your animosity until the kids aren't around. But when a couple never manifests the least hint of conflict, either no one's paying attention or someone's getting stepped on. Whatever the case with Mallory's parents was, she and her brother grew up without seeing how partners express and negotiate their differences. As a result, Mallory didn't know how to deal with conflict in her own romances. "In all of my relationships, in the beginning, if there was any kind of tension or fighting, I was really, really uncomfortable, and it felt as if it were the end of the world and that it was the end of the relationship, and we would never get through it. I have a fear that they're just not going to want to put up with it or bother with it if I really express my needs and feelings too much, that they'll say, 'I'm not going to bother with this.' So I've gotten into some situations where the focus of the relationship was me trying to meet their needs and not worry about my own needs. I think a lot of that is because I never saw my parents successfully argue."

Jyoti, a twenty-eight-year-old medical student whose Sanskrit name refers to the sacred flame, had a different problem: Her parents argued too much. Born and reared in Milwaukee, she grew up the only child of parents born in India and united through an arranged marriage. Their relationship was stormy, roiled by the father's belief that women should defer to men—a bias that cast the mother into a depressive cloud and Jyoti into a miasma of self-doubt.

"I don't feel he ever really taught me how to stand up for myself or to trust my own instincts, especially in relationships with other men," Jyoti said. "His advice was to give in and be more submissive, to let things go. He taught me to do that, and I feel like I've done that too many times in situations where I needed advice more in terms of 'Stand up for yourself, be independent.' He and my mom have had some rocky years, and I think he felt that my mom was too independent, had too many opinions, and he didn't want me to make what he considered to be the same mistake."

Aggravating the family's strife was Jyoti's father's decision when she was nine to bring his aging parents from India to live with them and their subsequent elevation to supreme status in the household. Jyoti's mother was entrusted with their day-to-day care, a role that demanded great exertion on her part and for which she received scant reward. "They didn't treat her very well and my dad never stood up for her," Jyoti said. "They were unappreciative of the care she provided, and she was doing 100 percent of the work when they first came. They treated her like a servant, but they treated my dad like a prince.

"He missed my high school graduation. Everyone came, and then my dad's parents felt a little cold, so he drove them home, which was about twenty minutes away. Coming back meant there was a forty-minute gap, so he ended up missing my graduation. I asked him, 'Why couldn't they sit inside? Why did you have to take them all the way home? If they had sat inside the school, you wouldn't have had to miss anything.' Then he told me I was being a brat, and it's never been forgotten. . . . I felt like I was more [like] a sibling with my grandparents because we were fighting over my dad, always fighting over who he'd spend time with. I felt like they were the ones I had to compete with growing up." When Jyoti needed comforting, she turned to her mother, who would bundle her into the car and drive to the grocery store parking lot, where they would sit in the car and talk. "That way she wouldn't get distracted by the grandparents or somebody saying, 'Do this. Do that.' We'd sit there and I'd tell her what I was upset about, and she'd listen."

My heart went out to Jyoti, who wept throughout the interview; by her midtwenties, she had already endured more rejection than many women do in a lifetime. Yet she had prevailed: She had come to understand that she needed to function as an equal partner in a relationship, not a submissive one, and had set about changing the ways she interacted with men. In so doing, she had deliberately rejected both her father's admonishment to elevate her partner's wishes over her own and his view that women should be obedient, complaisant creatures.

And she was studying to be a physician, which she described as the pinnacle of prestige for a child of Indian parents and the career her father had always pushed her toward. At first, Jyoti enrolled in a nursing program even though she really preferred medicine—"I resisted for a long time because if I didn't get in or if I failed, it would be the absolute worst failure and I'd never live it down"—but she had marshaled her courage, applied to med school, and gotten in. Not surprisingly, her acceptance raised her status in her father's eyes.

"Ever since I got into medical school, he respects my opinion. All of a sudden, I'm the smart person in my house. He gives me credit as an adult. That's never happened before. It's only since I got into medical school. But I don't feel like it's real. It's not because of who I am. Because I'm going to be a doctor, all of a sudden my opinion matters." Jyoti knew her father's newfound regard for her was not devoid of self-interest; as she put it, "My dad's self-worth rides on how well I do in my life," but I detected more than a bit of triumph in her voice. I asked her if getting his approval was important to her, and she said yes, it always had been. Which felt like déjà vu all over again: This daughter, like so many others, wanted to know that her father thought highly of her, even if she did not think all that highly of him.

Some successful women were uncomfortable when their
achievements eclipsed those of their dads

Financial success was common among the women I spoke to, as
were feelings of ambivalence about it. It wasn't that they regretted
their success. In fact, it was quite the opposite. They were proud
that they were doing well for themselves and eager for their fathers
to acknowledge that, preferably in a manner similar to Martha's
dad, who, you may recall, was blown out of the water at the boat
show by how much money his daughter made. In fact, the ambivalence didn't originate with the fathers as much as with the daughters, whose elevated financial status catapulted them to new
heights of emotional and familial complexity. It also seemed that
the higher a daughter leapt, the greater the complexity she
encountered.

Some stories were very dramatic; others, more modestly
so. One on the modest side was that of Joan, a thirty-year-old
married veterinarian whose income, along with her husband's,
significantly exceeded that of her parents when she was a child.
Even though her parents had more money now than they'd had
before, Joan still felt self-conscious about her prosperity, concealing from them the amount of her salary and what she paid for
things. When Joan's family needed a new car, for example, she
rejected her husband's suggestion that they buy a BMW. "I would
feel kind of awkward driving around in that," she said. "I feel if I
have that kind of money, I should give it to my parents."

On the more dramatic side was Nichelle.

Nichelle's story was unique among the ones I heard,
although I am certain there are others like it. I listened with wonder as this recent graduate of the University of Pennsylvania's
Wharton School of Business MBA program spoke about the
small investment start-up that she owns and runs, her dream of
becoming a venture capitalist financing entrepreneurs of color,
and a childhood spent shuttling back and forth between Georgia

and Nevada after her parents divorced. Her mother, who grew up poor and black in a shack with a tin roof, had graduated from high school with a scholarship to college. But instead of going, she had married Nichelle's father because, Nichelle said, he was building a house that would have electricity and indoor plumbing. He could neither read nor write.

"I'm just coming to terms with my dad being illiterate," she said. "I just got out of business school. I was talking to someone and was thinking, *It's pretty interesting that I'm here with people whose fathers are doctors or lawyers or professors. It's pretty wild that I'm here.* . . . We lived down a dirt road in a small town in Georgia. If you go to this town now, it probably looks the same. Black people live on one side of the tracks and white people live on the other."

Nichelle's relationship with her father, whom her mother left when Nichelle was four, was complicated long before she launched her own business (with the mentoring support, both financial and emotional, of an entrepreneur who saw her spark and kindled it). Nichelle described her relationship with her father as "not a bad one; we'll call it neutral. . . . I don't hate my dad and I'm not mad at him, but I don't have this overwhelming love for him. If he died tomorrow, I'm sure I'd be sad, but to be honest, I wouldn't be overwhelmed with grief." No other woman I interviewed sounded as emotionally detached as Nichelle did when speaking of her father, and I wondered if there was more going on than met the ear.

There was, of course. Not that Nichelle was harboring an uncharted well of affection for her father; she was sufficiently introspective to have ruled that out. But I do believe her relationship with him involved feelings that were far from neutral and caused her considerable conflict. She made it clear that she was helping to support her family Down South and felt responsible for their welfare. But her generosity with them did not assuage the guilt she felt about having a father she wasn't proud of.

"I just couldn't imagine bringing him to the city. It would

look like a movie; it wouldn't look real. At this point, I don't care
what people really think. My family is my family. But I can't imagine what it would be like to integrate him into that environment. I
tell people about the fact that he doesn't read or write. But it does
bother me to some degree, because I'd love for him to be a part of
whatever celebration. . . . This world is so different, I'm not sure it
would be healthy to bring him into this environment.

"This one student, his dad came in and he was a big-time
professor in Germany, an awesome guy who talked about modern
economic theory. I watched their interaction. He was cracking
jokes about his son, and the son was so proud to have his dad come
and speak to the class. I was thinking, *I could never have my dad
come and speak to a class, let alone invite certain people to dinner with
him*. I feel bad. It's my family and it's who I am, so I shouldn't be
ashamed. I will tell people about my dad not reading and writing.
But would I ever want to invite them to sit down to dinner with
my dad? Probably not."

Still, as with other daughters whose success overshadowed
their fathers', Nichelle wanted me to know that her father possessed his own brand of intelligence, and that she admired it. She
told me about an outing she'd had with her father when she had
visited Georgia the previous year.

"My sister took us to a discount store. I was interested in how
they had it set up—more like a warehouse—so I was walking
around the store and thinking about it. Ten minutes later, my dad
comes up to me and says, 'They're able to make money around
here because they have a lot of volume.' He said something that
was so business smart that it shocked me. I didn't expect that to
come from his mouth. Then I started to think about him and his
ability. He may have only a dime in his pocket, but he's not worried. He really doesn't worry about anything. I think that's savvy
of him, for someone who can't read or write. I think I get that
inner strength from him. He's been able to get through life and
sustain himself. He's very entrepreneurial in spirit. I do think I get

those characteristics from him." I found it instructive that despite her embarrassment about her father, this woman was eager to acknowledge the ways in which she resembled him and identify the positive qualities that were his legacy to her.

She was in good company. Remember Theresa, the TV creative director who took a lower-paying job despite her father's disapproval? Although he was more conservative than she was, Theresa's dad was still able to admire her sky-high credit rating (she spoke of having her credit report framed and presenting it to him as a Christmas present) and, not incidentally, the fact that she was making much more money than her musician brother. Still, like Nichelle, she found herself wishing she had a father whom she could acknowledge publicly with pride, much as her father was able to do with her. She described a visit to a comedy club two nights earlier.

"One of the comedians was hilarious. He mentioned having his twenty-two-year-old and twenty-one-year-old in the audience. I did feel this little bit of . . . What pride they must have to have this really funny, successful dad. It could be kind of fun to have that dad. My dad is funny in his own self-deprecating way. He tries to be witty, but he's not. It's like, 'Aww, dad, that wasn't that funny.' I do think there is something to be said about the dad who you just think is very charismatic." Might Theresa have wished for a more glamorous father even if she weren't making $100,000 a year? Perhaps. But I also think that her financial success had granted her access to people and places she might otherwise not have known, which in turn prompted her to reexamine who she was and where she had come from.

Some daughters struggled with loving their fathers even as they resented how they'd treated them as children

Numerous women expressed deep conflicts between their feelings about their fathers' behaviors while they were growing up and the sometimes grudging affection they retained for them as adults. Few daughters cited their fathers' bad behavior as the source of an estrangement; more often, they would start a sentence with "I love my dad, but" and finish with a description of an egregious episode from years earlier or a continuing pattern that still distressed them.

Julia, a thirty-three-year-old organic farmer and mother of two young children, said she grew up afraid of her father, a private school headmaster who was prone to unpredictable explosions of rage. "Growing up, there was a lot of stress with four kids; he had and still has a pretty incredible temper. You never knew when it would come. . . . It could be as silly as not being able to find the remote control. Growing up, he seemed successful, hardworking, really smart. So in some ways he was my hero. Yet he had this side of him that made him difficult to love. In some ways you tried to hide yourself from him, to not always show him exactly what was going on in your life. I still feel like it's that way sometimes. If he doesn't have his thing or his way, then nothing is right. I hear myself saying these things and they are true, but I feel bad about it. It's who he is. He can be warm and caring. Then he has this whole other side of him that is so intense and scary."

Compounding the conflict for Julia was relentless guilt; she said she felt that talking about her dad was "ratting him out" and that, after all, she had been reared well, cared for, and sent to college—all valid reasons for a daughter to feel grateful to her parents despite their flaws (and what parent isn't flawed?). Still, what resonated for me was the legacy of internal discord that her father's anger had bequeathed to her. "The thing that's unfortunate is you become an adult and you either choose to accept that this was your childhood and that although there were rough times, overall you were pretty lucky, or you can say, wow, he was really an asshole and he still can be, and I don't want anything to do with it." It was this ongoing struggle to reconcile past wounds with present needs that struck a recurring and poignant chord among the daughters I interviewed.

Tracy was another young woman struggling to conduct an adult relationship with a father and mother whose parenting she felt had been decidedly lacking (I had to agree). A thirty-four-year-old blog editor, Tracy and her sister were born in North Carolina to Filipino parents. Her father was an oral surgeon and her mother an office manager, both now retired. Tracy said her parents didn't have much time or patience for their children when they were growing up. When I asked who took care of them and their emotional needs, Tracy archly replied, "Our emotional needs? Are there such things?" She said tough love guided their parenting philosophy, adding that her parents neither understood American sensibilities nor were open to learning about them. She cited her prom night as an example.

"My father said I had to be home by ten o'clock at night. Prom didn't even start until ten! Leaving prom at the time it started—he completely didn't understand that. There was no reasoning whatsoever with my parents. I tried to explain to them about prom, but there was no reasoning whatsoever. So instead, I went out with some girlfriends with the intention of coming home by ten. At seven o'clock, I called my parents to let them know that I was having dinner with friends and I'd be coming home later. Since I couldn't go to prom, I thought that having dinner with friends was something, at the very least, that I could do. My father, who was never home, happened to be home that night. He picked up the phone and said, 'No, you are coming home right now.' 'But it's seven,' I told him, 'you said to be home by ten.' And my father said, 'Absolutely not. You are coming home right now.' I was upset, crying, irate, and I tried to express it to him, but I had no leverage whatsoever. His temper is amazing."

I was impressed by Tracy's resilience; here was a woman with not one intransigent parent but two who was trying to make a silk-purse adulthood out of a sow's-ear past. (She described how, during a trip to the Philippines when she was sixteen, she read a letter her mother had written to the family after Tracy's birth lamenting the fact that she had borne yet another daughter and vowing not to have any more children.) Still, Tracy was intent upon making the best of things, especially with regard to her father, whom she said was warmer and more nurturing than her mother. "I try to be grateful for every bit of interaction I have with him now, the conversations that we're able to have," she said. "I am in the process of applying to graduate school, so having my father, who has been through that process of arduous schooling and hard work and studying, is very helpful. . . . He's owned his practice for so long and he's seen so many different types of personalities. I appreciate the wisdom he's able to offer."

Some daughters' lives were stymied by their insistence on seeing their fathers as paragons of excellence rather than as human and flawed

There were several women whose initial glowing descriptions of their dads made it sound as if their fathers really did know best. But as the interviews continued, the glow faded and a less rosy image developed. All too often, the descriptions of these all-knowing fathers turned out to be idealized depictions of what actually were know-it-all types of men. And all too often as well, their adult daughters saw their dads through the wide, adoring eyes of the girls they used to be rather than the women they had become. This was yet another example of some daughters' need to idealize their dads even after they are adults. You've already read about Dianne, the woman whose husband commandeered her paychecks and, like her father, ran the family. Dianne's refusal (or inability, depending on how you see it) to recognize her father's need to control her induced her to marry a man just like him, to whose control she obediently succumbed. Another, arguably even more extreme case, was Sondra, the woman who believed her dad was always right.

Sondra grew up in New England, the eldest of two children. At thirty-two, she held a master's degree from an Ivy League university and was making a six-figure salary at a health insurance company. Dressed conservatively in a navy blue suit and white shirt, she gave an impression of buttoned-down competence, the kind of person whom you could count on to get a job done. "I started out very responsible," she said. "I was never the one who lost my mittens at school."

She described her mother, who did not work outside the home, as a supermom; when I asked about her father, a lawyer, she said that he'd "flip out" if he knew she were being interviewed for this book and that she'd been afraid of him as a child. Then, almost immediately, she began to stammer. "Not that I . . . in some ways I was afraid of him, and in other ways, I was very close to him. I think that's probably typical, or, I don't know, not uncommon." This became a pattern: Sondra would reveal a potentially unattractive aspect of her father, try to soften the effect, and then frame it as a characteristic shared by many other dads.

Sondra was a mass of contradictions. She said her father expected her to excel in school; when I asked if his expectations felt comfortable or onerous, she said they felt comfortable but knew that if she stepped out of line she would get punished. She mentioned her desire to attend a college that would be more politically diverse than her liberal prep school, then said the college she went to was affiliated with the Catholic Church and populated almost exclusively by white, religious, conservative, middle-class kids. When I asked if she ever felt judged by her father, she said her father evaluated her, he did not judge her. And when I asked if she valued his opinion, she said, "Yes, I seek his opinion routinely, often. Dad always knows the answer. I learned long ago that he is always right. It's terrible."

"Really?" I asked.

"It's true. He is always right. He always told me that he's always right, and as a teenager, I thought that was a load of baloney, but he is always right."

When a little girl declares that her father is always right, it's cute; when a thirty-two-year-old says it without a trace of irony, there's something amiss. In Sondra's case, what was missing was the ability to think for herself, so thoroughly had she subscribed to the myth of her father's infallibility. It was no wonder Sondra had no mind of her own, as she had no need for one. From what I could tell, she was content to let her father do her thinking for her. When I asked about her father's attitude toward working mothers, she replied, "He thinks it's fine. But he doesn't think that's what I would want. He always says to me, 'Oh, honey, you can think you're going to want to work. You're not going to want to work when you have kids.' I think if I had to work, that would be okay. He wouldn't see anything wrong with that, although he would prefer me to stay home."

Whether or not Sondra would eventually have kids was an open question, as her idealization of her father had made it difficult for her to sustain a fulfilling romance of her own. She had enjoyed a long relationship that began when she was fourteen and ended when she was twenty; since then, she said, she had attracted a string of successful, professional, straight-arrow types who were all oppressively possessive and jealous. "For some reason, I've always attracted these guys who love that I'm independent and smart and do all these things on my own, yet hate it because it means they can't control me."

Sound familiar? That's what I wanted to ask—but I didn't. I couldn't, not without exceeding the boundaries of our relationship. I was acting in my capacity as a research psychologist, not a clinical one. Sondra had not come for therapy, and it was inappropriate for me to offer my opinions. Instead, I asked her if there was anything she wished had been different about her relationship with her father when she was growing up.

"A lot of times, the answer to 'Why not?' was 'Because I'm your father, and that's it.' That always bothered me. I always wished he would sit down and have a conversation with me. I think it upset him when we fought and he just couldn't deal. There was one time when we totally butted heads. I don't even think it was anything important. I think we had just had it with each other. I was probably ten or eleven. I was upset, and my mother had to calm me down because I stormed out. But generally, that did not happen."

So Sondra had rebelled—dramatically on at least one occasion and sufficiently on others to infuriate her father to the point where he resorted to the because-I-said-so argument deployed by frustrated parents everywhere. But somewhere along the line, she had abandoned her mutinous outbursts, probably because her father's inability to deal, as she put it, made her uncomfortable. Eager to please her daddy and loath to provoke his wrath (as most little girls are), she set out to win her father's approval, relinquishing her powers of discernment and adopting his. Now she was attracting guys who tried to control her and whom she couldn't stand. I asked her why she thought this was the case.

"I am different with men than I am with my dad," she replied. "I am much more compliant, which I shouldn't be. I try to be a people pleaser; I am always trying to please somebody. When I'm dating, I am always trying to make the other person comfortable. As a result, I wind up with people who need to be made to feel comfortable and have a lot of issues of their own."

Sondra could see that her eagerness to please was creating unsatisfactory relationships—so far so good. But when I asked how much she thought her father's personality had affected her interactions with men, her self-awareness went only so far.

"I hold my father in very high regard, so I hold men to that standard," she said. "They don't have to be as great as my dad, but they have to at least attempt to be. I am attempting to be. He is my role model in a lot of ways. He's just an all-around good guy. It's hard not to love him."

For her, maybe, but not for me. I found it easy not to love this man who had established his status as idol-in-residence and perpetuated the folly even after his daughter left home. In reality, daughters like Sondra and Dianne continue to live in their fathers' houses long after they've left home. Some of them never leave.

Some daughters who outgrew the need to see their fathers as perfect were nonetheless disappointed by the imperfect men they found

Here were daughters who had cast off the naïveté of girlhood, gazed upon their dads with grown-up eyes, and were still sometimes disillusioned by what they saw.

Trisha, a thirty-eight-year-old holistic healer and massage therapist, said both she and her genetically unrelated brother had been adopted as infants and reared by parents who argued frequently. She described her adoptive father as more even-keeled than her adoptive mother and said that she sided with him because her mother yelled a lot, especially at him, which Trisha found deeply upsetting. She said her father was practical, loyal, responsible, somewhat shy and reticent, but overall, a "pretty sweet, pretty nice guy." She adored him when she was a young girl and said he sometimes took her and her brother away on short vacations while her mother stayed home. "He was kind of the fun, nice parent. I'm not trying to make my mom out to be horrible, but he would be the one that we'd want to hang out with," she said. Still, when I asked if her dad had encouraged her in sports, she replied that he hadn't, although he didn't discourage her. When I pressed her about whether her father had encouraged her in other ways, her disappointment began to show.

"He encouraged me to be how he envisioned a successful person to be, but he didn't necessarily encourage me to do things that I was inclined to do," she said. "I wanted to play the saxophone and he made me play the flute instead. To this day, I wish I had learned to play the sax. But that's okay, I'm not mad at him for it."

"Were you mad at the time?" I asked.

"I was mad. Definitely. . . . He would often start sentences with 'You should,' as in 'You should get a degree in nursing, you should become a teacher.' I can't recall exactly what he said to me as a child, but there was a lot about what I should wear, how I should be with people, things like that. He'd couch it in a kind or warm way. It's not like he was yelling at me, but there were a lot of shoulds."

Like some other fathers, Trisha's dad had encouraged his daughter to do and be things within the confines of gender stereotypes—why had he not urged her to become a college professor or a doctor rather than a teacher or a nurse, and why had he insisted that she take up the flute rather than the saxophone?—that were fraught with expectations that had more to do with a girl's potential than with the actual potential of the girl his daughter was. Trisha's father encouraged his daughter in his own way, as many dads do. And for this Trisha was grateful, as many daughters are. But just as some daughters wished their dads had urged them to aim higher and take more risks, Trisha wished her dad's vision of her had been more congruent with her vision of herself.

Sometimes a daughter's disappointment seemed founded less in her father's actual shortcomings than in her perception of him. In the case of Jordan, a thirty-one-year-old assistant business professor

at a large Midwestern university, her disparagement of her father
was matched by the high regard in which she held her mother,
whose moxie she admired for immigrating alone to the United
States from Hungary as a young woman. Once here, Jordan's
mother sent for her own German-born mother, who lived with the
family throughout Jordan's childhood, with the result that Jordan
grew up speaking German and Hungarian as well as English.
"The three women have always been very, very close," she said.
"The big joke was that my brother had three moms—me, my
mom, and my grandmother, so that was also another role that I
took on."

Jordan's parents owned and operated an audio production
facility in Minneapolis. Jordan described her father as being the
public face of the company and her mother as the brains of the
operation. "He was great with people, but he was the figurehead
while she was the one behind the scenes actually making things
happen. She managed all the money, but anytime negotiations
came, it was my dad who would be there at the forefront dealing
with the attorneys." When her mother grew tired of handling the
finances, Jordan said, her dad "took over and made a bunch of
blunders and ended up losing a lot of money and fighting with her
about that [because of] his stubbornness and very quick temper,
and he'd argue with my mom about whatever she said." Whenever Jordan spoke of her parents, it sounded as if her mother was
the hardworking, competent one, charged with undoing the damage wrought by her father.

Jordan's dismissive attitude toward her father seemed
incongruent with other things she revealed about him: He was
highly intelligent, had graduated from a prestigious university,
was willing to do chores and run business errands whenever his
wife asked him to, and was a voracious reader who would pepper
his kids with random facts, a trait that they teased him about.

Jordan said he was the one who taught her and her brother to swim and ride bicycles, and that he often took her out for ice cream after her brother had gone to bed. She talked about the ten-day trip the two of them took to visit colleges, how thrilled her father was when she got into graduate school, and how he had urged her to press on when she was having a difficult time during the program. Later, I realized that whereas Jordan recounted numerous details of these events, she never talked about how they made her feel.

It sounded as if Jordan's father was a decent man who had not only made a point of spending time with her when she was a girl, but had also put up with having his mother-in-law in the house for more than thirty-five years. He comforted Jordan when she was discouraged and let her know how proud he was of her. Why, then, did she sound so disappointed in him?

The answer lay, I believe, in the strong bond between Jordan and her mother. Describing their relationship as resembling that of sisters, Jordan said her mother routinely confided her frustrations with her husband, seeking Jordan's empathy and support. "I was in college and she would tell me, this is what's going on, this is what your father and I argued about, this is the dumb thing he did today, this is what he should have done or forgot to do—just the little daily gripes that people have." Getting daily updates on her father's alleged incompetence didn't do much to burnish Jordan's image of him, and in time her opinion of her father became indistinguishable from her mother's. The takeaway from this story? That a daughter (or a son, for that matter) may not be the most reliable witness when it comes to measuring the worth of a parent; it all depends on what else she (or he) has going on, and with whom. (If you think you may need to reevaluate your impression of your father, look at "Questionnaire: How Well Do You Really Know Your Dad?" on page 199.)

No matter how close they were to their dads, most women said
they more often confided in their mothers about emotional issues

What's newsworthy here is not that most daughters went to their
mothers when they wanted to talk about relationships, but rather
that some went to their mothers even when they felt a closer kinship with their fathers. Dana, a twenty-year-old college junior, is
a good example. The eldest of four children, Dana grew up with a
stay-at-home dad and a mother who supported the family on her
salary as the director of research and development for a Silicon
Valley technology company. When Dana was fourteen, she left for
boarding school because she fell in love with what she had read
about the place, whose attractions included assigning each girl a
horse to ride and care for; after graduation, she left for college on
the East Coast. Dana spoke lovingly of both parents, but perceived
them as having different gifts. She said her mother was highly
intelligent, both book smart and people smart, and always offered
her good advice. "She's great. I love my mom," Dana said. "I call
my mom and talk to her pretty much every day." Dana admired
her mother's business savvy, work ethic, and success and described
her as being "pretty darn close" to perfection, even if she did work
too hard and wear herself out. Her father, on the other hand,
sounded as if he were more fully present and engaged, and he set
more store by connecting with people—traits typically associated
more with women than with men. "I talk to my dad probably two to
three times a week. I usually just call him to chat. I usually call my
mom for something particular. I almost never call my dad with
something particular to say. That being said, I usually call him
sometime in the afternoon and we'll talk. Sometimes with my
mom I will give her a quick call to say hi and tell her what's going
on. My dad and I will just chat for an hour about my siblings,
about the dogs, about everything." I found this interesting in light
of Tannen's findings about women's connecting through talk:
Here was a daughter who connected with both her mother and her

father through talk, only in different ways. Curiously, Dana said she talked with her father about everything, whereas she'd call her mother to discuss something in particular. This may have been because Dana was reluctant to interrupt her mother at work just to chat, or because Dana felt a need to connect with her father more than her mother about the mundane aspects of everyday life. I began to suspect the latter after Dana's next remark.

"My dad is incredibly considerate," Dana continued. "He's friends with the butcher, the butcher's kids, the garbageman, the dog walker. He takes the time to listen to them and hear what they have to say. He gives everyone the time of day." Dana clearly admired her father's amiability and interest in other people, and I asked her if she was similar to him in this respect.

"I try to be. I think about people a lot more than I think my mom does. My mom goes a million miles an hour and zooms through everything. She is my role model in that I take after her in terms of ambition. My mom is the master of social grace, knowing what the right thing to do is in terms of etiquette, how to approach a situation, how to apologize, things like that. On a human-to-human level, a very personal level, I try to emulate my dad. Every relationship he has with someone is really mean-ingful. My mom doesn't chat with people like my dad does. . . . I think my relationship with my mom is a standard mother-daughter one, whereas my relationship with my dad is compli-cated but very deep."

"In what sense is it deep?" I asked.

"I haven't even told my mom this. They're not hidden so I don't feel that bad, but there are all these journals of his from col-lege, and . . . it's musings, poetry, random thoughts. I read them sometimes and I feel bad about it. I feel guilty. But it shocked me the first time I did, because it was literally exactly what I would have written in my journal."

This was strong stuff for Dana, discovering that her father's college-age meditations were identical to her own. So intimate a bond did she feel with him that she had resisted telling her mother about the journals. Still, Dana said, she would never, ever talk to her father about sex; the nature of their relationship would not permit it.

I asked Dana if her relationship with her dad had changed when she hit puberty and her response was instructive. "I think that's one of the reasons I'm glad I decided to go to boarding school. Looking back, I realize that I could feel my relationship with my dad becoming different," she said. In fact, the changing father-daughter dynamic was not the main instigator of Dana's shift to boarding school; a plague of middle school mean girls had more to do with it, as did living with three younger siblings, minimal privacy, and maximum noise. Still, Dana's remark about the awkwardness she felt with her father shed light on her reluctance to discuss romantic relationships with him. I think she felt uncomfortable around her dad when her sexuality began to blossom, just as he felt uncomfortable around her. This is not unusual. It's common for a father to avoid physical contact with his adolescent daughter for fear of the sexual feelings it might elicit, but the daughter then becomes confused when she goes to hug her dad and he shrinks back, afraid to return the embrace. Even now, as a college student, Dana still felt discomfort. When she had dated a boy in the summer after her sophomore year and spent the night at his family's house, she would tell her mom but not her dad where she was going. "In situations with boys, with my dad it's don't ask, don't tell. I lied to him all summer. It was hard for me. He was an incredibly nice boy and it was nothing I was ashamed of, but if my dad had known I was spending the night there, he would have been horrified. He doesn't think of me at all that way."

Dana was her father's soul mate, but only to a point—the point at which her sexuality began to emerge. That Dana's father stayed home with the kids while her mother went to work undoubtedly intensified Dana's bond with him and their mutual awkwardness when she hit puberty. I can see how their emotional closeness might have made it hard for Dana to freely explore her interest in boys, and difficult for her dad to balance his protective, possessive feelings with the desire to nurture his daughter's growing sexual identity. And I can see how being bullied by a bunch of nasty girls could inspire her to look kindly upon going away to high school (not to mention the whole horse angle).

But the point of Dana's story is that like other women I interviewed who felt closer emotional kinships with their dads than their moms, there were still things they chose not to share with them. There were limits to what daughters would discuss with their fathers, and in those cases, only mothers would do.

Daughters valued the good aspects of their relationships with their dads while acknowledging that they'd want better for their own kids

I was cheered by the emotional generosity of the many women who were able to appreciate the good in their dads while acknowledging that there were other aspects of the relationship they'd just as soon forget. Even when there wasn't much good to speak of, some women spoke of it nonetheless, even as they emphasized that they wouldn't want their own daughters to replicate their experience.

Listening to Suzanne's story, I found myself smiling and sometimes laughing aloud as she described what was not the cheeriest childhood. A thirty-nine-year-old entrepreneur whose line of skin-care products has made her wealthy in her own right, Suzanne was fiercely intelligent, articulate, and droll, as well as gimlet-eyed in her view of her father, his privileged background, and his abandonment of Suzanne's mother to marry his childhood sweetheart. "My dad is a very dynamic person," she said. "He's the guy you watch, whatever he's doing. He's extremely attractive and an unbelievable athlete. If he was batting, he'd probably hit a home run. If he was in tennis, he was the best dressed and the best player. My father's like out of *The Great Gatsby*. His father was a totally self-made and powerful man, so my father grew up with governesses. . . . He grew up sophisticated. They were very affluent."

As was the childhood sweetheart he left Suzanne's mother for. When Suzanne's parents split up (she was seven and her brother was four), her mother retained custody of the children, who would wait at their modest Brooklyn apartment for their father to pick them up for weekends at his much grander house in Connecticut.

"If my father was supposed to come at 1:00, he came at 4:00. We didn't want to go. I used to call it the spa, because all I would do was relax. I was the most rested human being in the world. It was eight miles to town from this magnificent home. There was a pond on the lawn and we used to ice-skate on it. . . . My stepsiblings were there. We're all very close in age, so we'd do things together. But it wasn't like I was going to make friends out there. Walking next door, you could get tired."

Unlike some daughters, Suzanne had no trouble seeing her father's limitations. "My father's a very selfish person. . . . He had a lot of money and he was cheap; he could have made things a little easier at times rather than making my mother work so hard. . . . He's a limited person. I was always in the school plays; I always got the good parts. Once he walked in and said, 'You were the best!' and I said, 'You came in as we were bowing. I saw you!'"

When I asked Suzanne where she got her humor from, she said everyone in her family was funny. "They're all so funny because you laugh or you cry, so everybody laughs." And she did, throughout the interview, as she regaled me with stories of shopping trips to Bergdorf Goodman with her grandmother (father's side), then shopping on her own in the East Village and dressing like a cross between Cyndi Lauper and Madonna. This was during her teen years, after her mother got remarried to a man Suzanne wasn't crazy about.

"I wasn't getting along with my stepfather, so I went to live at my father's for a month and a half, but they lived all the way out in Greenwich and I went to school in the city, so it was a terrible commute. So I got myself an apartment and a job after school, and I came home with the lease. It was a walkup and there was no sink in the bathroom. You had to wash your hands in the kitchen sink. Who lets a person get an apartment when they're a senior in high school?"

Suzanne was spot-on: How *do* you allow your teenage daughter to live unsupervised in a fleabag walk-up when you're living in a palace in Connecticut? Her humor notwithstanding, Suzanne harbored plenty of resentment toward her father: She said she didn't think she'd ever forgive him for abandoning the family, admitted that she was still furious about his stinginess, and remarked that she sometimes went for months without speaking to him. Still, she did not write him off. She credited him with motivating her to push herself, work hard, and feel she could do anything. "My father is a perfect gentleman. He definitely set the bar high for me for what I think about men, and he definitely set the bar very high for how I behave, because I have very high standards. . . . My father was like, 'I don't care what you do [professionally].' He was more about 'Be a success, be a success.' The reason he talks about me all day long—he has boxes of my press clippings—I am his girl because I am successful. He is very proud."

I confess that the emphasis on success didn't resonate as sweetly with me as it did with Suzanne. To her it was a clarion call to achievement; to me, it sounded like a celebration of superficiality over substance. But it had clearly worked for her, which is what struck me most about Suzanne and the other women like her: They were able to appreciate the good their dads had done for them while still holding their own husbands to a higher standard. "You know, I still hold him in unbelievably high regard," Suzanne said, "but I wouldn't want that for my child. I definitely wouldn't want that." Mission accomplished, I'd say.

Even when a father was damaged or flawed, his daughter found something of value in the relationship, felt loyal to him, or both

Imagine this: You're eight years old and sitting in the car with your younger sister and brother outside the house where you grew up. You're moving out because your parents are separating, and your father has dragged some furniture and household belongings onto the front lawn. As you watch, he hoists a red plastic container and douses the pile with gasoline as your mother tries to stop him, scratching his face and getting her finger broken in the process.

Now it's more than twenty years later and you're on the phone with a psychologist who's writing a book and asking you questions about your relationship with your dad. And you say— what? That you hated him? That he was a horrible person? That you would just as soon forget about him? Not necessarily.

"He was generally a pretty extreme character, but I loved my dad very much," said Abigail, who recently earned a PhD in biology after spending six years in Latin America working with children with AIDS. "I never felt like he didn't love us. He and I had a couple of moments that still affect me and will forever." I held the phone closer to my ear so as not to miss a word.

"Early on," she continued, "I remember he told me the only reason he and my mom had ever gotten married was because she had gotten pregnant with me. I think that's probably true. I think they did love each other, too. I think they were one of these couples where there was good and bad. They couldn't be peaceful together and find happiness. He told me that they didn't really want me, but he felt forced to marry her. I was seven or eight [when he told me this]. It was pretty weird to say something like that to me."

That was the understatement of the year.

At twenty-nine, Abigail was married, expecting her first child, and touchingly loyal to the memory of her father, a physician

who suffered from violent mood swings that were likely the result
of a mental disorder. He died of a heart attack when Abigail was
fourteen, after having relocated to the US Virgin Islands after the
divorce. She said he loved the outdoors and was a superb athlete,
and she credited him with inspiring her own varied athletic activities, which included swimming, deep-sea diving, skiing, and
snowboarding. Abigail's glowing memories of her dad alternated
with dark ones: He became very hurt and angry once when she
asked permission to shorten one of their scheduled visits so she
could play in a championship game with her softball team, and he
threatened not to attend her middle school commencement because
her mother would be there. Still, she persisted in recalling his
quirky, admirable qualities.

"He always said he would only be happy with no lower than
a B-plus in any subject except for religion, where he wanted us to
get Fs," she said. "In a lot of ways, he was a positive influence in
terms of my personal drive and my desire to change things. He
was instrumental in changing the health care in [the Islands] to
get more poor people seen by doctors at the hospital. I admired
him for a lot of reasons. . . . I don't know how to really talk about
my relationship with my dad, because there was an element of
fear. For a lot of time when I was young, I was kind of afraid of
my dad after some of the stuff when they first separated. But I
never felt like he didn't care about us or didn't want us. I was
scared of him and kind of reserved with him, but I really loved
him still."

No one would fault Abigail for abjuring her father's memory, yet she held it close to her heart, as did Ariel, the young
woman I mentioned earlier whose father suffered an emotional
collapse. Now thirty-two and a senior tax manager at an account-
ing firm, Ariel strode into my office and sat down, removing a
pillow from the chair and positioning herself without a lot of fuss.
I found her thoughtful, straightforward, and very likable, with

long, graceful fingers that she used frequently to emphasize a point or punctuate an emotion in a way that was both attractive and compelling. She said she was single, lived alone, and was almost completely estranged from her father because she found him combative and belligerent. But it hadn't always been this way: Until Ariel was twelve, her father had been an engaged and loving presence in her life, spending hours with her in bookstores and coaching her team when she was one of the few girls playing Little League baseball.

"There were probably three girls in the whole league," she said, three long fingers upraised. "And I could play. I remember the first time I went up to bat in a Little League game, it was a big deal that I was a girl standing at the plate. The coach on the other team was telling everybody to move in. My dad was standing at first base and I looked at him. He knew I was mad."

"How old were you?" I asked.

"I was in third grade. They stopped the whole game to move everybody in. He went like this"—she gestured with her eyebrows and sliced her hands through the air—" 'Let them do that if they want to do that, so don't worry.' I ended up hitting it right over the center fielder's head, which was great. But my father was very encouraging and positive. The kid who had no talent and the kid who was the best, he made everybody feel good." Ariel also spent time with her father in his home office, where he worked as an independent consultant helping women and minorities secure small business loans. "I used to come home and sit in his office and watch him work. I was fascinated by it. I remember seeing him at his desk, seeing the books, smelling work. I always liked coming upstairs, where he saw clients. I liked the environment. Even before that, when I was little and he worked for a bank, I used to love going to the office. Then when he started working out of the house, I remember clients coming in. I liked what he did for his work because people were coming who needed money for their businesses and no one would give them loans. They were distraught, but my father was very good with them. He'd build them up and get them money, and they left our house feeling better."

But everything changed one day when Ariel came home from school and learned that her grandfather—her father's father—had died.

"He had a breakdown of some sort and went into a depression for two or three years. What I remember the most during those times was he was in a robe, smoking cigarettes and crying a lot. He was on a lot of medication, and not available [for me] at all. . . . The first two years it was somewhat of an innocuous situation, because he had no energy and he was so depressed . . . but when he started to get his life back, it turned into anger. He shifted from being passive and needing to be taken care of to raging and being verbally abusive to my mother and me." Ariel said her dad kept it together enough to deal with clients, then would scream for hours, especially at her and her mother. Gradually, the family's dynamics became lopsided as each member's focus shifted inexorably toward the father's needs and away from everyone else's.

As Ariel's connection with her father further deteriorated, she developed debilitating bouts of depression, coming home from school and sleeping for hours. Despite this, she played sports, managed to keep her grades up, and went away to college. Her parents split up later and her father remarried, but relations between him and the grown children have remained strained due to what Ariel described as his self-centeredness.

Ariel's interview was more dramatic than most and many impressions remain. Two are particularly vivid. The first is that throughout her father's illness and despite the invective he hurled her way, Ariel retained her fascination with her father's business. "I actually worked in his office in the summers in high school, even when we weren't getting along," she said. "Even during the bad times, I used to read all his work stuff." That this connection prevailed despite his rages is astonishing: This young woman was drawn so powerfully to the world of her father's work that she said she could smell it. I do not think it's a coincidence that she has risen to the top of her company and has eighty people working under her. I believe her ambition and drive took hold at home, in her father's book-strewn office. There was something about the atmosphere in there—the phone on the desk, the stacks of forms, the clients who left looking more hopeful than they had when they walked in—that exerted a powerful pull on Ariel's imagination, propelled her desire to succeed, and convinced her of her ability to succeed in the world of work.

The second impression that remains with me is Ariel's unrelenting will to seek out the seed of hope in a morass of pain, hold it close to her heart, and let it root there and grow into something useful and true. It was consistent with the pattern I was seeing of women wanting and needing to glean the good from their relationships with their dads.

"I want women to know that there's a lot of good that can come out of a dynamic that's estranged on some level," she said. "You have to dig in there and unearth it all, but I know I would never be in the position I am in, managing the number of people that I am in the way that I do, had I not had such a tumultuous relationship. When you are constantly confronted with a negative interaction, you're able to remove yourself and look at it from a different perspective. It is not unsettling to me when people—men—get upset. I'm looking at the dynamic and thinking, *What's operating here? What is this situation?* That's a direct result of this relationship with my dad, no question."

Many women persisted in trying to build relationships with fathers who sounded undeserving of the effort

I left this one for last because it was the one universal theme expressed by every woman I spoke with, and it conveys what may be the last word on how daughters feel about their fathers: They just don't want to give up on them.

This was especially evident in cases where the family split up and the dad lived apart from his kids. Some of the women I talked to had parents who divorced when they were young, so visits with dad were scheduled, time-bound, and focused on fun rather than the day-to-day discipline and drudgery their mothers were dealing with. The result was that no matter how lacking a dad was in the parenting department, his daughter tended to remember him as the playful parent, the one who was free to hang out, relax, and have fun. The evidence from my interviews was anecdotal, but scientific studies have confirmed that fathers tend to engage with their children in markedly playful ways, even when the children are infants. In a multiauthored book about the role of the father in child development, editor Michael E. Lamb asserts that not only do "fathers tend to engage in more physically stimulating and unpredictable play than mothers do," but also that "since these types of play elicited more positive responses from infants, young children prefer to play with their fathers when they have the choice."[5]

I believe it's safe to extrapolate this preference beyond early childhood into adolescence and even beyond, as is confirmed by Tannen, who asserts that studies show that dads spend more time playing with their kids than tending them, with the result that even in adulthood, many women think of their dads as terrific company and lots of fun to be around.[6] The point is that some of the women I spoke to treasured fond childhood memories of their fun and playful fathers, only to find as adults that their halos had tarnished once they became aware of the subtler aspects of childrearing and child support. Now, in adulthood, the women yearned to reexperience the childhood joy they had felt in their fathers' company, unencumbered by the doubt and disappointment that came later.

Taryn, a twenty-three-year-old first-year medical student from Mississippi, was the daughter of two physicians who divorced when she was two years old. Angry with her father for cutting off financial support when she and her two sisters turned eighteen (she was one of a set of identical triplets, the other two of whom were also in medical school), she nevertheless remembered him as warm and loving when she was little and was struggling to find a way to reconcile her conflicting feelings about him. "He is turning seventy this year. It has made me realize that he may not be around for that much longer. I would rather enjoy my time with him now and put that in the past. Not necessarily forgive him for it, but move on from it, because I know him as a good dad."

The power of this tendency to remember a father as good, despite some of the memories, became evident after Taryn's next story.

"My sisters and I were five years old. This was after a massive hurricane in Biloxi, where my dad lived. My mom and my grandma were dropping us off at his house but it had been destroyed, so we were going to be living on his boat in the meantime. They were walking us around the back of the house onto the dock to put us on the boat. My dad had a girlfriend at the time and he started threatening my mom, saying, 'If you don't get off the property, I'm going to kill you.' He and his girlfriend beat up my mom, and they beat up my grandma, too. I was caught in the middle and I was hit by something. I don't really remember, but there are pictures of me in the police report. He was beating her up and then the police got involved." Taryn said this was the only memory she had of her father being violent. Still, it's a doozy. And still she remembers him warmly, with more than a hint of nostalgia.

"As a little kid, I thought he was the coolest dad ever. If we wanted to go to Disney World, he'd be the one saying, 'Let's ride all the roller coasters.' He would actively participate in the things we wanted to do. It was different with my mom. . . . He was more willing to let us hang out with friends of ours on the weekend. It was always more fun at our dad's house. As a parent, aside from the issues we went through past high school [when he cut off financial support], he was a fun dad. I had a fun childhood with him." The tenacity of Taryn's memories was instructive: Her father was a fun dad and she had a fun childhood with him, period. She didn't discount what came later; she wasn't forgiving him, she said, but rather moving on. But for Taryn, moving on did not mean demolishing the happy memories she had of her father. She had plenty of bad memories that wouldn't go away; why not hold on to the good ones as well?

Now, Taryn says, she speaks to her father once or twice a month. She says she calls him infrequently and when she does, it is for the express purpose of sustaining the relationship.

"I am the one who wants to spend time with him, and my sisters aren't as willing—but they'll do it," she said. "I am the one saying, 'Guys, we need to go see Dad and hang out with him.' I am trying to plan a family vacation with him this winter break, and my sisters didn't really want to do it. I had to convince them. I tend to be the more active one as far as wanting to hang out with him." I asked her what she hoped her efforts might accomplish.

"I'd like some sort of acknowledgement that he was wrong, but I know I'm probably not going to get that," she said. "At this point, I want him to know he shouldn't be afraid to tell me that, to admit that he was wrong, because I would forgive him. I would be okay with it. I don't think he's not apologizing because he thinks I won't accept the apology. I think he's not apologizing because he doesn't do that."

Clearly and poignantly, Taryn was yearning for her father to acknowledge how he had wronged her so she could forgive him. It wasn't sufficient that she forgive him in her heart; she wanted a living, in-the-moment connection with him that would convince her of his remorse and provide her with an opportunity to demonstrate her love by forgiving him. If apologizing was something her father didn't do, what greater proof of his love could there be than for him to break new emotional ground and tell her he was sorry?

The theme of forgiveness ran strongly through Kim's narrative as well. Kim is the woman I mentioned who I listened to, dumbfounded, as she recounted how she came home after a bad day in sixth grade and found solace in a vodka and orange juice provided by her father. Yet, as she sat before me, she said she felt no anger toward him. A thirty-one-year-old exotically beautiful brown-skinned woman with jet black hair and honey-colored eyes, Kim had steady work managing the office of a group orthodontic practice, had been sober for two years, and said she attended Alcoholics Anonymous meetings at least once and sometimes twice a day (she joined AA after she nearly drowned in the bathtub after polishing off three bottles of Champagne). A slight accent and eccentric phrasings permeated her speech, and her humor belied the veil of sadness that hooded her eyes. She said that even though she and her father lived far apart, she was still very close to him and they told each other everything.

"When I got sober, I thought things were going to get a little awkward," she said. "He actually supports my decision. When he was here—he stayed with me for a couple of months— he used to drink, and I used to sit with him and chat, even though I was sober."

"Does he admit he's an alcoholic?" I asked.

"He doesn't admit anything. He is color-blind, and he doesn't even admit that."

Born into a wealthy family in Mexico, Kim, the younger of two daughters, grew up surrounded by nannies, private tutors, chauffeurs, bodyguards, and alcohol. Her father was the youngest of twenty-one children and came from a very wealthy black family who disinherited him for marrying Kim's mother, who was white. Together, Kim's parents established a string of health spas that flourished—due to her mother's business savvy and hard work, according to Kim—and supported the family's luxurious way of life. The family moved frequently, relocating to different cities as they opened more and more spas. Running the business kept Kim's mother on the road; Kim's sister, Sonia, who was four years older, was rebellious and out with friends most of the time, so Kim was reared by nannies. Her father was a serious alcoholic who spent a good deal of time at home with a handler of sorts—"my father's nanny," Kim said—who accompanied him everywhere to help him up when he fell and keep him from hurting himself.

After that fateful day in sixth grade, Kim began drinking with her father every afternoon when she got home from school. When she was not quite thirteen, she dropped out of school, preferring to study at home with tutors. Kim was thus free to drink with her father earlier in the day. Her nanny disapproved, but because she was employed by Kim's father, she wasn't in a position to say anything to either of them. And so it was that Kim became her father's drinking partner. She said that, in the beginning, they would sometimes talk when they drank, "but then we got so wasted there was nothing to talk about." Her father would then black out, and Kim would be left to her own devices.

"I used to spend lots of money, take the car and go away for a couple weeks at a time without telling him—hoping he would notice I wasn't home or call me and ask me what was I doing," she said. "When I turned fifteen, he gave me my first car. Two weeks after I got it, I took the car—I had a driver at the time—and went to Belize. By the time I got back he was like, 'Oh, I haven't seen you.' He didn't even notice I was gone for two weeks."

Sequestered inside the house with her father, nannies, and tutors, Kim had no real friends until she was sixteen, when a boy the same age moved in next door. They shared a crippling sense of social isolation; Kim said he also struggled with depression. "He was from another city and moved to my town. I had a terrace on my bedroom and he had a terrace on his bedroom as well. He was very lonely. We used to go to the terraces at nighttime, and we started talking. We got really, really close." When Kim was nearly eighteen, she was on the phone with him one evening when he put a gun in his mouth and pulled the trigger. She was in her bedroom and he was in his. Kim was devastated by the loss, which galvanized her to change her life. She decided to go back to school. Within three months her mother had enrolled her in an ultraconservative Catholic academy.

Kim's life in Mexico sounded like a treatment for an action movie, complete with expulsion from aforementioned academy ("I was making too many questions for them"), admission to a university where she drank too much to keep up with the work ("I used to pay my teachers to pass me"), and being shipped north to the United States when her sister Sonia was kidnapped—*twice* ("The first time they targeted me, but I had a flat tire that day, so she passed [by them] first"). I absorbed Kim's story with an ample dose of disbelief, so alien were these events to my way of living. Equally alien to me was Kim's capacity to forgive a man who had wreaked such havoc on her life. This was what I wanted most to understand.

"Do you admire your father at all?" I asked.

"No," Kim replied. (This I understood.)

"What would you say is your greatest disappointment in the relationship?"

"The alcohol. I was eleven when he gave me my first drink!"

"Then how do you love him, and how are you able to not be angry with him?"

"Because I really think he didn't know any better."

This, then, was the key: Because her father hadn't known any better, because he had not meant to addict his daughter to alcohol, she could forgive him and remain lovingly connected to him. (Kim said she spoke to her father, who lives in Mexico, at least two or three times a day.) The logic was impeccable, if astoundingly benevolent. And I marveled at Kim's capacity to separate her father's dissolute ways from the ways he showed his love for her.

"Last year, I started getting these hives," Kim said. "They ran all kinds of tests and everything came out negative. It was stress related. The fourth time I ended up in the emergency room, my father dropped everything he had in his hands and took a plane to be with me for a month and a half. I really know that no matter what I am going through, he is going to be right here if I need him." (Kim said her father's nanny came, too.)

So imagine your father is a very wealthy man who has chosen to spend most of his life in a drunken stupor and got you hooked on booze when you were eleven. Do you continue to love him? Do you talk to him several times a day? Do you even maintain a relationship with him? And if you do, does he deserve the effort you'd have to put into it?

Who's to say?

Both Kim and Taryn said yes. To reconcile a parent's destructive actions with his loving ones requires not only a compassionate, forgiving heart but also an unsentimental head; Kim and Taryn had both. Both women were survivors and had found a way to embrace the good in their fathers without denying the bad. Kim summed it up at the end of the interview when I asked her which of her parents she felt most similar to. She said, "Neither. I see in them what I don't want in my life, let's put it that way."

I couldn't have put it better myself.

[PART II]

Daughters and Fathers:
When Something Goes Right

The thing to remember about fathers is, they're men.
—PHYLLIS MCGINLEY, AMERICAN POET AND AUTHOR (1905–1978) [1]

It doesn't matter who my father was; it matters who I remember he was.
—ANNE SEXTON, AMERICAN POET (1928–1974) [2]

CHAPTER 3

Fathers Don't Have to Be Perfect to Be Good Dads

I N this section, you will read about six women for whom something went very right when it came to what they got from their fathers. When I say "something," that's what I mean: *Something* went right, not everything, not most things, not even necessarily a lot of things. But in my view, something these fathers did, whether deliberately or not, mindfully or not, lovingly or not—imbued their daughters with autonomy, sense of self, confidence, motivation, appreciation of their bodies, delight in their minds, and a capacity to love and be loved, in any or all combinations therein.

I chose to explore these particular daughters and fathers because there was something in each man's contribution that fomented a distinct outcome in his child. One father conferred authority on his daughter by granting her a title in his business and insisting that she accept it despite her misgivings. Another made his daughter feel seen and significant by always listening to her, which meant so much to her that she chose a career in which

she listens to people in order to help them (which she finds rewarding). These fathers' contributions stood out not because they were
utterly unique in the annals of childrearing; quite the contrary.
The things these men did were organic outgrowths of who they
were and what they had lived through, things available to any
father taking an active interest in his daughter's growing self.
These contributions stood out because, in each case, something in
the dynamic between father and daughter accrued to the daughter's advantage in a singular, identifiable way.

Which is not to say that mothers had no influence over their
daughters' lives. All the daughters profiled in this section had
mothers who undoubtedly made their own singular contributions
to their children's upbringing. Whereas some of these mothers
enjoyed their daughters' admiration and respect, others' accomplishments were perceived by their daughters as less noteworthy
than their fathers', usually in cases where mothers had forsaken
careers to stay home with the kids. While most mothers figured
prominently in their daughters' perceptions of what made them
who they were, a few sounded almost marginal, exerting much
less influence on their daughters' self-concepts than the fathers
did. But whatever a daughter's perceptions may have been and no
matter how much or how little they may have comported with
reality, my scant attention to the distaff side of the equation does
not indicate a lack of acknowledgment of, or respect for, what a
mother brings to the profoundly rewarding and exhausting process of childrearing. Even though my kids are now officially
grown, I am amply aware of all I did to rear them, just as I am
aware of how much mothers all over the world do every minute of
every day for their children.

That's precisely the point: Most of us are aware of the innu-
merable, immeasurable things that mothers do for their kids, an
awareness bolstered by reams of scientific research, critical essays,
and an array of women's magazines offering tips on how to prepare

quick and delicious low-fat meals your family will love while nursing your infant, working from home, and helping your future Rhodes scholars with their homework. But few of us are aware of the things that fathers do for their children beyond tossing the legendary football around the backyard and running behind the wobbly two-wheeler after the training wheels come off. One woman I know who occasionally traveled for business when her sons were little described the startled looks she'd get when she'd mention that she had two preschoolers at home. "People would ask, 'Who's taking care of the kids?' as if I'd left them tethered to a tree in the front yard with a box of Lucky Charms. When I'd tell people they were with their dad, they'd look flummoxed, as if it had never occurred to them that a father was capable of supervising an excursion to the potty or whipping up a pot of macaroni and cheese." But wait, you may be thinking—weren't people just responding to the idea that the father was probably at work all day and unable to tend the kids? To which I say, hooey! When a man travels for business and mentions his kids, do people get all concerned and ask him who's taking care of them? No, they do not, because they assume they're at home with their mother who, it is also assumed, can satisfy any professional obligations she may have and take care of kids at the same time. It's a bias we hold dear to our child-centered hearts: When it comes to kids, no one is as competent as a mom; a dad will do, but only when a mom isn't available. It's a view I became aware of when my kids were little and have become increasingly familiar with.

Throughout my son's and daughter's childhoods, folks credited me with doing the bulk of the childrearing tasks, which was accurate: My husband's career limited the time he could spend at home, requiring him to travel extensively and work long days and occasional nights and weekends for many of his fathering years. Twice, when he started new jobs, he lived on one side of the country for months at a time while the kids and I lived on the other, with him shuttling home on most weekends and holidays. But when my daughter was twelve and my husband was between jobs for a while, he became part of her life in ways that hard-driving businessmen don't always get to experience. It was a wonderful thing for them, if not always for me.

This loving, energetic father was suddenly encroaching on my turf. The time he spent with our daughter—joining her for breakfast, chaperoning class trips, driving her to practices—those bonding experiences had heretofore been hers and mine alone. I was the one who knew she liked a bagel and cream cheese in the morning. I was the one who accompanied her class on its annual visit to the San Francisco Exploratorium. I was the one who reminded her to stuff her shin guards into her backpack. I was the one, period. Worse, having grown up without a committed father figure in the house, I had no intimate knowledge of how two-parent families functioned when rearing a girl. I'd helped bring up a boy fourteen years earlier, but this was uncharted territory. The more time my husband spent with our daughter, the more it felt as if it was a competition, him versus me.

My husband soon took another job and I resumed my rightful place in the exclusive society of mothers and daughters. But our family's brief sojourn as a mom-and-pop operation yanked the blinders from my mommy-centric eyes: My husband had brought plenty to the table, including a new ritual of visiting a certain coffee bistro near our house to which he and our daughter would repair for early morning java infusions, hers heavier on the milk than the java. This was something I had never done with her; my husband was not substituting for me, but creating an original experience with our daughter that was of their making alone. I had no part in it, nor was my presence missed.

That's what made this time so uncomfortable for me, and so instructive. My husband wasn't acting as a stand-in because I wasn't available, bumbling about ineptly as fathers typically do on

TV and in commercials to the delight of gullible audiences every-where. Instead, he was offering our daughter something I could not: the experience of interacting with a man whose energy, per-ceptions, and way of thinking were different from but no less valid, compelling, and praiseworthy than mine.

That was then. Now, fathers are far more involved in family life than they were even when my kids were little, taking parental leave when babies are born or family members become ill; some-times declining to work late and leaving early to attend class plays, concerts, and soccer games; agreeing to be the trailing spouse when their wives relocate for new jobs more lucrative and satisfac-tory than their own; and insisting on joint custody of the kids rather than two weekends a month when negotiating divorce set-tlements. Fathers are not only highly present in their children's lives, but also mindful of the value of a masculine presence there. When best-selling author Bruce Feiler was diagnosed in 2008 with a rare, life-threatening cancer, his greatest worry was that his young twin daughters might grow up without him. "Would they wonder who I was?" he wrote. "Would they wonder what I thought? Would they yearn for my approval, my discipline, my love?" In a recently published memoir, he described how he dealt with this worry by enlisting six of his closest friends—"the men who traveled with me, studied with me, have been through pain and happiness with me"—to compose a council of dads to stand in for him in his daughters' lives should he not be there himself.[1]

But there is also a downside to fatherly involvement. Fathers are now venturing into the no-man's-land formerly reserved for mothers, that nether region of conflicting obligations, torn loyal-ties, and the sinking feeling that no matter how late you work or how much you do, you're doomed to mediocrity as both a parent and a professional. It's a feeling working mothers have long been familiar with. But some new research indicates that it is becoming all too familiar to fathers, too.

According to a 2008 report from the Families and Work Institute in New York City, in families where both partners work outside the home, 59 percent of fathers said they felt some degree of conflict between work and family demands, compared to only 45 percent of mothers.[2] That a greater percentage of fathers than mothers admitted to feeling conflicted could mean any of a number of things, among them that compared to moms, dads are feeling the stress more keenly as opposed to actually enduring more stress. I can easily imagine this being the case. Working mothers have been torn between business and family obligations for decades, are more inured to the accompanying angst, more familiar with ways to relieve it, and may have a higher threshold for the feeling than their male counterparts.

Or it could mean that working dads are actually more stressed out than working moms. I can imagine this as well, especially when the father is the main wage earner in the family and knows that it's his paycheck and not his wife's that covers the rent. Here's a man who wants to be a good provider for his family and a loving nurturer to his kids; how is he supposed to keep his supervisor *and* his family satisfied?

"'The conflict is newer to men, and it feels bigger than the same amount of conflict might feel to a woman,'" said Ellen Galinsky, president of the Families and Work Institute. "'Women have been doing it for a longer time, and they have more role models.'"[3]

Men also are less likely than women to ask for time off from work. In *The New Dad*, a 2010 study from Boston College, researchers found that men were far less likely than women to ask their supervisors outright for time off to fulfill family obligations. Instead, men ducked out of work to pick up kids from day care or accompany them to doctor's appointments.[4] The reasons for this are as yet undefined, but I suspect they include our professional culture's lack of regard for workers who attend to family responsibilities during business hours. Women have long borne the brunt of this bias and suffered an erosion of their professional reputations and prospects as a result. It's no wonder, then, that men are reluctant to be tarred with the same brush. It's bad enough when a woman acts like a mom at work, but far worse when a man acts like a dad. Better to fulfill his fatherly responsibilities without calling attention to himself.

Which may be the reason that some of men's household contributions go unnoticed, especially where kids are concerned. New research is offering scientific proof of what women have known for years: Fathers interact differently with kids than mothers do. But what's new is the value now placed on the ways fathers interact with kids—for example, by working on cars while their sons or daughters look on. In the past, women typically saw this as yet another three-hour bonanza their husbands squandered working on the jalopy, whereas now we are recognizing that this is a legitimate bonding activity between fathers and their kids, albeit one that usually doesn't involve mom. Which, not incidentally, probably accounts for its having been discounted for so long: If an activity wasn't obviously child-oriented and didn't involve a mother, it didn't really count as kid friendly.

"'Dads tend to discipline differently, use humor more and use play differently. Fathers want to show kids what's going on outside their mother's arms, to get their kids ready for the outside world,'" said psychiatrist Kyle Pruett, MD, about a 2009 study he coauthored on how to encourage low-income fathers to become more involved in their children's lives.[5]

Philip A. Cowan, PhD, emeritus professor of psychology at the University of California at Berkeley and another coauthor of the study, made the point that fathers are routinely sent the message that involvement in children's lives is women's work. "'The walls in family resource centers are pink, there are women's magazines in the waiting room, the mother's name is on the files, and the home visitor asks for the mother if the father answers the door,'" he said. "'It's like fathers are not there.'"[6]

The same might be said for what goes on at back-to-school

nights across the land. One working mother I know described how she would show up with her husband at these events and, after being exhorted by the teacher to volunteer in the classroom, would see "Room Mother" emblazoned at the top of the sign-up sheet. "It drove me crazy," she said. "Every year, I'd cross it out and write 'Room *Parent*.' It was such a double-whammy: Not only are mothers guilt-tripped into feeling obligated to volunteer for the job, but fathers are discreetly informed that they're not wanted."

Not that dads have any more spare time than moms to devote to volunteering. Today, couples work an average of 63 hours a week between the two of them, compared to 52½ hours in 1970. Only four couples out of ten have one partner at home full-time, compared to seven out of ten in 1970, when that partner was almost certainly the wife.[7] Everyone is racing to keep up with work while trying to keep the household running, and today's husbands are doing a lot more laundry and diaper changing than they saw their fathers do. Still, they are neophytes compared to their wives. In couples where both partners have paying jobs, the man logs about sixteen hours a week on housework compared to an average of twenty-eight hours—75 percent more—for the woman.[8]

So, yes, women are still spending more time than men on household chores. And a lot of that time is psychological: planning meals; creating shopping lists; remembering which kid needs to be dropped off, picked up, or otherwise transported from one location to another. These exertions are as invisible as they are frequently unacknowledged. A man may spend time grilling hot dogs and burgers for his kid's birthday party but not realize how much time his wife spent planning the menu, the guest list, party games, and goody bags.

But it works the other way, too. All too often, women are oblivious to what their menfolk do to help out. "'Women consistently underestimate how much their husbands do,'" said Stephanie

Coontz, PhD, a marriage historian. "'Women don't necessarily give his contribution the same value as theirs. They don't always recognize that what he does with the kids is a form of care, too.'"[9]

Which is what this part of the book is about: the forms of care that dads provide their daughters that often go unnoticed and unacknowledged. The fathers profiled in this section were present in ways that their daughters noted and remembered, in detail and with fondness, and for which they were still grateful—in some cases, extravagantly so. Even so, there were frustrations and complaints, much as you would expect in any such relationship: One highly accomplished woman, beset by tragedy both as a child and as an adult, said she never felt she achieved enough to please her dad; another woman, in whose life religion and spirituality play a significant role, expressed impatience with her father's conservative politics and what she considered intolerant religious views. Still, each woman emerged from her girlhood into full, expansive womanhood, sure of herself in ways that her father helped define. I had always wondered how fathers managed to do this. These women's stories gave me a clue.

CHAPTER 4

A Father Who Encouraged His Daughter to Take Risks and Think for Herself

He always gave me a little more freedom than I was comfortable with.
—FRAN, 32, PHYSICIST

T HERE'S a greeting card designed by a comic genius named Eric Decetis that always makes me smile. It shows a generously proportioned woman kneeling in the sand, slathering her little boy with sunscreen as he prepares for a day at the beach. He stands motionless, sun hat on his head, ointment on his nose, face obscured by sunglasses, arms thrust akimbo by inflated water wings, torso engulfed in a life jacket, right ankle secured to a beach umbrella by a short, thick cord. As he holds his mouth in a straight, stoic line, his beaming mother coos, "There you go, honey. Have fun."

It's a hilarious send-up of the culture of protection—many would say overprotection—that pervades our childrearing ethos. When I was growing up, kids walked to school, rode city buses and bicycles outside their neighborhoods (sans helmets), traveled in cars without seat belts, and usually survived to adulthood without being disinfected several times a day with antibacterial soaps and wipes. Parents let kids out of the house without coating them with sunscreen, and let themselves out for the evening without benefit of cell phones and pagers. "We'll be at Wing Luck," they'd tell the uncredentialed twelve-year-old who showed up to babysit for fifty cents an hour. "Call the restaurant if there's an emergency." But now we worry about everything, and we are passing the legacy on to our children. Two women I interviewed castigated their fathers for failing to apply sunscreen to them during postdivorce visits. There was no mistaking their indignation: Their fathers had neglected to protect them adequately, and they neither forgot the lapse nor forgave them for it.

Don't get me wrong, I have nothing against sunscreen. I have applied it over the years to all members of my family and use it myself. But we sometimes go too far in trying to protect kids from any and all harm, and I believe we crossed that Rubicon a while ago. When high school sophomores are required to wear goggles during earth science class—to handle *rocks*—you've got to wonder what it is, exactly, that we're trying to protect our kids from. ' In that class, what they were protected from was a close look at what they were supposed to be looking at: a slab of granite or some equally fearsome substance that most sane people, parents included, would declare perfectly safe. In short, they were overprotected from living their lives.

Which is something that Fran's father made sure didn't happen to her.

"In Southern California there are these hills that are green for about two weeks of the year and brown the rest of the time," Fran told me. "We loved to go hiking up them. I think parents these days would never consider letting their kids do this, but when I was ten or eleven, my parents let us pack a lunch. My brother and I and some of the other kids in the neighborhood who were our age would go hiking. They made us wear these whistles, and the idea was if we ever got hurt, we would whistle really loud and they'd come find us. These hills weren't dangerous, but we saw rattlesnakes and there were coyotes around, though not during the day. One time, our friend fell down between these two boulders and hurt his ankle badly. There were about six of us there and we blew our whistles together over and over. To this day, I'm amazed at how fast my dad showed up. He came bounding up the hill, Paul Bunyan–like, running to see what was wrong. It's maybe not as far away as I thought when I was a kid, but it was probably a good half a mile from where our house was. They trusted us to do that. That's the only time I ever remember anything going wrong, but he was there very quickly. You could tell he'd been listening. People these days might think it was negligent parenting. But it taught us to have a sense of adventure and independence from our parents."

I envisioned a clutch of red-faced girls and boys, cheeks puffed and eyes a-squint, blasting their whistles and asked myself, what is right with this picture? Lots of things, I decided, not least the liberating effect it had on the woman who was telling the story. Of all the elements of her upbringing that Fran described, I believe her father's emphasis on independence, both in thought and action, catalyzed her will to shape a life conforming to her truest, purest self.

The elder of two children, Fran was born in California, where the family lived until she was fourteen and her brother was twelve. Her father, an architectural carpenter, crafted fine wooden pieces for upscale homes and restaurants along the California coast; her mother stayed home with Fran and her brother, with occasional stints as a preschool teacher and purveyor of Tupperware products. (Fran noted that her mother has since gone back to college and completed her degree. She now works as a certified occupational therapy assistant, the career she'd had her eye on before deciding to marry and have kids.)

Fran said she enjoyed a close relationship with her mother

while she was growing up, with one exception. "As a teenager, I was probably closer to my dad than my mom," she said. "I would say the ugliest, snottiest things to my mom—total attitude. I thought, *I am so nice to my teachers and my friends. I am never like this to anyone else. Why am I so awful to my mom?* You know a mother's love is not going to waver, so maybe you feel you can take it out on her." (Note to women who are either currently mothers of teenagers or contemplating a future as such: Tattoo that on your memory. They're awful to us because they know we love them. Repeat as required.)

Still it was Fran's relationship with her father to which she attributed her interest in science ("We had an aboveground pool. When we had earthquakes, I remember him running to the back door and calling us over to come look and see if water was splashing out"), her sense of humor, and her passion for original, independent thinking.

"I had a real curiosity about the world around me, especially that questioning attitude that my dad taught us," she said. "I took physics on a whim when I was a freshman in college. I didn't have it in high school, and in some ways I am glad I didn't, because I didn't develop an aversion to it like so many people do at that age. When I took it, it really clicked with me as being so interesting, as being a way math can be applied to find out about the world around us. To me that was exciting, to have mathematical equations that corresponded to real things." Of all the ways I've heard physics described, Fran's description made it sound the most appealing and approachable. A physics professor I know says that when he meets people for the first time and they hear what he does for a living, nine out of ten groan and say, "Oh, I hated physics!" and the remaining one says, "Oh, I hate you!"—ostensibly because she or he finds incomprehensible what the beleaguered professor finds as easy as, well, pi. But who bears responsibility for perpetuating this bias? How many of us—girls and women especially—have avoided science in general and physics in particular because we have been told over and over again that it is impossible to understand? And how many of us, refusing to be intimidated, have sallied forth onto the fields of scientific inquiry to see for ourselves whether or not we can handle it?

Fran did. Here was a woman open to the notion that she could handle a college physics class and, once she was there, found a way of conceptualizing the material that enabled her to understand it. Understanding led to fascination, which blossomed into passion, which motivated Fran to earn bachelor's, master's, and doctoral degrees in physics, with time off after college to do something completely different. "When I graduated with my bachelor's degree, I went on a road trip and then got a job landscaping. That was a good mental break, and I enjoyed the manual labor." Fran said she learned years later that her dad had been nervous about her taking time off between college and graduate school, but that he kept his misgivings to himself. My guess is that he didn't want to second-guess her decision: He was the one, after all, who had taught her to think for herself. He was also the one, as you may have guessed, who had taught his daughter that the sky was green and the grass was purple. Another thought I had was that he understood that people who work with their heads also need to work with their hands, wisdom his daughter would find useful in her career as a rocket scientist.

"One thing I learned from my dad was what one of my professors somewhat pejoratively called 'a penchant for manual labor,'" Fran said. "My dad has an extremely hard work ethic. He kept up the yard, the cars, his boat. In my day-to-day goings-on at work, sometimes I'm in front of my computer, but sometimes I am on my hands and knees in the basement running cables or plumbing hardware to run gases to a model. I really enjoy that hands-on part of the job. When I was little, my dad would let me come into the garage with him to help him work on cars. I'd hold the light for him or bring him his tools when he asked for them. When I walk into a Lowe's or Home Depot, I like that smell. It brings back good memories for me of trips to the hardware store with my dad."

It's an image I love, this father trolling the aisles of a hardware store with his little girl who, twenty years hence, would be a physicist at one of NASA's aeronautical research facilities.

"I work at a wind tunnel, several wind tunnels, in fact, with a group that does measurements," Fran continued.[2] "Some people do measurements where they're looking at surface heating, heat flux, or surface pressure. Our group looks at the flow around the model, so we are interested in turbulent phenomena, especially in hypersonics, which is roughly somewhere more than Mach 3 or Mach 5." I was with her so far. Sort of.

"What's a wind tunnel?" I asked.

"When you want to test airplane models or space models, you can build flyable models, but especially for supersonic speeds, it's easier to test a smaller model on the ground. On one side, we essentially have a reservoir of really high-pressure gas—imagine the kind of tanks that you fill helium balloons with, but just a lot of them and a lot bigger. On the other side we have these giant vacuum spheres—they look kind of like mini–Epcot Centers—where they suck all the air out of them down to a vacuum. The wind tunnel is the portion in the middle, between the high pressure and the low pressure. As the name implies, it's really windy in there. The wind tunnel I'm currently working in is a Mach 10. So they're able to test these models for various things, like aerodynamic forces or various interactions of shock waves. They test to see if experiments agree before building full-scale models."

I was still with her—not that I could quantify the difference between Machs 3, 5, and 10—but I could picture the wind tunnel and understand the technology behind it. As much as I'd like to attribute this to my familiarity with the laws of physics, I think it's more likely due to Fran's picturesque description, which used imagery rather than equations to convey its essence. It was, it seemed to me, a description minted in the mind of someone who liked to work with her hands.

Fran spoke admiringly of both of her parents, crediting them with making her feel valued not for what she achieved, but for who she inherently was, and praising their respect for their children's autonomy. "They always had this sense of us being independent people," Fran said. "It wasn't their job to form us, but rather ours to figure out who we were. I think I benefited from that. Whatever I set my hands to, they encouraged me to do. They signed me up for piano lessons and I did that for a while. It wasn't my favorite, so they let me give it up after a year or two. I was a dancer for a while. I regret that I gave that up, but I hated getting ready and putting on my leotard, although once I was there, I loved it. I feel like I could have chosen any path and I would have had their blessing." This was instructive: Fran's parents encouraged their daughter's interests, yet allowed her to abandon them when her enthusiasm waned. Some parents would reject this philosophy, arguing that children don't know what's best for them and that it is a parent's job to introduce, encourage, and enforce those interests they think are best for their kids. Plenty of adults regret never having learned to play the piano or speak a foreign language when they were young, and they don't want their own kids to make the same mistake.

But Fran's parents weren't worried that she might regret dropping piano and ballet lessons; somewhere along the line, they decided it was their daughter's responsibility to pursue her interests, not theirs to foist them upon her. And Fran got the message. Her way of describing her fledgling ballet career—"I was a dancer for a while. I regret that I gave that up, but I hated getting ready"—places herself at the center of the decision: She was the one who gave up ballet, and she is the one who regrets it. I heard not a hint of resentment or any suggestion that she thought her parents should have done anything differently. What I heard was an adult holding her childhood self responsible for a decision she had made and later came to regret.

How does someone become this way? How does it happen that some people see themselves as the directors of their lives while others see themselves as mere extras who are told what to do, where to move, and what to say? How did Fran, who never took a physics course until college, end up with a PhD in the subject and working as a physicist in a top research laboratory, loving the work and holding her own among scores of men?

I think her father had a lot to do with it.

"I think that all the time I got to spend with my dad doing things like camping, sailing, working on the car, working in the yard, and learning how to use power tools made me very comfortable working with men," Fran said. "It is most decidedly a predominantly male workplace, but luckily, I feel at ease working in that environment. I've never felt out of place in my chosen field.

"One thing my dad noticed early on was that I was extremely competitive and very strong-willed. That can be a positive thing or it can be a negative thing. As a kid, I remember when we would play games—Monopoly or anything like that—he would never let us win, my brother or me. He always played the best he could. It's surprising to me now to watch parents play with their kids and let them get the advantage. I remember beating my dad at checkers for the first time at seven years old and I was very satisfied with that because I knew I'd won it fair and square."

This put me in mind of the self-esteem culture that informs kids' sports today: Every kid gets a trophy, no matter how well she plays or how poorly the team does. The team can lose left and right and never make it to the playoffs, let alone the championship, but no matter; every kid gets a trophy. It's supposed to make them feel good, but I believe it makes them feel something else: that they are entitled to praise and recognition for merely showing up. Making an appearance is good, but in real life you don't get rewarded for just showing up. The rewards come when you work hard and accomplish something, and I don't think we do our kids any favors by teaching them otherwise.

Fran's father taught her to own her accomplishments. And by not talking down to her, he implied that he trusted her ability to grasp concepts that often elude adults. "One day, I asked him how TV worked," Fran said. "I was probably five or six years old. He gave me a pretty in-depth explanation for my age, explaining how things were filmed; how the signal was broadcast through the air; how the antennae picked up the signal; how the picture was decoded, reconstructed, and projected onto the back of the TV screen with an electron gun. When he finished, I looked at him, smiled, and said, 'Oh, Daddy! Mom, how does TV work?' It must have sounded too much like magic to me, images flying through the air and all that. He'd made me a good skeptic. And, of course, being a good skeptic is essential to being a good scientist."

I am convinced that this father's belief in his daughter's intelligence fueled her urge to compete and emerge victorious. When Fran finally beat her dad at checkers, she knew the win was real, that she had actually played better than he had, and that's what made her feel satisfied. Had he established a precedent of playing less than his best and allowing her to win, Fran would not have been able to trust that her eventual triumph was real; the trophy would ring hollow. But because she knew she had beaten her dad fair and square, she was primed, at the age of seven, to trust her competence and own her success.

Which is not to say that she was always eager to take risks. This was another area in which Fran received more than a casual nudge from her parents generally and her dad specifically. This story dates from a couple of years after the family relocated from

California to Colorado, and it made me feel like an amateur in the urge-your-daughter-to-take-risks sweepstakes.

"One thing they did for me was, they always gave me a little more freedom than I was comfortable with," Fran said. "When I was sixteen, I had had my [driver's] license for all of a month. My brother really wanted to go snowboarding. He was fourteen or thirteen. Our neighbor was his age and wanted to go, too. My parents weren't in the mood to go skiing that weekend, so they said, 'Why don't you take them?' I was like, 'It's going to be mountain driving, with snow.' They said, 'We trust you.' My dad took me out and we drove in some parking lots. I learned how to recover from a skid. We did a little driving on some curvy roads around town. I remember going on that trip, driving on roads with no guard rails, thinking, *I don't have to do anything to kill all of us in this car; all I have to do is* not *do something. If I just don't turn the wheel, over the side we go!* I was thinking, *This was a lot of responsibility they gave me. A lot of trust.*

"My dad, I think it was partly his sense of humor and partly his parenting technique [that] I never had an established curfew, but if I was going out with friends, he'd ask, 'What time do you expect to be home?' I'd say, 'Probably ten, ten thirty.' He'd say, 'Well, be home no later than eleven fifteen.' He'd always tack on a little time. The deal was that when I came home, I had to come in and kiss my mom good night and close their door. If I was going to be more than fifteen minutes later than what we had said, I was supposed to call and update my time, with the understanding that if I didn't show up, they would start looking for me. And that happened exactly once. My car broke down. They started making phone calls when I was about fifteen minutes late. This was the era before cell phones, of course. They came looking for me. I was a good kid for the most part, and I don't think I ever broke their trust. They were willing to hold the reins very loosely as long as I didn't."

I confess that allowing a sixteen-year-old to drive her kid brother and his friend across the Colorado mountains in the snow falls a little outside my own parental comfort zone, but I suppose that was precisely the point: Fran was outside her comfort zone when she did it, too. It was because her parents said they trusted her—and because her father supervised her skidding hither and yon in assorted icy parking lots before she embarked on the drive—that she was able to muster her courage and self-confidence, fulfill their high expectations, and take the boys snowboarding.

After the interview, Fran uploaded photos from her wedding several years earlier on the banks of a river in a wooded state park. The groom (tall, dark, and handsome in an unstudied way) sported a loose dark suit and black Birkenstocks; Fran wore a white satin gown that she had sewn herself. About five foot ten with her dark blonde hair looped in ringlets atop her head, she smiled with a vigor that leapt off the screen, especially in a shot where she canted sideways clutching her veil, which, tossed by a gust of wind, had caught on something as she walked to meet her groom. There was an unself-conscious energy to the gesture: This wasn't a frothy, ethereal bride but an earthly one, grabbing at the headdress lest it yank her hairdo out of whack (as might happen in, say, a wind tunnel). There was also a shot of Fran and her father walking toward the wooden platform where the bridal attendants, groomsmen, and groom waited. They were both grinning. The photo captured a feeling of exuberance and intimacy, public cheer and private understanding. It wasn't maudlin or teary, nor was it staged. It was a candid moment between father and daughter, and it looked real.

Fran met her husband, a medical evacuation helicopter pilot, when they were both undergraduates. Today, on the eve of their fourth wedding anniversary, they are parents of an eighteen-month-old daughter and sharing child-care duty. Chris's work schedule calls for him to be at home three days and four nights a week, so on the days he is at home, Fran puts in ten-hour days at the lab; when Chris is away, she works from home. She said she enjoys the support of her supervisor and coworkers, who foster a flexible environment that enables young scientists such as herself to have both a family and a career. She also attributes some of her marital accord to what she saw at home as a child.

"I'm grateful for the relationship that I now have with my husband. I attribute a lot of it to the way I saw my dad treat my mom. He still opens doors for her. It's half a joke between them, because she doesn't care, but he wants to play the gallant part. They still hold hands when they go on walks. I've never heard him belittle her in any way or criticize her in front of other people. Even though I can tell that sometimes something she says has irritated him or vice versa, he's always been very respectful of her. I think I grew up expecting that from the men in my life."

To me, Fran is a perfect example of a woman whose competence and self-confidence are directly traceable to her relationship with her dad. So thoroughly did he urge her to have a mind of her own that he now occasionally finds himself on the business end of her intellect over what she sees as his growing conservatism. Fran, who described herself as a nondenominational Christian, said that the conservative trend in the United States was frustrating to her. "One of the things Jesus did was reach out to people who the religious establishment had rejected: the woman caught in adultery, the tax collectors, people like that. So my dad and I have gotten into it over issues of gay marriage, for example. He's started listening to talk radio. He'll tease me a little about moving to the East Coast and becoming a liberal. I feel like if I could talk to my dad from fifteen years ago, he would agree with me more." Fran allowed that maybe she's the one who has changed rather than her father, but she remained adamant about her interpretation of her faith. She said that when she was growing up, religion had had a

negative connotation for her because it implied a ritualistic adher-
ence to a set of doctrines and practices, but now, it felt more
organic. The biggest way religion was influencing her life, she
said, was that she and her husband were involved in an outreach
program for the homeless in their area.

Fran was living as a Christian and practicing her faith, yet had
a different take on it than her father did. This struck me as the apo-
theosis of the green-sky, purple-grass training he had put her
through. When she first told me about this eccentricity of her father's,
I asked where she thought he'd gotten the idea from. Her answer
was, now that I think about it, an articulate description of the philosophy that guided her upbringing and shaped her life.

"He wanted to teach us to question what we were told, in a
respectful way. When we came home from school, he'd ask us
what we'd learned. If we told him something, he'd say, 'Do you
think that's true?' I'd say, 'My teacher said so.' He'd say, 'It's good
to trust your teacher, but what do you think?' You should question your elders in a respectful way, you should find knowledge
for yourself: That was bred into us from a young age. That has
been one of the biggest influences in my life. The way I look at the
world is with that mind-set: Have knowledge for yourself, especially in matters of faith. It's surprising, as I've gotten older, the
number of people who just accept what their parents believed or
just continue going to the same place their parents went. My parents, especially my dad, drilled into us pretty firmly that these are
our beliefs, but you have to discover what you think about the
world around you—particularly about something like God. That
is not a transferrable kind of knowledge."

CHAPTER 5

A Father Who Answered His Daughter's Endless Questions

I have a mouth. I've always had a mouth. My favorite question was "But why?" Whereas my mother would take it as me talking back or trying to be flippant, my father would answer my "but why" questions.

—JACQUELINE, 42, FAMILY THERAPIST

I T makes complete sense, I suppose, that a girl who grew up questioning everything should end up listening for a living. If you were the youngest of four daughters, as Jacqueline was, you got to see a lot of what a girl's life was like before you got to actually live your own. Unless, as was the case with Jacqueline, you also got to spend Monday afternoons with your dad when you were in kindergarten. Then you found out something about what a man's life was like, too.

"When I was dating my husband, he told me I could hammer better than a lot of men," Jacqueline said. "My sister Toni will pick up a hammer to hang a picture, but putting a bookshelf together, no, she's not going to do that. And Sharon or Gwen? No. They'd be shopping instead." A trill of laughter rippled across the telephone line.

Jacqueline grew up in Detroit, where she still lives with her husband of eleven years, a diagnostic medical sonographer and photographer ("He'd just say photographer," Jacqueline said), and their sons, ages nine and six. I was charmed by her self-effacing sense of humor, which surfaced in the first thirty seconds of the interview when I asked some routine questions.

"So, Jacqueline," I said, "what are your race and ethnic background?"

"My race is African American. Ethnicity is a mix. I'm a mutt: I'm African American, Native American. And please call me Jackie—everyone else does."

"Okay, Jackie. What is your political affiliation?"

"I'm a big Democrat."

"Are you religious?"

"I'm Christian."

"Are you a practicing Christian?" (What I was after here was whether or not she attended church regularly.)

"I try to be." Laughter on the line. Point taken.

I interviewed Jackie over the telephone in two segments: The first, at her office, had to end when a couple arrived for a therapy session; the second took place the next day when she was at home and the schools were closed because of a snowstorm. When speaking from her office, she was spontaneous, lively, and open; the next day, at home, she seemed more measured and guarded, which may have been because her sons were within earshot of our conversation. Both times she was poised, articulate, and self-confident. She laughed easily and often; sometimes, it seemed, to defuse discomfort engendered by a question I had asked. For the most part, however, her responses felt spontaneous and candid.

Jackie's father was well into his eighties and retired when we spoke, but he had owned a restaurant when Jackie was growing up, a small, busy neighborhood place that catered to the lunchtime crowd during the week and families on the weekends. I asked her if her father had been around when she was growing up.

"He worked a lot," Jackie said. "He worked long hours, but he was a phone call away. Literally, I called him five or ten times a day, so I was constantly talking to him when he was at work."

"What kinds of things would you call him about?" I asked. Jackie laughed.

"'Can I cook a hamburger?' 'Can I go outside?' 'Can I walk to my cousin's house?' 'So, Dad, whatcha doin'?'" I asked Jackie why she hadn't just asked her mother instead.

"I really wanted to talk to my dad. And my mother went to work when I turned five. She worked at a store called Hudson's, which then became Marshall Field's and is now Macy's. When I went to kindergarten, I was on half days, and on Mondays my dad would pick me up from school and I'd spend the rest of the day with him because the restaurant was closed on Monday."

"You felt more comfortable with him than with your mom?"

"I think I felt equally comfortable with them. But I think I just felt like dad understood me more, and it was easier to call him. I didn't have to go through a switchboard like I did with my mom; he would pick up the phone himself."

"What do you mean that you felt he understood you more?"

"I have a mouth. I've always had a mouth. My favorite question was 'But why?' I wasn't trying to be disrespectful, but I questioned everything. Whereas my mother would take it as me talking back or trying to be flippant, my father would answer my 'but why' questions. My mother's the type where if I said, 'But why?' I'd get in trouble because it was talking back. If I went to her an hour later and said, 'Mama, I really just wanted to know,' then she'd say, 'Okay, I'm sorry, I didn't mean to yell, but I thought you were talking back.' To this day, she is the same way.

She would never hesitate to apologize if she was wrong and would say, 'If I am wrong, let me know.' But my father didn't take my curiosity as disrespect. He answered all my questions."

"Did you feel satisfied with his answers?"

"Yes, I did."

"So, you really spoke to one another? You had a conversation going?"

"Right, we really talked, growing up."

That's what went right between Jackie and her father: He listened, he answered, and they talked. No matter how many questions she peppered him with, he did not find her impertinent or disrespectful, nor, from the sound of it, did he ever act as if he was too busy to take her call. He accepted his daughter's relentless queries for what they were—manifestations of her curiosity—and provided answers that satisfied her need to know. Also, by answering her with patience and sincerity, he implicitly validated the ardor of her inquisitiveness. Jackie's father let her know that acquiring knowledge was a noble pursuit, and that it was worth both her time and energy and his to enable her to pursue it to her heart's and mind's content—which she did a great deal of when they were together.

"He would pick me up from school on Mondays. We'd go have lunch and then do any errands he had to run—the bank, you know, he had to take care of all of his transactions on Monday, because he worked from Tuesday through Sunday afternoon, when the restaurant closed at three. So Monday was the only day he had where the banks were open, or if he had to drive somewhere to pick up stuff. So I went wherever he went on Mondays. It was just the two of us, because my sisters were older and in full-day school. So after he picked me up and we got something to eat, we'd do all of his stuff. He also did odd jobs for a friend of his who had rental properties—doing plumbing and kitchen repairs, that kind of thing. So, we oftentimes went to the hardware store so he could get his stuff, and if he had to do any work on these rental properties, sometimes I would go with him."

"Did you feel special?" I asked. Jackie laughed.

"Of course I did! My sisters didn't want to go. There's an age difference. Sharon is eleven years older than I am, so when I was five, she was sixteen. She was doing what sixteen-year-olds do. Toni was fourteen so she was involved with her friends, and Gwen was eleven and wanted to stay at home to watch TV or talk on the phone. My dad and I did that stuff. . . . I don't think he preferred me to my sisters, but I was the one who learned how to hammer a nail, saw, and put things together . . . and take them apart. I was possibly the boy he didn't have. I was fine with that, because I wanted to know how to work with tools and stuff."

I was reminded of Fran's saying she loved the smell of Lowe's and Home Depot because it reminded her of going to the hardware store with her father, and how his teaching her to work with her hands had influenced the pleasure she took in her work. I believe a similar connection was forged between Jackie and her father, whose forbearance with the onslaught of her endless questions engendered her own talent for listening and fascination with human nature. This emerged frequently during the interview, often when she would talk about her father, who was adamant about the importance of education, and her mother, whom she loved and respected but said focused more on the domestic sphere.

"My dad wasn't able to complete a full high school education, so the things he learned how to do and the skills he acquired along the way, he did all of that without formalized education after eighth grade. He grew up on a farm in South Carolina and had to work the farm after his dad died. He wished he could have gone to school and gotten a degree, so he made sure that all four of us knew the importance of education. School, that was all. School. 'Get your grades. Let's get this lesson done. Let's read a book.' School. School. School."

"Did you feel pressured, or that he cared about you?" I asked.

"There wasn't any pressure, but there was 'Turn the TV off. Let's get a book. Let's figure out how to do this and that.' That was just the way it was. We did these things together. And even with my kids now, when my older son has homework and is over there, my father sits down and does homework with him, and then will even make up math problems with him."

"It doesn't sound like you were ever angry with your father."

"No, because I didn't have a reason to be. He always listened to me and didn't shut me down or accuse me of talking back or being flippant when I said 'why?'"

"Did you ever feel he was judging you or critical of you, or that he didn't love you?" I asked.

"No. Even when I screwed up. Never."

"How about your mother?"

"Oh, yes. Oh, yes. My mom instilled different things in me. She pushed education, but not as much as he did. Her thing was showing me how to do domestic things. To this day, my mother irons all my father's clothes and runs the household, keeping things organized and neat. Growing up, I knew that there was an expectation that I would do my laundry, clean my room. If it wasn't done, I would hear about it—but, it never really wasn't done. The only thing she said that I could leave undone was if I was running late for school, if I didn't make my bed up because I ran out of time, I didn't get in trouble for that. If I would even attempt to go out of the house without my hair being combed or with curlers in my hair, I would hear about it from my mom. My father bridged a lot during those rough teenage years. That was the roughest time between my mom and me, me trying to be more independent and her saying, 'No, you can't go to the movies with your friends.' He would come in and say, 'It's okay. You drop them off and I will pick them up.' So that worked.

"I remember in maybe fourth or fifth grade, one boy and I were very good friends. We hung out, we talked on the phone. In third grade, it was me, this girl Sheree, and this boy, whose name was Ben. Well, Sheree moved, so in fourth grade, Ben and I remained friends, through fourth and fifth, and then in sixth grade, he went to another school. In fourth and fifth grade, I remember him calling the house and my mom saying, 'Jacqueline can't talk to boys on the phone.' I was like, 'But mom, he's just my friend. It's like Sheree, but Sheree is gone.' I remember having that discussion and me finally talking to my father, saying, 'You know, we are just friends. I'm not liking boys like that. We're just friends.' Then I remember my father saying it was probably okay. I also remember Ben being the only boy that could call me. We stayed in contact via phone through sixth and seventh grade. He was the only boy that would call the house. Even when I got older and my mother and I clashed more, I remember my dad bridging several gaps. When I moved back home and transferred colleges and the curfew thing came up, he bridged that gap as well."

It sounded as if Jackie had enjoyed a more tender relationship with her father than with her mother, which was not uncommon among the women I interviewed who had modeled themselves on their dads. A common characteristic of this kind of father-daughter bond was an element of gentleness on the father's part, which was used, it seemed, to counterbalance a mother's strictness or less affectionate personality. For Jackie, her father's tenderness manifested in his practice of giving her baths when she was little, a ritual that ended abruptly when adolescence approached.

"My dad used to give me my baths and he played with me in the water. We used to splash and he used to shampoo my hair. When puberty started for me and he couldn't anymore, I cried. I must have been eight or nine when he stopped."

"Was it devastating?" I asked.

"I don't know that 'devastating' was the word, because he

was still there. We still did our activities. I still hung out at the restaurant after school. In the summer, I still went with him to do all his running around, and I still went with him when he had to work on the rental properties. But I knew that [the baths] weren't appropriate anymore. I don't remember us talking about it. I just remember it not happening anymore. My mother, she said, 'We're not splashing. I'm not shampooing your hair in the bathtub. We're going to do it at the sink.'"

"She wasn't nurturing like your dad?"

"In a different kind of way. It was a different kind of nurturing. She was cleaning. She wasn't doing all the cooking, because they shared that responsibility. But as far as all of the housework, taking care of the inside of the home, she did all that. She's one of sixteen kids. Her dad always prayed with them. Her mother was the disciplinarian, but very loving. I think she has modeled her parenting style after her mom. But my mother played games with me. She showed me how to play checkers. She played cards with me. To this day, we'll still sit down and play cards. She is more social. My father's more of an introvert, kind of quiet. If you're not listening, you're not going to hear what he's saying. I heard him raise his voice one time in my life, and that was at my mother. I remember they were yelling at each other, and I cried, and they both told me it was okay. When my father put his foot down, you knew that was it. He wasn't a yeller and still isn't."

Implicit in Jackie's reminiscences was an awareness of her parents' histories and what may have made them into the people they were. All too often, we are unable to imagine our mothers and fathers as the all-too-human women and men they were before they were parents; it's disorienting to think that there was a time when they were utterly indifferent to the idea of our existence and lavished love on other people, none of whom were us. But if we can put our parents and ourselves into perspective, we begin to see that they, just like us, are products of the families, cultures, and times they grew up in. And once we see that, we can begin to unravel the tangled mass of passions, mysteries, and contradictions they sometimes seem to be.

Jackie was good at this. When she spoke of her father's obsession with education, she tied it to his grief that his own schooling never progressed beyond the eighth grade. In describing her mother's more pragmatic, less playful parenting style, Jackie understood it to be a result of her mother's own upbringing in a household teeming with children. She looked at people as interconnected elements of an organic system rather than discrete entities bouncing off one another, and I believe this resulted in no small part from her feeling of connection with her father. She admired him, so she strove to be like him. And because he, in Jackie's words, bridged the gulf of understanding between her and her mother, she grew to bridge the gaps between her family members, and sometimes between them and their loved ones as well.

"Growing up, I was the one who, if my sisters and my mother were having an issue, I was the one who was called," Jackie said. "One of my brothers-in-law is, well, he's not the easiest person. He yells, he screams, he talks too loud. He and my niece, who is twenty-one, they don't have the best relationship. I'm the one my sister calls to talk to her husband. I'm the one my niece calls when she's fighting with her dad. I am the one who is called about everything."

"Think about that for a moment," I said. "Why do you think that is?"

"I don't know. Maybe because I'm a therapist, they feel I can handle it. I know how to get people to see reason without pissing them off."

"Do you feel it had anything to do with your relationship with your father, that he listened to what you said, that he valued your questions?"

"Probably. A big reason I am the way I am is because of the way he is. I try to make sure that I'm open, and if I don't understand, I ask questions. I guess I would describe myself as a peacemaker. I found my role because it was needed. My sister Toni, I don't want to call her a troublemaker, but she got in trouble. Gwen, she's extremely passive and lets things go. Me, I am going to speak my mind in a peaceable way. You're not pulling one over on me. I'm going to let you know what it is and the way it should be, but I'm not going to yell and scream about it, and I am going to be very assertive in a very nice way."

Something interesting came up toward the end of the interview, when I asked Jackie which of her parents was more likely to have comforted her when she hurt herself as a child.

"They both did," she said. "And another piece of it, my father's brother came to live with us before I was born. He stayed with my parents until he died. I can't remember what year my uncle died. He was in the home until he retired, as well. I remember being on my bike and falling, because there's a hill. I remember being bloody. There was this huge rock. Why I thought I could run over this rock on my bike, I don't know. I was really messed up—cuts and bruises everywhere. Both of my parents were at work. My uncle Teddy was there, and I remember being downstairs, on the couch, and him bandaging me up and taking care of me until my parents got home. I remember calling my dad on the phone, of course."

I don't know why Jackie neglected to mention her uncle Teddy sooner. It was probably because he was a fixture in the household whose presence didn't warrant special mention for our purposes. She didn't say any more about him, so I don't know why he came to live with his brother's family, or under what circumstances he remained there for the rest of his life. But it did seem significant that Jackie grew up with not one but two kindhearted men in the house (her sisters were all older than her and therefore had Uncle Teddy as a housemate for less time than Jackie did). It must have seemed perfectly natural to her that men should be nurturing and protective; indeed, when she told the story of her daring bicycle stunt, she said it was her father, not her mother, that her uncle called when she got hurt. When I asked Jackie if she had chosen to marry a man who was like her father, she said, "The ironic thing is I married someone who is very similar to my dad in a lot of ways. He's from South Carolina. He's very handy with his hands. He cooks well. And he used to be soft-spoken, like my dad. Then we had children." Jackie laughed, and I joined her. I knew how that went, too.

What Jackie's father may have lacked in formal education, he had more than made up for in wisdom. Somehow, he had had all the answers. And by passing them on to his daughter, he had imbued in her, and in his other daughters as well, a sense of ownership of their own selves.

"He raised me to believe that 'You can do this by yourself. You don't have to be in a relationship to do A, B, C. You can take care of yourself.' Being independent. All four of us were instilled with 'You don't have to put up with any guff from anybody. Get your education and you can stand up on your own two feet.' None of us puts up with any guff from anybody."

CHAPTER 6

A Father Who Bestowed a Mantle of Power Upon His Daughter

He felt it was important that people know that when I walk into the room, I can make a decision. So he gave me a title so that the outside world would look at me and see a decision maker.
—NINA, 30, EXECUTIVE VICE PRESIDENT OF FAMILY-OWNED EYEWEAR BUSINESS

NINA arrived half an hour late for the interview. She was tied up, she said, on an overseas conference call with her brothers and it ran long. She apologized, extended her hand, and smiled warmly. At about five foot five with straight, dark hair and blue eyes, she had a clear, direct gaze and the charm of a woman who is confident without being overbearing. During the ninety or so minutes we spent together, she gave the impression of considering each question before answering it and of speaking from her heart without censoring herself. A hint of a Southern accent flavored her speech.

I soon learned its provenance. Nina grew up in Tennessee, where her parents still lived. Her father, who was approaching seventy, ran the eyeglass frame business he had founded before Nina was born; her mother had been working for the business for a little more than a decade, since the younger of Nina's two brothers had turned sixteen. All three children worked for the company.

Nina, as executive vice president, ran the New York City office and held the highest position next to her father's. Each of her brothers was a vice president based in Asia, where the business had opened several manufacturing plants. Nina said her father had waited to build factories overseas until she and her brothers were in college because he didn't like being away from the family. "He always had a rule that he would never be away on the weekend," Nina said. "Part of why we never opened any factories in Asia until we were all grown up was because he didn't want to have to be somewhere else for two to three weeks at a time. He felt it was important to at least get home by the weekend. The things that mattered to him were my relationship with my brothers, with my grandparents. Family was very important to him."

The primacy of family was heightened, no doubt, by the fact that Nina's was the only Jewish family in the Tennessee suburb she grew up in. Her parents moved there from New York shortly after their wedding because Nina's father had located a suitable factory there for his new eyewear business. "When he chose it, he thought he would live in New York and commute," Nina said. "My parents met and got married in six months. It was quick, love at first sight. My mom grew up in Germany. She moved to New York, spoke English, but didn't know anybody in the city. After the wedding, my dad was like, 'I'm going to Knoxville on business. See ya!' She was like, 'What am I going to do all week?' She actually said, 'How bad could it be down there? Let me go check it out.' She always said that when she got married, New York was bankrupt, the city was filthy. She might not have left New York today, but when she left it, she thought she was doing a good thing."

It turned out to be a good thing for the business, but not so good for Nina's mother, who, as a German émigré, felt far more foreign in Tennessee than she had in New York. Nor did it help that Nina's parents were fairly religious, which meant that they did not drive or attend social gatherings or sporting or school events from sundown on Friday to sundown on Saturday, the Jewish Sabbath, which prevented Nina and her brothers from joining friends in a variety of activities. She said she didn't encounter any overt prejudice: "It wasn't anti-Semitism, but there was this, 'Oh, you're *Jewish*.' They'd never met a Jewish person. They were just uneducated, unaware. They just didn't know.

"It bothered me. I used to feel it wasn't fair. The big thing in high school and even junior high was Friday night football games. In the South, everybody from school goes, and your whole social life revolves around it, so it really upset me. After I got bat mitzvahed [at age thirteen, the ceremony by which a Jewish girl assumes religious responsibilities], they made this whole thing about now you are an adult and can make your own decisions, so I went to my parents and was like, 'I am my own decision maker now, I am responsible for myself, and I want to drive [on the Sabbath].' It was a whole big thing. They were like, 'But we don't drive.' We debated it for a while, but in the end, they finally said, as long as I was home for dinner on Friday nights, if I wanted to [drive], I could make my own decisions. So, I would have dinner with my family, then I'd go to the football game. They wouldn't drive me. I had to get someone else's mom to pick me up. I'm sure it upset my dad. It was really his family that was more religious. But I felt like he let me make that choice for myself, and to this day, I still drive [on the Sabbath]. My husband's like, 'Not when your dad's here. He feels bad!' But my father knows it makes me a happier person. He doesn't hold me to live the way he chooses to live."

Several things stood out in this anecdote. One was that Nina's father respected her autonomy, even when she was thirteen years old, and even when the results of her autonomy went against the family's religious practice. (At thirteen, Nina would not have been driving herself as she said. She would have been driven by a friend's parent. Still, a religious Jewish family would refrain from attending a football game or riding in a car on the Sabbath.) When you're the only family in town who's of a certain religion, it takes more energy to follow your faith than it does when you're surrounded by people who believe as you do. If you're Jewish and growing up in New York City, you don't have to worry about missing school on the High Holy Days because the schools are closed in honor of them. But when you and your siblings are the only Jewish kids in the school and you need to attend synagogue on the High Holy Days, you not only miss classes; you may also miss an important exam that you'll have to make up on your own time, not to mention lose the chance to earn a perfect attendance record. It was easy to understand how important it was for Nina's father to instill in his children a sense of their religious identity, so I appreciated his generosity of spirit in allowing Nina to make up her own mind about driving on the Sabbath (interestingly, she said both of her brothers chose to preserve the no-driving rule; she was the lone dissenter in that department).

I also appreciated how this generosity would endear him to his daughter. It showed he was willing to bend his principles out of respect for hers, especially in light of her having become a bat mitzvah, received into the Jewish community as an adult, and newly charged with making her own decisions. Had he insisted that Nina observe the Sabbath on his terms, she might have perceived this as hypocrisy: How could he usher her into adulthood in the Jewish religion yet treat her like a child when it came to deciding how to observe its rituals? By compromising with her—allowing her to go out with friends on Friday nights as long as she ate dinner with the family—he acceded to her demand for autonomy.

He also supported her when it came to sports, after a fashion.

"I played soccer," Nina continued. "My father came to all of my games and was very dedicated like that. They were always on Sunday and he would always come. I used to get upset because he would come to the game, which was sweet, but he would always bring his work. He didn't really care about the rest of the team. He wanted to watch me play and nobody else. So he would bring a briefcase full of paperwork. The mom of one of my friends on the team would tell him, 'The ball is going toward Nina,' and he would stop working and watch. When I was nowhere near the ball, he was doing his work! I told him, 'Dad, it's embarrassing.' So then he wouldn't do it, but he'd get so behind that he would bring it. Then I was sort of like, 'I guess I don't really care,' but none of the other dads would do that. Growing up in Tennessee, there was not a big Jewish community then. I was always very harried by feeling so different. I didn't get to play in Saturday games. One thing my dad always taught us was to be proud of who we were, and to be who you are and not worry about what someone else thinks. As I got older and understood that, I didn't care as much. When I was ten or twelve, it bothered me." I could see how it would. I imagined the other fathers cheering on their daughters but also being involved in the game for its own sake. And there was Nina's dad, hunched over his paperwork, getting nudged by other moms (Nina's mother did not come to her soccer games) when his daughter was about to make contact with the ball. To Nina and others as well, he must have seemed the epitome of otherness.

The theme of feeling different—not liking it as a kid but growing to appreciate the sense of individuality it conferred upon her and the closeness it conferred upon her family—recurred throughout Nina's interview. Of all of the women I interviewed, she seemed the most grateful for and satisfied with the closeness of her family, which developed a tight-knit, self-sufficient identity during Nina's childhood.

"We didn't have a lot of people around growing up, because we were very different from everybody else," Nina said. "Truly, we were a group of five. We're very happy with each other. We all get along great. We laugh and have a good time. We don't need others. My parents didn't have a lot of friends. We [the children] had friends, but it was different. On holidays, you didn't think to invite the neighbors; you weren't friends with them in that way. There's a closeness and tightness. If I need something, I call my parents or my brothers before I call a friend."

This sounded curious. When speaking of the closeness of her family, Nina used both past and present tenses. When saying she'd call her parents or her brothers if she needed something, she spoke in the present tense. But Nina was married. Why would she not call her husband if she needed something?

"If you have a big problem that's troubling you, whom would you call first?" I asked.

"Now I'd call Ethan, my husband. But it took a while. I definitely went through a phase. Up until the wedding, I probably would still call my dad. Even if something good happened, instinctively I wanted to call my dad. Then we got married and I felt like I was supposed to call my husband first. I went through this guilt over who I was going to call first. Now I don't even think about it."

"How did you work through the guilt?"

"I knew the right person should be Ethan. If I didn't want to call him first, then I shouldn't have been married to him. On the other hand, you have this history of calling your dad for thirty years. I made the decision that my dad would be upset if he knew he got the call first. He'd be like, 'Why did you call me first? You should call me second.' If I asked him, he would say that, so I would just go with that. Little by little I got into that habit, and now I don't even think about it." I marveled at Nina's bifurcated perception of the situation: Her rational side believed that a husband should supplant a father in a healthy marriage, even though her emotional side didn't completely buy it. So she remedied the conflict by doing what she thought she ought to be doing and letting the emotional underpinnings catch up later—which they did. Whether she knew it or not, Nina had enacted a textbook example of cognitive behavioral theory: She had used her thinking self—her cognition—rather than her emotions to dictate her behavior. By changing her behavior, she changed the underlying emotional structure that was causing the conflict.

I was fascinated not only by Nina's handling of the situation but also by the close bond between her and her father that it spoke of. I pressed on.

"You would call your dad before calling your mom?" I asked.

"I guess I always wanted to be more like him than my mother," Nina replied. "Even from a young age, I observed him and thought, 'That's how I want to be.' My mom has some great qualities, but I was so busy not wanting to be like her when I was young that I wouldn't have even seen those. I was very focused on my dad. Anything he did that I thought was good, I tried to copy."

I was so busy not wanting to be like her. . . . I was very focused on my dad. And I was very focused on the phenomenon of a daughter emulating her father's example and abjuring her mother's. Why did Nina reject her mother? How had it happened that, from a young age, this girl had admired her father so much more? I could see why Nina was drawn to her dad, given his respect for her independence. What was it about the family chemistry that made her mother so unappealing?

"I guess I felt like he had it together and my mom didn't," she said. "That was the key. As a kid, I thought she was not as open. My father would always hear me out and make a decision. My mother was much more 'I said so.' When I would say, 'Why can't I do it?' she'd say, 'I don't owe you an explanation.' My dad was never like that. Looking back on it, she grew up in pretty complicated circumstances. Her parents are Holocaust survivors, and they weren't really there to parent her given what they'd been through, so I don't think she knew how to handle it. Apparently, we had a fight when I was twelve or thirteen and I told her, 'You need to see somebody. You have all these issues.' She actually did [seek therapeutic help]. I think she was much better with my brothers as a result. I think she probably didn't have any clue about how to deal with any of this, because nobody was around to tell her what to do; she just did what she wanted. But my dad didn't explain that either. He's not that analytical. Even though he knew this was going on, he just compensated for it more than he took the time to figure it out."

Nina compensated at least as much as her father did, mostly by taking charge of tasks her mother might have done had she felt up to it.

"I was definitely the go-to person for everything," Nina said. "I used to book our family vacations. I would book the airlines. My mom, even to this day, she is not good with having to make decisions under pressure. So if we were going somewhere and the airline tickets had to be bought, and we had to plan when to leave and when to come back, my dad and I . . . by the time I was twelve, he would stay up with me at night and say, 'These are the dates. Call and get the tickets.' So I was sort of the organizer. I remember telling my mom, 'It's time for braces. I need braces.' 'Oh, okay, we'll go get braces.' With my brothers, I was like, 'Mom, they need braces, too.' I was making sure everything would happen when it was supposed to. If my dad needed gifts to be bought for his customers, he always had me doing it."

"Even at a young age?" I asked. Nina nodded.

"How did you know what to do?"

"That's the thing he did so well. He always made us feel we could do these things. I don't remember the first time, but he taught me how to buy a plane ticket. In those days, there wasn't the Internet. You call the travel agent, you go over the dates and the possibilities, and you do it. Same thing for gifts: 'Here is the

Tiffany account. You call Tiffany and these are the kinds of things you get for this or that occasion. You get it shipped. This is the kind of card you write.' And I did it."

Nina did it because her father needed her to do it and expected that she could do it. She lived up to his expectations—which, in my opinion, were lofty, considering her youth and inexperience. Here was another real-life manifestation of Pruett's theory of fatherly nurturing in action: By urging his daughter to operate outside her comfort zone, Nina's dad instigated her mastery of both numerous challenging tasks and her own diffidence. She learned by doing. I asked Nina why she thought her father had not asked for her mother's help instead.

"I think she was overwhelmed," Nina said. "The way she explains it today is she felt her mother never recovered from the trauma she went through. [My mom said] there were days when my grandmother just wouldn't get out of bed. My mom didn't get up in the morning, either. I would get up and make myself breakfast, get dressed, and go to school. I thought all moms slept until ten or eleven o'clock. Once, I came home from school after an exam, and I was leaving on a trip. I got home at noon and she was sitting in her bathrobe. I was like, 'Mom, what have you been doing?' She was almost confused, like she didn't know it was wrong. I don't know what she did all morning—drank her coffee, laid around, read a book? She didn't get up and do anything. She just didn't get these things."

It was clear why Nina chose to model herself on her father, who woke up in the morning, got dressed, went to work, and came home in the evening in time to greet his kids and dine with his wife. (Nina praised her mother's wifely traits, mentioning that she prepared two dinners every night, an early one for the children and a later one, served in the dining room, for herself and Nina's dad.) It also became clear as the interview progressed that Nina had begun to feel more sympathetic toward her mother than she had when she was younger, alluding to her mother's growing role in the business and mentioning that she had designed a line of new, rimless eyeglass frames that were selling well even though she, Nina, didn't care for the look. But it was her father whom Nina had focused on, and it was his legacy that stood her in good stead as an adult. I had garnered some insights into what drew Nina to her father; this story provided another.

"When my brother turned sixteen, he got a car, and it came with a defective sunroof," Nina said. "He decided he wanted to sue the car company because he felt he'd been mistreated. My dad said 'great' and helped him find a lawyer that would take it on. Everybody else was like, 'This is nuts. You don't sue Ford. You settle.' My dad took the day off from work. It didn't go to court, it went [into arbitration]. They took the day off, they drove three hours to where this was going to be, and my brother ended up with a new car. And it was because my dad told him to go to the library, do the research, and find out what he needed to know to win, instead of saying, 'You're crazy. Settle, okay? Just settle.'"

Nina's father believed. He believed in justice, in doing the right thing, in the power of the individual. I saw how this had captured Nina's imagination and earned her respect. Her father was an idealist. When something didn't go the way he thought it should, he took action to make things right.

"When I got my PSAT scores, they were not as good as he had hoped," Nina said. "He went into this mode of 'We can fix this.' That's his attitude: Everything is possible. They have [private test preparation centers] down there and I went to one of their programs, but he decided that wasn't enough, so they hired a special tutor that came to the house three days a week, and it worked. If there is a problem, he finds a solution. I joked that it was the phase of the tutor, because we'd never had tutors before, and then my father thought, *This a good thing*. My brother had a bar mitzvah tutor. We got a dog and the dog had a tutor that came over and trained the dog. It was tutor time. It was always, *If there is a problem, there is a solution*. My father always thought I could do anything. He was such a positive thinker. It wasn't just me, but anybody. He thinks no matter what you say you want to do, it is possible. My mother's a more negative thinker. With my father, I felt the sky was the limit. My mother probably wouldn't have thought that at all."

What had gone right between Nina and her father was that he had imbued her with a belief in the power of a person to change a situation, to make things happen. He respected authority, but none more than the moral authority of each person to do what he or she thought was right. Nina, having absorbed this from a very young age, grew up believing in her own agency, her inherent power to not only think for herself, but also act on her own behalf. "I will never forget that when I went to college, all my friends would call their parents and ask, 'When am I coming home for Thanksgiving?'" she said. "Their parents had booked the tickets. How could your parents know when you should leave? You know your schedule. So I feel like I learned a lot and my brothers learned a lot that maybe we wouldn't have if my mother had been more involved."

During her student years at Barnard College in New York City, Nina applied for a summer job in Manhattan's garment district. Her father asked her why she wasn't working for him instead. After all, she had volunteered at the business since she was ten years old. "I was in charge of answering the phones," Nina said. "It was so much fun. I got to answer the switchboard and would page whoever the call was for." But Nina had never gotten a salary. She took a deep breath and told her father that she wanted to make money.

"He told me if I came to work for him in the summer, he would pay me. He said, 'I'll pay you like I pay any other salesperson.' I had a big head and thought I should be able to sell eyeglass frames better than anybody else, so I started. I literally cold-called. He told me to go to this building on the Avenue of the Americas [in Manhattan], go to the top floor, knock on every door, and start walking down. That's how I started. In the beginning, I called him eight million times a day with questions. Then I'd bring him to New York to meet my customers, and he was always amazed. He didn't know anybody in these companies."

Nina's father told her which building to go to, but she did the rest—just as she had when he taught her how to talk to an airline reservations clerk over the telephone. When she graduated from college, her father hired her full-time and put her in charge of marketing.

"He felt that if you go into a meeting and you are the marketing manager, people think there is somebody else, that you don't have the power to make a decision. So he felt it was important that people know that when I walk into the room, I can make a decision. For him, that was really the point, to make me feel empowered enough to do that. My very first title was director. I was like, 'How can I be a director? I'm twenty-one years old!' He said, 'You've been in the business your whole life. When you go into a meeting, you don't want people to think you have to ask your boss.' So he gave me a title so that the outside world would look at me and see a decision maker.

"Anything related to New York, I have final say on—even with my father. I am hiring some people right now, and one person I want to hire will cost a lot more money than we had originally budgeted for that position. He's like, 'If that is what we need to spend the money on, go ahead and spend it.' When it comes to New York, I have the say."

The old man had not yet handed over the reins—Nina was in charge of New York, not the entire company—but of the three children, she held the highest position, ostensibly, she said, because she was the eldest and had been working for the company the longest. This sounded logical and fair, but it was also unusual until fairly recently. Traditionally, when a family ran a business, it was the sons, not the daughters, who joined the company and eventually succeeded their father as CEO. When Joel Russ changed the name of his New York City appetizing shop to Russ and Daughters in 1933, it became, as far as they could tell, the first business ever to mention daughters in its name. (The store, which opened in 1914 on the Lower East Side and still thrives today, employed all three of Russ's daughters at various times and has been dubbed "a part of New York's cultural heritage" by the Smithsonian Institution.)[1]

Of all of Nina's reminiscences, the most vivid for me was the one in which her father thrust a title upon her over her objections. Nina felt she was too young and inexperienced to be a director of the company; in her view, she had to earn the title before she could use it. But her father had a different perspective. He knew how men perceive, deploy, and respond to power and didn't want his daughter to be at a disadvantage when dealing with them. To this end, he bestowed power upon her by granting her a title, believing that in business, what you see is what you get. You see a marketing person, you get an underling who needs approval from a higher-up to make a decision. But you see the marketing director, you get someone who can make a decision right there on the spot, so you deal with her. Voilà!—instant authority.

This struck me as a distinctly male tactic: You want power? Take it. You want authority? Assume it. It's not about hoping others see you as you want to see yourself, it's about putting yourself where you want to be and convincing yourself that you deserve to be there. Like many women, Nina felt she needed to prove her worthiness—to herself and others—before she could assume the mantle of authority. Her father knew better; in his world, first you assume the mantle, then you prove you are worthy. By draping the mantle on Nina's shoulders, he conferred upon her the authority she was unwilling to claim for herself. He made her a company director and expected her to grow into the role. And she did.

This, then, was Nina's legacy from her father: By entrusting her with responsibility, he taught her to rise up, learn on the fly, and derive satisfaction from what she accomplished. She held a position of responsibility in the family business and knew her father respected and relied upon her. Nina said she and her husband hoped to have a child in the next few years, and she was mindful that she would probably have to adapt her work schedule and responsibilities to accommodate a family. Still, she valued her position in the business and had no intention of giving it up.

"It's not so much that I want to make a difference in people's lives, but for my company, I do. It's not like I am saving the world. But when I go to work, things happen as a result of it. That is what I think is the important thing."

CHAPTER 7

A Father Who Always Knew What His Daughter Was Feeling

In high school, when we would drive together, he would always sign his cards, "Love, your copilot." He's my copilot. It's not that I need him; he needs me, too. Everyone needs people.

—KELLY, 31, SPEECH PATHOLOGIST

W HEN a father deliberately sets out to teach his daughter the ways of the world, he changes how she sees herself in it. Fran, Jackie, and Nina said their independence, ambition, choice of career, and sheer joy in working were founded in great part on their fathers' nurturing of their confidence and intelligence. When I listened to them recount stories from their childhoods, they as often as not spoke of their fathers' influence as intellectual, citing exhortations to think for themselves, study hard, and make well-considered decisions, among other things.

Kelly's comments were a bit different. It wasn't that her father wasn't intellectual, but quite the contrary: He taught English at a community college until Kelly was twelve, at which point he changed careers and became a freelance college advisor, helping high school seniors choose where to apply and prepare their applications. He was intelligent, educated, and articulate. But the sense I got was that his greatest gifts to his daughter issued from an emotional rather than an intellectual place. This was a man who connected with his daughter with spontaneous empathy, who had a gift for knowing what she was feeling and responding in a way that made her feel encouraged, emboldened, or simply understood.

"We would walk," Kelly said. "There was a forest behind our house in New Jersey and we'd collect frogs. He used to practice sports with me. There was this road we had to take to get to the supermarket—the bumpy road—and I remember just my dad and I driving in the car. There were bumps on the road, and usually there were not many cars on it. My dad would always make it fun. He would go a little faster. There were never any cars around, and I would always ask him to go faster. I remember he taught me how to catch the beat to a song. That's an early memory I have of the music on the radio in the car on the way to the supermarket. I don't have a great memory, but I remember songs from those car rides."

Kelly called up these memories less than a minute into the interview. I noted the variety of experience she described: walking, frog catching, playing sports, riding in a bumpy car, listening to music and finding the beat. These were sensory memories, vivid and enlivened with feeling. I also noticed that she was mindful of the portrait she was painting of her father, taking care to mention that she was the one who provoked him to speed up and that there were no other cars on the road when he did. She was loath to give the impression that he was irresponsible (which, for the record, I would not have thought he was), and I wondered what factors might have conspired to foster her protective attitude toward him.

Kelly was a speech pathologist in private practice on the Upper East Side of Manhattan. She held bachelor's and master's degrees from the New England Catholic college from which her father had also graduated. She looked like the quintessential all-American girl: tall (about five foot eight), with a solid, athletic build and long, straight hair pulled back with an elastic band. There was a fluidity to her movements that lent her an air of competence; later, when I learned that she had played Little League baseball, basketball, and volleyball and rowed in college, I understood whence it came ("Both my parents would drive up to my college, which was four hours away, for a crew race that would take eight minutes, and then they would drive four hours home," Kelly said; now, that's devotion for you). She responded to my questions honestly if prudently. As manifested in the way she described the bumpy car ride, I sensed that she was aware of the impression that her remarks might make on me, and concerned that she present her thoughts with both candor and circumspection. In addition, Kelly's responses contained an element of introspective inquisitiveness. It was common for her to answer a question and then wonder aloud about the nature of the response, weighing its aptness or its depth. She gave the impression of being intelligent, thoughtful, and truthful.

Kelly had two brothers, one older and one younger, with whom she said she'd competed for her parents' attention. "I used to always try to argue that I was getting shortchanged because I was the girl. My parents both made it very clear, in any argument I would give, that that was false, I was being ridiculous, and they would correct whatever accusation I made. If my brother was going to basketball camp and I wanted to go to basketball camp, then I got to go to basketball camp. I think I would just make these things up. I think I was just testing." It sounded like classic middle-child business as usual, and to Kelly's credit, she knew it. When I pressed her a bit about whether she ever got her father's full attention, she said that she did, especially when it came to sports. Because the college where he taught was near Kelly's elementary and middle schools, he would drive her to class, which gave them time alone. Also, because he was often done teaching by midafternoon, he coached basketball for a while at Kelly's future high school and would take her along.

"I used to sit in on their practices when he would coach," she said. "Later, when it became time for me to play, he would practice dribbling, passing, and things like that with me a lot. He would teach me things, to use your mind, use your feet, to look at positioning. He took a lot of time with that."

"Did you feel he was tough or critical?" I asked.

"He was tough, but he never made me cry," she said. "I was tough, too. I don't remember. I remember watching him as a coach and he was tough. He'd throw chairs and get angry at his players. He was mostly a calm man, though. I don't remember him being too tough. I don't remember him being really tough on me. He just encouraged me to go out there and get the ball. Dive for the ball. Be alive, be alive. He wasn't a mean-spirited tough type. He taught me to be aggressive. He taught me to be confident with my body positioning. Basketball's a funny sport, because it's contact. I think that sport gave me a lot of confidence. I was usually playing with my brother or his friends and a lot of times I was the only girl. It gave me confidence to be able to physically box someone out and go after the ball. He taught me to do that. In eighth grade, I was in a game, and a girl put me in a headlock and flipped me onto the floor. I looked up at the stands and everybody was looking down at me. I was shocked and shaken up, but I got up and ended up being okay. I wasn't a dainty little thing."

The demise of daintiness as a sacred female trait is perhaps most obvious in the fierceness with which American girls and women have embraced competitive sports. It can be traced to Title IX, a 1972 law enacted by the US Congress forbidding any educational program or activity receiving federal funds to discriminate on the basis of sex, which led to greater funding of girls' sports programs.[1] Whereas the interrelationship between daughters, fathers, and sport is a new field for researchers, some preliminary findings indicate that a father has a tremendous influence on his daughter's decision of whether or not to take up a sport, as well as how much she enjoys the experience if she does decide to play. In her study of Australian female footballers—soccer players, to us—Nikki Wedgwood, PhD, a research fellow at the University of Sydney, writes that because childrearing is still largely women's work in Australia, playing soccer affords girls contact with their fathers they might not otherwise have. "For some of these young women, as well as for some women in the adult league, wanting to play is directly linked with their desire to inspire love and admiration in their fathers the only way they know how."[2] I'd like to think that in America, fathers' greater involvement in their daughters' lives provides girls with avenues other than sports through which to inspire their love and admiration. Still, there is no doubt that when an American father and daughter are both into sports, it's a fertile ground in which their relationship can grow and flourish.

Or develop strain: A study by Nicole Willms, an adjunct professor at the University of Montana, of twenty-two female athletes at a large, private West Coast university found that fathers' involvement in their daughters' sports activities was a double-edged skate blade, sometimes leading to dads offering unsolicited instruction and advice; becoming overinvolved in matters of training, scheduling, and nutrition; foisting motivation on their daughters in the form of emotional or verbal abuse; behaving badly at competitions; and unduly influencing their daughters' decisions about which sports to play.[3] Apropos of this, I asked Kelly if she liked having her father at her sporting events.

"Oh yeah," she replied. "He was a coach when I was younger, so he knew a lot about the game. After the game, he would give me feedback if I wanted it. He understood me. If I didn't want anyone to talk to me, he understood that."

"He backed off?" I asked.

"Oh yeah. In high school, he coached my summer league games. He was involved."

"What were your signals to him to back off?"

"Oh, just my mood! He knew. He always knows."

"And he responded?"

"Yeah."

He knew. He always knows. Again, I was struck by the empathic nature of Kelly's connection with her father. Although many women had spoken of the kinship they felt with their dads, few had expressed the degree of simpatico Kelly routinely described with hers. It seemed that their connection transcended whatever situation they were in. Even when it came to sports, a traditionally masculine enclave, Kelly and her father connected in a traditionally feminine way, through intuitive feeling. When I asked about her dad's attitude toward her schoolwork, she conjured a memory laden with emotion.

"I have a picture on my desk that I love. It's my dad and me on the couch. I have my phonics book open, and he used to help me with phonics, because I remember that was hard. Or spelling, he would quiz me on spelling. We would take these drives, and since he was an English teacher, he would quiz me on grammar while we'd be driving to school. Or, we would just talk about it. He always wanted me to do well. When I was younger, we would get rewards for our report cards and chores around the house. We'd have a list and gold stars. I know my dad wanted me to do well in school because he cared so much. . . . I remember wanting to drop a physics class in college, and I had a hard time doing that but felt like I wasn't getting it, and I didn't want it to screw up my GPA. My dad had minored in physics, so I felt bad about that, but I remember him talking me through it. I thought I let myself down and I let him down. But I remember standardized tests were very nerve-racking for me—SATs, PSATs. I used to get myself all worked up with anxiety. He said, 'What do you think we should do about it?' I ended up taking a course and then getting a private tutor. That really helped."

"Why do you love that picture so much, of him teaching you phonics?" I asked.

"It sounds so stupid. He would sit there with this cup of tea and he always spoiled me with time. It's a perfect example of his constant support. That's why I love that picture."

"What's stupid about it?"

"That he's drinking tea!" Kelly laughed as she said this (I suppose she thought coffee would have been more acceptable). It seemed that what she remembered and felt most deeply was that her father made her feel that she was worthy—worthy of his energy, his attention, his time. I asked her if they still spent time together, now that she was busy with her career, living on her own, and engaged to be married. Kelly said they would go to museums and learn about art together, and that they had begun to garden together.

"When we were done he said, 'Kelly, thank you so much for doing this, because I wouldn't have done it if you weren't here.'" Kelly bowed her head, inhaled sharply, and pressed her fingers to her forehead.

"Why does that make you cry?" I asked.

"Because I think it's too bad that my mom's not there to help him do that."

The story emerged: It turned out that a year earlier, after thirty years of marriage, Kelly's mother had decided to separate from her father. The divorce would soon be final.

"What troubles me is that not only did my mom want a divorce, but that she wanted the house that we grew up in," Kelly said. "Some people would say she's entitled to that. She wanted to sell our house. My dad wanted to die in that house. He loved that house. He wanted to grow old with her in that house. I feel like if you want to leave, just leave. Don't leave and take. She has her own apartment now. She didn't get it herself. She had to take half the house from my dad to get it. I don't really respect that." I said that it sounded as if Kelly was more sympathetic to her father's position in the conflict, and she readily agreed. I asked her why.

"Because my dad did not want the divorce or separation. I don't think he did anything wrong. My mom wanted things that he couldn't provide, but I don't see why my father had to be punished for it, or our family has to be destroyed because of it. I've only seen my father cry twice. One was when my aunt passed away, and the second time was when he had to tell me what was going on with him and my mom, that they were separating. I don't see him as vulnerable—well, I guess a little bit, yes. I never really worried about him before, but he'll be okay. He's strong."

This explained the protectiveness toward her dad that Kelly had exhibited early in the interview. She loved him for his steadfastness and loyalty and, I believed, was struggling with how much to look up to him versus how much to look after him. And she loved him fiercely for always seeing her as someone worth taking seriously.

"I remember saying I wanted to run away when I was really young, and my dad said okay. I was probably seven or six. He helped me pack my bags and brought me to the train station, which is not in a nice part of town, and dropped me off and drove away. He drove around the block and then came back and picked me up. I remember being scared." Kelly laughed as she spoke, even when she said she was crying by the time her father returned. I pictured this frightened little girl with her suitcases, standing in a train station in a bad part of town. I felt many things: compassion for her fear, worry for her safety, and a twinge of surprise that her father had left her there all by herself. Wasn't he worried about her? Didn't he care about her feelings?

Yes, and yes. He did worry about her, which is why he came

right back. He did care about her feelings, which is why he took them seriously and brought her to the station. I might not have made those choices, but that's the point, isn't it? Fathers do things differently. What this one did was respond to his daughter as if her wish to run away were reasonable, which was precisely how she saw it. He didn't mock her or try to talk her out of it, or try to point out that a seven-year-old couldn't get very far traveling by herself. He didn't try to quell her anger or point out the absurdity of her urge to flee, nor did he assert his power to end the whole episode by sending her to her room or just saying no.

What he did was treat her with empathy: He looked at the situation through her eyes and responded as if she had a point. So what if she got scared? So what if she changed her mind and decided she wanted to come home? So she experienced some discomfort—is that really so terrible? Which is also the point: We all learn best from our own mistakes. Not that I think Kelly made a mistake by wanting to run away; she was angry and frustrated and needed to act on her feelings. Sometimes you just have to feel the emotions, endure the pain, survive the fear, and come out on the other side a little wiser than when you went in, even if you are only seven years old. There's a prejudice now against pain; we don't want to feel it ourselves, and we sure don't want it for our kids.

Which harks back to the trophies-for-everyone mentality, in which we're so busy handing them out to every kid that hardly any of them are learning that yes, losing feels crummy, but it isn't fatal. And, not incidentally, that it's only after you lose a bunch of times that you feel how glorious it is to win. Which is what Kelly's father was allowing her to do. By helping her pack and driving her to the station, he was giving her the power to live out her wishes, albeit to a point (the one at which he came back for her). By the time he got back, she had thought better of it and was ready to go home. But her desire to go home grew out of her desire to run away in the first place; she had come full circle, on her own steam and her own terms.

Kelly told the story with humor and seemed fond of the memory; there was no sense that she resented the way her father had handled the situation. Interestingly, when I asked her what had happened to cause her to want to run away, she said she didn't remember, but that her father would. This wasn't the first time Kelly said she didn't remember something; throughout the interview, she protested that she had a bad memory and couldn't recall details. Which was not always the case. She remembered, for example, that her father used to drink tea when they sat on the couch working on phonics and that she thought it was stupid. It seemed to me that she remembered things well when they were bound up with feeling, which is probably the case for many of us.

Kelly was grateful for something that several other women also appreciated: Her father treated her with the respect and regard that he accorded to adults. "Since maybe I was thirteen, he's always made me feel more of an equal, not younger or on a lesser level," she said. "In high school, when we would drive [to school] together, he would always sign his cards, 'Love, your copilot.' He's my copilot. It's not that I need him; he needs me, too. Everyone needs people."

Throughout her childhood and adolescence and now in her adulthood, Kelly's father made her a part of his life. "When he was a teacher, in the summer he would paint houses and I would go with him and watch him work really hard around these beautiful homes," she said. "I would just sit and play with the rocks. Then when he would teach or coach, he would bring me to school and I would sit in the back. When he was a consultant, I would go to his office. Yeah, he brought me to work a lot." Here again, a daughter whose father inspired her remembered the experience of accompanying him to work. Not only did these daughters get to see, hear, touch, and smell the environments in which their fathers labored every day, they also got to see their fathers as others saw them: men involved in pursuits that did not involve their families, talking, laughing, and working with strangers who knew nothing about their kids or how they looked in their pajamas, yet who saw their fathers as people to respect, people who were good at something and whose presence was valued because of their competence and skill.

Can mothers not similarly inspire their daughters? Of course they can, and they do. Some of the women I spoke with cited their mothers as examples of professional competence and success, and many praised their mothers' capacity to be all things to all people while managing the household and sometimes a career as well. But other women, such as Nina in the last chapter, failed to be inspired by their mothers, sometimes for obvious reasons. Kelly's reasons emerged gradually.

"She provided a role model for me in the home things she would do," Kelly said. "She was kind and loving. She gave me tools. I will be a very good mother to a child and a baby. I got that from her. My mom's very funny and outgoing. She is social. That is why she's complicated. She has this side that is not very confident, yet she is beautiful, can talk to anyone, and is working in a fancy boutique on Madison Avenue. It's a complex dichotomy there. I remember going off to college, and I didn't have any older female cousins. My brother's friend's sister went to college and finished. She did it. But I didn't have a model so that I could say, 'My mom did that. I could do that.' She wasn't as confident. I can't remember my mom giving a toast, things like that, that I wish I had and could get from her."

It was clear that Kelly was working through conflicting feelings about her mother. On one hand, she said she loved telling people about the celebrities her mom was meeting in her new job in Manhattan; on the other, she wished her mother had been more polished and sophisticated when she was growing up and had taught her more about how to make her way in the world. Still, there was a fundamental difference in the way Kelly talked about her parents' contributions to her life. Whereas she could acknowledge that her mother was kind and loving, there was an intellectual cast to the way she described these traits, as when she said, "she gave me tools." But when it came to describing her father's legacy to her, there was plain, raw feeling. One poignant example involved Kelly's quest for the perfect prom dress.

"I wanted the perfect prom dress," Kelly said. "I remember driving, honestly, to a number of different stores. Any store I wanted, we went to! I mean, we covered New Jersey—Short Hills, Rumson, Livingston; he took me into Manhattan, even out to Long Island. I wanted the perfect dress. I remember him driving me."

"Patiently?" I asked.

"Oh yeah. Oh yeah." Kelly's face creased in a smile; her face glowed. Usually it's the mother who runs around from store to store to store, accompanying her daughter in this most feminine of pursuits. But in this case, it was the father who indulged his daughter's dream of looking beautiful for the prom, driving her what was probably hundreds of miles (and spending hours in what was probably horrendous traffic) around the New York–New Jersey metropolitan area. Again, it bespoke a deep empathic bond, as did this next story.

"I have this image in my head that I will never forget. This was about six years ago. I was engaged to a gentleman, and out of the blue—well, I thought it was out of the blue, but obviously it wasn't—out of the blue, he ended the engagement. I was home with my roommate in our apartment in Queens. I called up my parents and I was crying. I was so heartbroken. My parents came right to my apartment. I was on the floor crying. My dad picked me up like a little girl. I was twenty-four. He picked me up and just held me. He brought me into my room and put me on my bed. I'll never forget that. He used to do things like that. When I was little, I used to pretend I was asleep on the couch and he'd take me up to my bed. I remember asking this guy, my former fiancé, 'Did you ask my dad for my hand in marriage?' He was like, 'No.' He obviously didn't understand me that well, and I didn't know him that well. I said, 'You didn't ask him? My father and I are so close. How could you not?' I remember being so taken aback."

There was a lot going on here: the shock of the broken engagement, Kelly's despair, her parents' hastening into the city to take care of her, her father's physicality in gathering her up from the floor, Kelly's disappointment that her fiancé had not asked her father for her hand in marriage. (Also, Kelly's referring to her former fiancé as a gentleman—a gallant gesture, I thought, considering that he had broken her heart.) But the image she said she would never forget was that of her father picking her up and carrying her in his arms, just as he had when she was a girl.

Now Kelly was engaged to Tommy, an associate director at a Manhattan investment firm, with whom she shared an apartment now that they were formally affianced (she declined to live with him until they had actually set a date). She spoke warmly of Tommy and declared them both very independent people by way of describing how their relationship differed from that of her parents. "Tommy and I communicate a lot," Kelly said. "I'm very open. I'm older [than when engaged for the first time] and I am very aware. I can say anything. I am not afraid to fight. I never saw my parents fight. I know they probably fought behind closed doors, but they kept it away from us."

Kelly also differentiated her relationship from that of her parents by emphasizing that she did not see marriage as a way to secure her financial future. In fact, she had no need to: Her practice was thriving and she was bringing in more than $100,000 a year. So it piqued my interest when, after touting the open lines of communication she and Tommy shared, she said that she did not know his annual income until relatively recently, long after their engagement.

"I was saying to Tommy that I had to fill out an application for the apartment and I didn't know how much money he made, and I needed to know," Kelly said. "He said, 'Oh, I make this much.'"

"And you also told him how much you make?" I asked.

"I think he already knew. I'm pretty sure I already told him."

Well, this was interesting. If he knew Kelly's income, why didn't she know his? I asked her why she hadn't asked him earlier.

"I didn't want him to think I was judging him by his money," Kelly said. "There are a lot of women in New York City who do that. I didn't want him to think I was one of those girls who is after that. I didn't want that to be an issue."

"I'd like you to think about something," I said. "Was there, just maybe, a part of you that didn't want him to know how much money you were making, too?" Kelly gazed out the window before answering.

"No, I didn't care about that. I'm very proud of how much money I make."

As were, I imagined, her parents—the very people whose financial arrangement had shaped their daughter's fierce pursuit of financial independence. It seemed to me that Kelly's commitment to self-sufficiency was rooted in her mother's dependency on her father for financial support. The fact that her mother lacked a college education and a career—in other words, the independence that Kelly prized—rendered her less than inspirational to her daughter. Kelly's ambivalence about her mother had curdled into distaste and rage when her mother demanded that they sell the family home so she could afford to buy her own apartment. There was no way that Kelly was going to allow herself to get in that position.

Kelly's relationship with her father continues to evolve. Because of the impending divorce, they spend more time together than they use to, visiting a museum every few months rather than once a year. But their growing closeness has its difficulties as well.

"He wanted me to go with him to this tavern near his house and have a drink on a Sunday night. I said, 'I just don't really . . . This isn't fun. I don't want to be the going-out buddy. You have all of these other friends. Go call them. That's not fun for me.'"

"You told your father that?" I asked.

"Yeah, I told him, 'This isn't fun for me.'"

"How did you get up the courage to say that?"

"As soon as a child feels forced to do something, it's no longer fun. Sometimes it was a drag. I was holding that in, and then I told him. But for the most part, it is fun for me."

"How did he feel when you said that?"

"He said, 'I understand.'"

"Was it hard to say that?" I assumed it was, but I wanted to hear what she had to say.

"It had built up so I just had to say it, and once I said it, I felt better. I think it has to be said, what's going on. You have to be conscious of everything. He understands."

That is the gift that Kelly's father gave her: He understood. He understood her when she was little, and he understood her now. In so doing, he made her feel seen and known.

Toward the end of the interview, I asked Kelly if she thought there was a connection between her father's expectations of her and her hopes for herself. Her answer started out in one place and ended in another, as many of her answers had.

"He doesn't expect me to do anything, but he does expect me to go as far as I want to go. I want to go on and get my doctorate. Be the best I can be. He was the one who first taught me how to set goals."

"Did he encourage you socially, too, toward friends? To be popular?" The question sounded, as I reread it in the transcript, somewhat prosaic. But Kelly's answer bore a touch of the poet.

"It wasn't so much popular," she said. "To give an example, he has a really great group of guy friends from college. Every summer we would go up to Cape Cod to one of their houses and get together with their families. The friendship among these men is so amazing that that was part of the reason I ended up going to the same college my dad went to. I wanted friends like that. They all have the same values and are nice people. I witnessed that. I wanted that."

[CHAPTER 8]

A Father Who Inspired
His Daughter to Persevere
and Succeed

There's this balance between giving me the feeling that I'm capable of anything, but always making me feel like I haven't quite gotten there yet, I'm not quite doing enough. There's this little holding back of his final approval, and it makes me strive that much harder to achieve more.

—JUSTINE, 38, NEUROLOGIST

FIVE days ago, I opened the *New York Times* and read the headline "Boy, 8, Dies in Brooklyn Fire." "An 8-year-old boy was killed and five other children were seriously injured when a fast-moving fire broke out in a residential building in the Midwood section of Brooklyn on Wednesday." There was more. Two families lived in the building: One, which occupied the basement and two lower levels, was sitting down to dinner to celebrate the Jewish holiday of Sukkot when one of the daughters cried out that the roof was burning. The parents of the other family, which lived on the top floor where the fire broke out, were in the backyard preparing for dinner; their six children, ranging in age from one to ten, were upstairs. The father ran back into the house, frantically pulling the children to safety, but the eight-year-old became trapped in a room whose window was fortified metal burglar-deterrent bars. Firefighters struggled to free the child. "They broke the glass and cut the gate," a young witness said. The children were

taken to the hospital, where all but one survived, albeit with critical injuries. [1]

I put down the paper and stared at nothing, as I do when I
read about such things. I thought of the children, their parents, the
smoke, the heat, the horror. I tried to imagine the clawing feelings
of panic, desperation, helplessness. But I couldn't; it's overwhelming. It is literally unimaginable.

Yet it happens every day; open a Web browser or newspaper
anywhere in the world and you are confronted with the unimaginable: earthquakes, landslides, tsunamis, fires, tornadoes, explosions, floods. Buildings fall, villages perish, families are broken
and reconfigured. I think about the parents, their bottomless
grief, their profound, immeasurable loss. I think about the children who lose sisters, brothers, mothers, fathers, who are themselves hurt, who grow up and go through life with calamity seared
into their memories. How do people recover from such loss? How
do families go on? How do you marshal the brute force to wake up
every day, pull on your clothes, and engage with life as if nothing
bad could ever happen to you again?

I got an idea when I spoke to Justine.

I met Justine through her father, a neurologist with whom I
had consulted some years before on a professional matter. We had
since become friendly and would chat about work and our families
when we saw each other. Early in our acquaintance, I asked about
his family and he said he was married and had had ten children,
but three had died. He offered no explanation and I could see in
his eyes that he wished to go no further, so I said something about
being terribly sorry and let it go at that. When I saw him most
recently and told him what I was working on, he suggested that I
interview his daughter Justine, who was also a neurologist and
shared his practice in Princeton, New Jersey, where he worked the
one week out of the month when he was not at his Philadelphia
office. I had never met Justine and agreed to call her. When I did,

she was enthusiastic about participating and offered to come into Manhattan for an interview.

Justine arrived exactly on time and rang the bell. When I opened the door, she smiled, shook my hand, and was unselfconscious about asking if she could use the bathroom before we got started. Justine was about five feet six inches tall and of medium build, with wavy, light-brown midlength hair and hazel eyes. Her clothes were classic in style—tweed woolen slacks, a silk blouse, and low-heeled leather pumps with buckles on the toes. She came off as a no-nonsense, can-do kind of woman, an impression that was borne out when she emerged from the bathroom to find me struggling with the tape deck I use to record interviews. After observing my unsuccessful attempts to get it going, she extended her hand, asked if she might take a look, and, in about seven seconds, had the thing working again (I had unwittingly slid the pause bar and frozen the machine). When I muttered something about being technologically challenged, she dismissed the comment with a wave of her hand. "I use these things all the time to dictate notes," she said, "so I'm pretty good with them." There was something intimidating about her matter-of-fact skill and confidence in an area that baffled me. From that moment on, I wanted to understand where she got her confidence and what role, if any, her father had played in its development.

The first thing I asked was if her father had been around when she was young and if they had spent any time together, just the two of them.

"When you're one of seven kids," she said, laughing, "it is hard to do the exclusive thing, but I always felt it anyhow. I felt a special attention from him. He was a doctor, so he worked his usual doctor's hours. He'd come home after work and just about the first thing he would do was play with the kids. We all had dinner together every night. I would say my mom organized us for bedtime, but he did the story reading—he was a great story

reader. Weekends were for family, so we would spend it doing one
activity or another together, with my dad present. I certainly
never thought, 'Oh, I don't get to spend time with my dad.' Put it
this way: I felt he was around a lot." It struck me that even with six
siblings, Justine felt as if she had received special attention from
her father. She also was the only one who had joined him in his
profession and his practice.

"Justine," I said, "your father once told me that there had
been more children in your family, that some had died. Can you
talk about what happened?"

"It was a pretty horrendous time. It was three sisters who
died. I was seven and the only girl to survive. We were six children at the time: four girls and two boys. One of the boys was a
newborn. All three of my sisters died; I was the only girl left. I
definitely went through all the survivor guilt. My parents were in
complete shock, as was everybody, but as a very perceptive child,
I got that my parents couldn't take anything more on their plate,
so my route was to keep it to myself. If I was upset, I cried, but I
cried by myself. My parents took us to a psychiatrist at some
point, as a family, to see if everyone was coping okay. The psychiatrist was like, 'Yeah, everyone seems to be about appropriate.' That was it. So, yes, it took me a very long time to work
through it, but maybe that's why I worked through it so well—
because I just had to do it on my own, in my own time, in my own
way." I noted Justine's perception that she had healed herself. I
detected no resentment in her tone, no petulance at not having
received more adequate professional care or more attention from
her parents. Quite the contrary: As she described it, it was she
who had recognized that her parents were overwhelmed with
grief and appointed herself guardian of their recovery by declining to burden them with her own sadness. And she was seven at
the time.

"What happened?" I asked.

"It was a fire."

"Were your parents at home?"

"No. My brother had been born five days earlier. It was my parents' first night out to celebrate the birth of their child, so we'd been left with two babysitters. A freakish electrical fire started in the house, and not everyone got out."

"Did the babysitters survive?"

"Yes, both of them did."

"Did your sisters die at the scene?"

"It was smoke inhalation. One died at the house before the ambulance even got there. One died in the ambulance on the way to the hospital, and one died in the hospital. They had originally wanted to put me in the ambulance with them, but some instinct in me said no way, and I fought it. I wouldn't go with those people. Thank god I didn't."

Those people. That's how she said it. I wasn't sure if Justine was referring to her sisters, the medical personnel, or both. Either way, the inference was clear: Justine's childhood self associated the ambulance with death, and she wanted no part of it. The three little girls with whom she lived, ate, played, and probably shared a room were no longer her sisters; they had joined the vast gray ranks of those who were no longer of the living, no longer of this world. I was astonished. Where does a seven-year-old get the wherewithal to say no, she's not going in the ambulance, she's not going with *those* people—those people who were but are no longer her sisters, whom she loves, but whom she somehow knows are already different from her, apart from her, separate from her in a brutally irrevocable way?

"Do you feel there was something magical about choosing not to go in there? Choosing in some way to live?" I asked. "No, I wouldn't say that," Justine said. "I just know it would have been a horrific experience had I been in there. Since I can remember, I've been a person who listens to my instincts. Sometimes that takes you the right way, and sometimes it takes you the wrong way, but I really listened to that little voice. It was there. My little voice is very loud, so I just listened to it."

She sat and looked at me, unperturbed. Her composure was complete, intact; mine, a bit less so. I was rooted to the sidewalk next to the ambulance, watching a defiant seven-year-old refuse to climb in with her doomed sisters. The adult Justine, however, was sitting on a sofa in my book-lined office, present and accounted for, attentively awaiting my next question. I came up with something.

"Do you think you were born with a strong will?"

"Yeah. A strong will, but I was a complete and utter people pleaser. Up until seventeen or eighteen, my goal in life was to keep everything okay and be the peacekeeper. And I did so willingly. I felt good when I could achieve that, but I was definitely in that role." I asked Justine if keeping the peace was related to her father in particular.

"My father is actually very predictable, stable, and even-tempered," she replied. "You knew exactly where you stood with him at all times, so it was quite easy. My mom had a lot more swings in mood, probably because she was pregnant nonstop. My dad said she was much different after she had children. Before-hand, she was much more of a free spirit, and less so after. I guess that happens with a lot of people. I think hormonally, she was probably going in waves all the time."

While I found it curious that Justine did not mention the violent loss of three daughters as a possible contributor to her mother's mood swings, I was still impressed by her assessment of her memories, which issued from an adult perspective rather than from that of the child she was when she was living them. Throughout the interview, she spoke of the losses she had endured—and there were many—with the detachment of someone who had not forgotten the anguish so much as developed an emotional distance from it. She was consistently able to discuss personal devastation in the language of a compassionate, if somewhat aloof observer. My take wasn't that Justine didn't care, but rather that she cared very, very much: She knew that she would not be able to survive her losses were she to cultivate an intimacy with them. It was an effective survival tactic, exemplified by her rejection of her connection to her sisters when they were bundled into the ambulance. This woman possessed a fierce and individuated sense of self, a self whose right to exist and prevail she embraced without question. I wanted to learn as much as I could about how she came by it.

As we spoke, I pieced together a picture of how Justine had borne up under her losses and came to believe that her position in the family had a lot to do with it. After the tragedy, she was the only female child left and, as such, was enlisted to help with her new siblings—four in all—as each was born. "I was kind of a full-time sister, part-time babysitter [when I was] growing up," she said. "I was helping to change the diapers and bottles and feed the kids from a pretty young age. I felt honored to have the responsibility. I didn't feel resentful until about age sixteen, seventeen, eighteen."

"Do you see your family, and your father in particular, as having influenced you to become the way you are, and your siblings to become the way they are?" I asked.

"My dad is a very successful person, and I think a lot of us have grown up wanting his approval and respect. I think we want it from my mom, as well, but my dad, in some ways, because he is out in the world—he's been in a career his whole life—that holds extra import."

Here it was again: A daughter citing her father's being out in the world as an inducement to please him and earn his respect. And she had, enough to have been invited by him to join his practice. I asked what, if anything, her father had had to do with her career choice.

"My dad was very smart. He didn't push. Initially I wanted to be a doctor, from a young age, and went to college planning to start my sciences to become a doctor. But I hated the undergrad science courses, while I loved this course I took on political philosophy. This famous philosopher took me under his wing, and I decided to switch majors. My dad was like, 'What are you going to do with that?' I said, 'I don't know. I'll figure something out.' I'm sure he didn't approve, but he didn't really make a big deal about it. I said, 'Look, this is my chance to get an education. Maybe at the end of this, I am going to decide to go to medical school, but I want to get an education now.' At the end of it, I decided not to be a philosopher, and I decided to go to medical school after all. I had to do a postbaccalaureate [premedical program], and then I went to medical school.

"My dad was very supportive through it all. Financially, he supported me through it. And he didn't push when it came to choosing what field I would go into. At first I chose obstetrics. He did push for me to at least go through a rotation in neurology. He encouraged me to come into the office from a young age. Starting when I was twelve, he let me help him do tests on patients." A twelve-year-old doing tests on patients? I tried not to look startled.

"Really? What sorts of things did you do?"

"Well, the first thing, which I actually did when I was younger, was to test people's reflexes by tapping their knees with a little hammer. I loved it when I learned where the right spot was to tap and their legs would swing up. That was really fun. Then, my father showed me how to test whether a person could feel pain by pricking them with a safety pin. Not hard, of course, but he taught me to gently prick their hand or arm to see if they could feel it. And then he taught me about proprioception, where you test a person's ability to sense the position of parts of their bodies by holding their fingers or their toes and moving them up and down and seeing if they can tell what you're doing."

"That's called what?"

"'Pro-prio-ception.' And he also showed me how to shine a penlight into a person's eyes and check how well their pupils constrict. So, yeah, I was doing a lot with patients when I was still a kid."

"He had confidence in your ability?"

"Yes, he did."

"Do you feel you would be as successful as you are professionally and have felt comfortable to explore your creativity if it weren't for him and his support?"

"I'm sure that the opportunities my dad has provided for me throughout my life have made it much easier and much more likely for me to get to where I am."

"But some people have opportunities and they can't or won't take advantage of them."

"Yeah, I have some siblings like that," she said. "I always felt like I had a lot of my dad. I think—I know—that some of my younger siblings didn't feel they had as much of him. For some of my siblings who didn't do quite so well, I know they felt they didn't have his approval. They went to college and never graduated because they were playing around. I think he was pretty predictable in that respect, as well."

"Do you think there might be some envy that you are like him and you work with him? That's a pretty special position to be in." Justine thought for a moment before speaking.

"I think there probably is some envy, to some degree. It's been spoken of a couple times, and my response is always 'Dad made it really clear that any one of us who wanted to join him in his practice could join him. Any one of us who wanted to go to med school, he was willing to pay. *Any* one of us. He would help us to do it. I am the one who is here because I chose it. I chose it in a very roundabout way, but I did end up choosing it. So, if you want to do it now, he would still support you.' I'm kind of like, don't cry me a river. If you want to go back to school and go to medical school and go into this practice, I will welcome you with open arms." I believed her, but there was steel in her eyes.

"I'd like you to think about something," I said, as I often do. "How do you understand the role of your emotional connection with your father?"

"We are both open books, whereas some of my siblings are much quieter and keep things to themselves. They are more reserved, some of them. Some of them are not. But my father and I, I feel like we speak the same emotional language. From a young age, I was a tomboy. I was really skinny with virtually no breasts. We would be up at the farm and all the boys were taking their shirts off, and I would take my shirt off, too. Even when I started to get some breasts, I was like, 'Why do I have to wear one of those uncomfortable bikini tops? They're uncomfortable and pull on your neck!' So I pranced about topless. At one point my dad came out to the pool when I was lying there topless, and I remember him being like, 'Oh, sorry.' I remember going, 'Dad, what's the big deal? You're a doctor,' or something like that. A couple times he came into my room when I was getting dressed or undressed, and he would back out quickly. I'd be like, 'Dad, what's the big deal?' I was very casual about it. I understood why he was a bit uncomfortable, but I was like, I am not letting this be a problem."

This was certainly not typical: an adolescent girl who, rather than heightening everyone's awareness of her budding body by concealing it, challenges them to ignore it and cavorts about shirtless like one of the boys. Provocative? Sure. Exhibitionistic? I think not. I believe Justine was asserting her desire to be identified with her father and the boys in the family rather than with her mother and the girls. I remembered that it was three sisters who had perished in the fire; both of Justine's brothers had survived. I could imagine how Justine might associate tenacity and survival with maleness, especially in light of her description of her father as a very successful person. I also took note of Justine's remark that she and her father spoke the same emotional language, as it invoked the primacy of talk in forging connections between women and those close to them. Continuing in this vein, I asked Justine if her father ever told her he was proud of her.

"It's interesting," she said. "There's this balance between giving me the feeling that I'm capable of anything, but always making me feel like I haven't quite gotten there yet, I'm not quite doing enough. There's this little holding back of his final approval, and it makes me strive that much harder to achieve more. So although I know he is very proud of what I've done in the practice, how my patients improve and all of that, he's still there with 'You need to write more. You need to speak more.' He does always still push a little, and sometimes I'll be like, 'Is there ever going to be a time when it's enough?'"

I detected perhaps a ripple of resentment, though mostly there was a rueful, matter-of-fact description of a familiar feature of their relationship: Father pushes daughter to do more, daughter wishes he would be satisfied for once but understands that he's doing it only so that she will succeed and so resigns herself to the behavior. It seemed clear that Justine yearned for her father to express delight in her accomplishments, yet stoically accepted that he would probably always push her to do more. I asked her if she had ever told him how this made her feel and she said no. I then asked her why.

"Because he will say, 'Justine, you do what you want to do. I'm giving you advice on what I think helped make my career. I know it worked well. I'm giving you that advice for the benefit of that experience. If you don't want to do it, you won't do it. You seem to be doing well without it.' I know his response."

"As you describe it," I said, "he's not really tuned in to how you feel when he pushes you a little more." Justine flicked her hand as if to swat away the idea.

"I think he actually does know I feel that way," she said. "It's just that there's no point to the conversation. That's why neither of us has had it. I think he thinks that he's giving me good advice, and he knows that makes me feel like I haven't quite done enough, and he thinks, 'Well, it's good that she feels that way.'" She laughed mirthlessly.

"But is it frustrating for you sometimes?"

"Occasionally, but usually not. I know that everything my dad does is good intentioned. I have never been angry at him for having done something—even if it ended up hurting me—because I know he didn't intend to hurt me." A confirmed pragmatist, Justine accepted her father's admonishments as evidence of his faith in her abilities, which enabled her to absorb the disappointment they inevitably provoked. She cited intent as the crux of the matter: Even though her father's lack of praise hurt sometimes, she could not be angry with him, she reasoned, because he did not intend to hurt her. As ever, a daughter's capacity to empathize with her father's intentions and forgive him won the day.

Would I recommend that fathers motivate their daughters by withholding praise and prodding them relentlessly to do more? No, probably not. And yet it had not done Justine any harm; according to her, her father's high expectations made her strive harder to achieve more. This is a classic example of paternal nurturance, according to Pruett, who asserts that a father's tendency to teach his child mastery of frustration "plays a supporting role in the development of a trait many children feel is more classically related to father care than mother care: the expectation of achievement."[2] Justine was a textbook example of this phenomenon, especially in light of the fact that she emulated her father rather than her mother, whom she loved and respected, but for whom she expressed less admiration than she did for her dad.

"From a pretty young age, I think I got it," she said, referring to her understanding of her mother's foibles. "I think I saw my mom as a person at a much younger age than most of my friends [saw theirs]. My friends were railing against my parents for being overprotective and strict. I would just wheel around and say, 'I think if you had three daughters who died, you might be protective of the ones that were around.'" I was struck again by Justine's reliably adult perspective on things, which required that she look at them from various points of view and not merely her own. Many people never transcend the hurts they received at their parents' hands. Right or wrong, their perspectives remain those of vulnerable children at the mercy of their all-powerful parents. Which is the child's truth: Parents, however damaged and flawed, are more powerful than their children. But Justine was one of those adults whose inner child was but one aspect of her identity. The adult Justine insisted on seeing her mother as someone who did her best and her father not as an all-knowing, all-powerful authority but as an imperfect, well-meaning man, a man who had prevailed over devastating loss to remain a devoted husband and father, as well as a highly competent physician who supported a large family.

It seemed to me that Justine's circumspect point of view was the result of something that had gone right between her and her father, even if it was her gimlet-eyed pragmatism that deserved much of the credit. Justine's dad cared more about building her competence than burnishing her self-esteem. He was a realist about the world and knew that to succeed in it, Justine would have to focus more on her skills than her feelings. He brought her to work when she was a child, taught her some basic procedures, and let her work with patients; he supported her emotionally when she decided to major in philosophy, then supported her financially when she had to make up some courses to apply to medical school; when she graduated, he made her a partner in his practice. Now, as her mentor, he told her the truth as he saw it, declining to sugarcoat reality to spare her feelings. If he thought she should pursue speaking engagements, he said so; if he believed she should be writing articles, he said so. But Justine understood that he was merely offering advice based on what had worked well in his career, knowing that Justine would take it only if it suited her and that she was doing just fine without it. He was telling her what he thought she needed to know to succeed; he was also aware that she was succeeding already. They shared a practice, after all: He had held out his hand to her, and she had taken it.

I could stop writing here and you'd probably come away impressed, as I was, by Justine's preternatural confidence, the blind trust she had in her instincts, and the little voice she said she always listened to. You would probably wonder why some people have to suffer as much as Justine and her family did, and perhaps feel a measure of comfort that she had emerged from the maelstrom of grief and loss into a secure and stable life.

But there was more.

When Justine was a resident in neurology, a few colleagues invited her to join them and some friends for dinner one night when her shift was over. When she arrived at the restaurant, she spotted them at a table in the corner and, as she approached, found herself looking into the eyes of the most beautiful man she had ever seen. His name was Omar; he was from Egypt, where his family still lived, and was a neurobiologist doing research at a neighboring medical center. Justine said she remembered little of the dinner, so mesmerized was she by his intelligence, his wit, and his beauty. He engaged her in conversation, asking about her parents, her siblings, and her work, listening intently as she spoke and making her feel as if there was no one in the room but her. He asked for her phone number as they were leaving the restaurant. "I froze," Justine said. "He was just so gorgeous, I didn't quite trust that he was really interested in me. I said something about working a lot of hours and that he could look me up at the hospital. Before he could say anything, I turned and hailed a cab. I never thought I'd see him again."

But Omar was persistent. He kept calling, and Justine finally relented and met him for dinner.

"It was, literally, love at first sight. I had never felt anything like it. I was completely overwhelmed, and he seemed to feel the same way. It took me a while to believe it. He was so charming, so smart, so gorgeous, he could have had anyone—why did he want *me*? But he did." Justine shook her head; her mouth curved in a small, private smile. "He did want me. I still can't believe it happened."

If Justine was ecstatic, her parents were less so. She did not elaborate more than to say that they never quite trusted Omar's intentions, even when the couple started talking about marriage and children. "It was the way he looked," Justine said. She meant to be cryptic and I went no further, but inferred that his startling good looks and exotic background rendered him fundamentally unknowable to her parents, who might also have feared that his passion for their daughter was stoked by the prospect of obtaining American citizenship. Justine was disappointed by their reaction but undeterred: Her small inner voice told her that this was her beloved, and she trusted it implicitly. "The odd thing was, he was actually a lot like my father," she said. "My dad loves topaz, and Omar did, too. And as pragmatic as my father is, Omar was the same way." When Omar proposed marriage, she accepted. For the first time in her life, Justine knew bliss.

It was short-lived. Several months after the engagement, Omar fell while he was jogging. He said it felt as if his leg simply collapsed beneath him and attributed it to having done several long runs the week before. But when it happened again, he became concerned and went in for tests. The results were devastating:

Omar was diagnosed with amyotrophic lateral sclerosis, also known as Lou Gehrig's disease. A degenerative nerve disorder, ALS attacks motor neurons, gradually weakening muscles until the patient is paralyzed, although the brain remains intact. The patient eventually dies when she or he can no longer breathe. Survival rates vary, but most ALS patients die within three to five years after they are diagnosed.

The irony was lost on neither Justine nor Omar: Here they were, a neurologist and a neurobiologist, helpless in the face of the diagnosis. Still, they decided to go ahead and live as fully as they could. New drugs were being developed every day, after all; they had nothing to lose. Justine decided her work hours were monopolizing too much of her time, took a leave of absence from her residency, and went to work for her father, who offered her a job as his head nurse for as long as she needed it. She gave up her room in a housing complex for medical residents and moved into Omar's tiny studio apartment, where they were soon joined by his mother, who came over from Cairo to help care for him.

Justine's parents knew that Omar was ill, but they did not know the severity of his illness. Because her father was a neurologist, Justine knew that he would quickly figure out the nature of Omar's condition if she provided too much information. Loath to give them any reason to lobby against the wedding, which was fast approaching, Justine told them that Omar was suffering from a mysterious constellation of neurological symptoms but that he was responding to treatment. A little more than a year after they met, they were married.

Omar's symptoms worsened dramatically during the honeymoon. Within months, he was seriously disabled; a year and a half later, he died.

Justine said she fell into a depression that lasted nearly three years; at its worst, she was suicidal. Three times she underwent in vitro fertilization treatments using sperm Omar had donated and had frozen after his diagnosis; three times, she lost the fetus.

"The only thing that kept me from killing myself was the thought that Omar might not be waiting for me on the other side," she said. Her eyes brimmed with tears. "That, and that he would have wanted me to live. What Omar and I had in three years, most people don't have in a lifetime. Even though he was sick for a lot of it, I still had him; we had each other. It sounds so corny, so ordinary. But it wasn't; it was extraordinary. Every moment I was with him, I felt more alive, more conscious, more—" she clenched her eyes shut and held her hands open, as if holding her heart—"more fully engaged in life than I ever had before or since. I didn't want to live without him, but I knew he would have wanted me to go on. So I did."

Justine continued to work for her father until she felt ready to complete her residency, after which she joined his practice. Throughout her ordeal she continued to work, showing up every day, seeing patients, forcing herself to function in the midst of life while yearning for oblivion. She managed to go on as I imagine her parents—especially her father—had after they lost their children: by turning her vision outward toward the living and away from the dead and disciplining her mind to focus on work and the matter at hand. Even so, on the evening I interviewed her several years ago, she said that she was still struggling mightily with depression and that, quite frankly, she did not particularly want to live.

And yet she did live, and is in fact now flourishing. When I ran into her father recently, he told me that Justine is now the mother of two-year-old twins, a girl and a boy who look exactly like their father. They are beautiful, he said, beaming, very much the doting grandfather. He said the children had changed Justine's life: Every time she looked at them, she saw Omar, young, healthy, bursting with life. The children went to daycare, he said, so Justine could continue to work at the practice. "But she takes time off whenever she needs to be with them," he said. "Her boss is in love with those kids."

I included Justine's story here because of her resilience and strength. Although her life was riven by tragedy, she is not a tragic figure. Much of this is due to her unshakable faith in herself and her inner wisdom, the little voice that told her not to go in the ambulance with those people who were dying, but to stay outside with these other people who were alive. This woman is possessed of a self-certainty that is both rare and of her own making. I believe that Justine was the architect of her survival, and that her life is an edifice erected by triumphing over adversity.

But I also believe that Justine's resilience was nurtured and fortified by her father, whose faith in her intelligence, talents, and judgment buttressed her natural strength. In speaking of her late husband, she enumerated the traits he shared with her father, implying that choosing Omar was an affirmation rather than a repudiation of her dad.

Justine's relationship with her father was far from idyllic; I watched her face as she talked about his relentless prodding and could see that she wished it were otherwise. But his belief in her galvanized her faith in herself, and I saw that, too.

CHAPTER 9

A Father Who Taught His Daughter Everything He Would Have Taught a Son

My dad taught me how to change the oil in my car. . . . He made sure that . . . I learned how to drive stick shift, because no other female in our family other than my mother knew how to drive a stick shift. He prided himself on his girls being able to do anything that a boy can do.
—ISABEL, 31, CORRECTIONS OFFICER

Listening to Isabel, I began to appreciate how hard it might be to be the daughter of a cop. Or how lucky.

"There was this guy that I was dating that my dad did not approve of, and he let me know. He told me, 'There's something about that guy. That guy is shady.' It was his law enforcement side coming through. I appreciated it in the long run, because that guy did end up being shady. He was deceptive as far as what he was doing, who he was talking to. He was secretive as far as his child was concerned; he had a daughter from a different relationship. We dated for about a year and he never let me meet his daughter. He was secretive about what he was doing on his weekends. I was being understanding because he had a kid, but yeah, he was just secretive and sneaky. I saw that later on. I tried to make it better. My dad told me, 'I don't think he's being honest with you. I think he is two-timing—seeing someone else on the side.' He would tell me relationship pointers, like 'If that guy is being shady with you now, it will just get worse if you guys become more serious.' He definitely gave me relationship advice."

I noticed that Isabel said she appreciated her father's input "in the long run," implying that she might not have received it warmly when it was offered. She probably didn't want to hear it at the time. She was trying to be understanding when her boyfriend was being cagey, trying to make things better between them—in other words, trying to make the romance work despite her boyfriend's disingenuous behavior. Like many women, she was doing what our culture had taught her to do in matters of love (and many others): She was being caring, empathetic, complaisant, understanding—and hoodwinked, from the sound of it. And all the while, who was there, interpreting her boyfriend's behaviors and telling her what was really going on? Her dad.

"He let my sister and me know that we weren't able to have boyfriends until we were fifteen," Isabel said. "He set ground rules for us because he wanted us to be successful, to finish school, go to college. He was up front with us: 'If you're going to have a boyfriend, you can't have one until you're fifteen, and even then, you have to have group dates where you go out with other friends until I feel comfortable that it's okay for you to be one-on-one with the boy. You have to bring him to meet your mom and me. We will meet him and know who he is. We'll be familiar with what he looks like.' Being in law enforcement, he always let us know that that was very important. So he was up front with us as far as what he expected from us as we got older and dating started to happen.

"He made sure my sister and I went together if we went to parties. As long as we were together, both he and my mom were okay with the idea that we'd go to parties or go to an all-ages club here in Houston. He'd drop us off and pick us up, and he'd even be the taxi for our girlfriends if a bunch of us wanted to go dancing. He was the dad who would talk to the other parents, meet the

other parents, and say, 'Okay, I am taking the girls to this location, dropping them off at this time, and I'm picking them up at
this time.' As long as he knew where we were and who we were
with, he was okay with it."

I interviewed Isabel over the phone when she was on a break
at her job in Houston. She said she had lived all her life in Texas
and described herself as Hispanic, a practicing Catholic, and a
Democrat. She said her father was fifty-six and her mother fifty-
two, and it occurred to me that Isabel's father was rather young—
he was twenty-four or twenty-five when she, his first child, was
born—so he was still in his thirties when he established the rules
for dating his daughters. Isabel's mother was younger still, having
borne her when she was only twenty or twenty-one years old. So
he was departing from the path he and his wife had chosen when
he insisted that his daughters were going to go to college and
complete their educations before getting too involved with guys.
He knew what young men are like—he was still one himself—
and he was not standing idly by as his daughters came of age. All
of which intrigued me, because I had assumed (incorrectly, it
now seemed) that Isabel's father might have sought to influence
his daughter to replicate the choices he had made for himself.
They were both in law enforcement after all, a career in which
women are still a distinct minority. As I had done frequently over
the course of conducting these interviews, I reminded myself not
to assume too much.

Isabel was engaged to a sheriff's deputy ("The fact that my
fiancé is in law enforcement, he and my dad have that in common,
so they talk about that at times") and on hiatus from her job as a
correctional deputy in a Houston prison to participate in a new
leadership program. Prior to that, she had been a recruit training
officer, teaching new recruits defensive tactics, how to deal with
and communicate with inmates, officer safety, first aid, cardiopul-
monary resuscitation—everything they needed to know to work

inside the prison, as she said. She held a bachelor's degree in criminal justice and was also a graduate of the police academy. Law enforcement seemed to run in the family, and I asked if she had always known she wanted to be a police officer.

"Actually, no," Isabel replied. "Initially I wanted to go into forensics. I knew I wanted to get into law enforcement but had a different idea of which direction I'd go in. When I realized I had to get into chemistry, I changed my mind. I was able to do some volunteer work with the sheriff's department because my father was still employed at the time and he knew a supervisor in one of the units there, and he said, 'My daughter is looking to do some internships for college.' That is how I got on board with the sheriff's department. Through word of mouth as to which positions were available, and having realized I didn't want to go through the forensics training after all, I decided to try the positions that became available in the sheriff's department, and I eventually landed the position with the academy. I wanted to become a correctional deputy, and I realized that if I wanted to have a promotion, I was going to have to go through the academy. That made my decision for me as far as what I was going to do. That's how I landed in corrections."

"Was your father a big influence on your choice of career?" I asked.

"Yes, he was," she replied. "He was in law enforcement for thirty-plus years. He worked at the academy at one point; he trained special agents. I saw what he'd bring home as far as work was concerned, and I saw the ethics that he himself held and instilled within me and my sister, and I felt that it was a very respectable career. Living in a law enforcement home, having that influence, it became somewhat natural that it was something I'd get into myself. I didn't necessarily want to do what he did, though he did ask me to go that route. He started as a border patrol agent and he wanted me to be at the academy for border patrol, but I felt like that was not what I wanted to do—but I knew I wanted to do something within law enforcement."

"Was he disappointed that you didn't do that?"

"I don't think he was disappointed; if he was, he never voiced it. He did want me to go sworn, meaning to work out in patrol, to carry a weapon. My current position does not entail that. I am not sworn, I don't carry weapons. He did voice a little . . . it wasn't disappointment, but he felt I wasn't going to enjoy working inside a facility. Toward the end of his career, he was assigned to work inside of a jail, and he didn't enjoy it himself, so he thought that I wouldn't enjoy it. He felt like, 'You might be making a wrong decision, but it's your decision. Do what's going to make you happy.'"

As was often the case, the father-daughter relationship that was emerging was more nuanced than it had first looked. Yes, Isabel's father projected some of his feelings about their profession onto her, but that was hardly without precedent. Nina's father persuaded her to follow him into the family business and once she was there, he pressed her to assume the mantle of authority he thought she should have; Justine's father was only too happy to usher her first into his specialty and later into his practice. It seemed to me that Isabel's father was doing much the same thing, guiding his daughter's progress in a profession she had followed him into. But he also seemed to know where the boundary lay between his life and hers. According to Isabel, he had expressed his feelings about the job but counseled her to obey her own, which seemed both fair and reasonable. It also revealed a degree of restraint on his part. It made sense to me that a father would fear for a daughter whose profession put her in harm's way, and I thought it admirably circumspect of Isabel's dad not to browbeat her into making the decision he would have made. What a contrast with Sondra's father, who, you may recall, sought to influence his daughter's thinking by replacing it with his own. As Sondra said, "He always says to

me, 'Oh, honey, you can think you're going to want to work.
You're not going to want to work when you have kids.'" I saw a
distinct difference between the ways these two fathers dealt with
their daughters: Isabel's father acknowledged her autonomy; Sondra's father denied hers.

I harked back to what Isabel had said about her father wanting her to "go sworn" and carry a gun and asked her why she
thought that was.

"He thinks that I can do it," she said. "It's not that I feel I
can't. I feel it's not what I want to do. He feels I might be selling
myself short, that there are more opportunities and possibilities
for me having a sworn career versus having a correctional career.
And it's true—there are more opportunities that sworn officers
are provided within the department. But I knew I would not be
happy going that way."

"What made you know that?" I asked.

"At one point in the various positions I held with the sheriff's department, I was what we call a community service officer,
and you pretty much aid the patrol deputies in the field. I held
that position for two months, and I did not enjoy what I did during that period, so I knew that if I didn't like the position as a
person assisting the patrol deputies, then I wouldn't like the position as patrol deputy."

"What didn't you like about it?"

"Honestly, I didn't feel very safe. The area I worked in was
high crime. I was working nights. As a community service officer, I didn't have the training that the sworn deputies had. Sworn
deputies go through a six-month academy prior to working at
patrol stations. As a community service officer, it's hands-on
training—you learn as you go. I didn't like that aspect of the job.
I didn't feel very safe with that job at all. All I carried was a can of
pepper spray and handcuffs. That was not desirable for me. I
didn't feel safe at all." Three times in thirty seconds, Isabel had
asserted that she hadn't felt safe in the job.

"But your father felt you were selling yourself short?"

"In my current position at corrections, he feels I am selling myself short, yeah."

"But not as a community service officer, the job you didn't like?

"Correct. He felt that I didn't give it enough of a shot because I only did it for two months. After the two-month training period, I said, 'No, I don't like this. I don't want to continue.' He definitely felt I didn't give it enough time to determine if it was for me or not for me."

"Did you feel bad that you were disappointing him?"

"I did, definitely. I didn't want to disappoint him, because I respect my dad and I respect what he thinks and his opinion of what I do. I want him to be proud of what I do. The fact that he felt that way did make me feel bad, but at the same time, I realized and knew that the bottom line was he wanted me to do what would make me happy."

This was interesting: Isabel was emphatic about not feeling safe armed with a mere can of pepper spray and so had resolved not to become a community service officer, despite her father's belief that she hadn't given the job enough of a chance. Yet she rejected the idea of carrying a gun, which would have made her feel safer and which her father would have preferred she do. She said straight out that she wanted her father to be proud of her and hated the idea of disappointing him, yet she stuck to her guns by refusing to carry one, if you will. There was more than a little push-and-pull between this father and daughter, but, at least from what I could tell, it seemed to be working for them. I thought of Justine's father, who dispensed advice to promote her medical career while acknowledging that she was free to reject it, and saw a similarity with Isabel's father. Both of their tactics amounted to "Here's what I think; now do what you want." But I didn't get the feeling from Isabel, as I had from Justine, that her father's advice was freighted with higher expectations than she felt she could fulfill. Isabel seemed able to follow or decline her father's advice with equanimity. In my view, this betokened a trust on her part that his opinion of her did not depend on whether or not she followed his advice. I asked her if she felt he understood her.

"He and I were definitely able to have sit-down conversations and talk to each other at the end of the day, whether I came home from a day at school or a day at work," she said. "We had open conversations about what happened that day, what we thought was important. We had an open relationship."

"You felt you could talk to him about personal feelings?"

"Absolutely, yes."

"Your mother, too?"

"Definitely. However, my mom would say I'm a daddy's girl. She does think that my dad can sit down and be calm with me and speak with me. If he's angry at someone else, he says I bring a calmness to him, where he and I can speak. But I'd be able to confide in either one of them equally." This was different from what other women had said about feeling more comfortable discussing feelings with their mothers.

"Were you able to bring a sense of calm to him more so than your sister was?"

"Yes. My father and my sister are so much alike that they would butt heads. It's 'my way or no way' for the both of them; they both feel very strongly. And my dad and my sister didn't have the same relationship growing up that my dad and I had. Me being the older one, my dad instilled in me that I had to set the example for my sister, and I just went along with it without question. My sister is the younger one, so she's more rebellious. When she was told no, she'd do it just because of that, so he got after her more. So they had a harder relationship. I guess she felt she couldn't confide in him as much as I did."

"What did you feel, want, or wish for from your father that he might not have known or understood?"

"Sometimes I wished he would hear my sister out more. For

whatever reason, if he was disappointed in her or felt her choices were wrong, he was quick to be angry with her, so she was quick to be angry with him. I saw that and was very much the mediator in the house. I wished that he would try to be more understanding with her and deal with what he saw as disappointments in her in a different way."

What had gone right between Isabel and her father had gone awry between him and her sister, whose relationship lacked the give-and-take that characterized Isabel's connection with him. I inferred that Isabel's sister, unconstrained by needing to set an example for anyone, may have made a few decisions that caused her (and probably her parents) some grief. Rather than feel she could compromise with her dad, as Isabel did, the sister felt honor bound to defy him, undoubtedly sabotaging her own best interests here and there along the way. What Isabel and her sister had in common was a need to assert and differentiate themselves from their father's expectations—a good thing, to be sure. But their ways of differentiating themselves were markedly different and yielded varying results.

Along the continuum of father-daughter dynamics, this was a recurring theme: a father wanting to guide his daughter in the direction he thought best for her, and the daughter having to decide how to deal with dad's advice. Would she embrace it without question, as Dianne did when she relinquished her autonomy so as to remain daddy's little girl? Would she accept it grudgingly, as Maureen did when she dutifully became a teacher while harboring a fantasy of attending law school? Would she flat out reject it, as Isabel's sister did, and predictably and repeatedly incur her father's wrath? Or would she consider it, as Isabel did, and balance it against her own judgment and use the best of both to point her in the right direction?

What enabled Isabel to decide what was best for her was due in large part, I believe, to the feelings of mutual respect and regard she and her father shared. The respect was engendered throughout her childhood when they had those sit-down, open conversations she described. I believe that those conversations established a pattern of exchanging ideas, which evolved into the emotional give-and-take that enabled Isabel to take from her father what she felt was helpful and give herself permission to decline the rest. Like Jackie, whose endless questions elicited patient, thoughtful answers from her dad, Isabel's conversations with her father established an atmosphere that welcomed inquiry and discussion. And like Jackie, Isabel also found herself the mediator of the family, the one who could be counted on to keep a cool head, see everyone's point of view, and help resolve disputes.

When I asked Isabel if she felt guilty about being her father's favorite, she demurred, saying that he treated her and her sister alike.

"He didn't treat me any better," she said. "He provided the exact same to me and to my sister. If I got a new car, she got a new car. If he gave me money, he gave her money. He gave us the exact same thing. I think he smiled upon me more [because] he preferred my actions and my choices more than he preferred hers." In this I heard echoes of Justine saying her father had issued to all her siblings an invitation to join his practice, though she was the only one to take him up on the offer. I wondered if there existed in Isabel, as I felt might be the case with Justine, a twinge of guilt at having found more favor in her father's eyes.

"What do you feel you've gotten from your father?" I asked.

"My sense of loyalty, not only toward my career but also toward individuals. My sense of fairness. He is a very fair man. Like I said, whatever he gave one child, he gave the other. A sense of honesty. In law enforcement, that's what you pride yourself on, being honest. Hardworking. My father's definitely a hard worker, whether it was at work or at home. He used to have a garden. He's very hospitable, as well. Those are qualities that I share and pride myself on. I'm all those same things."

Loyalty. Fairness. Honesty. A strong work ethic. Hospitality. These were the qualities Isabel admired in her father and cultivated in herself. By embodying these ideals, he gave her the central tenets on which to model her life. He also, however, had some qualities that Isabel chose not to emulate.

"My dad is heavy into video games," Isabel said, "and I have not gotten that from him. He sits there for hours, playing against himself or online, against people all over the world. I am not into that at all and that's fine by me." Isabel said her father's gaming is a source of strife in his marriage and that her mother has even considered divorce at times, but ultimately relented. I asked Isabel if she ever tried to talk to him about it.

"I did when I got to the point where I saw my mom was so unhappy that she was talking about leaving my dad. I told him, 'Mom's not happy. You need to make some changes.' He and I sat down and talked about that, and he said, 'You're right. I do need to make some changes. I'm going to try.' He tried for a while, but eventually went back to gaming. I think they fought for so long that my mom got tired of the fighting and she just accepted it."

"Did you feel in some way that you had to parent your dad at that point?"

"In that particular instance, I would say yes, because I had to make him see what he wasn't seeing, as far as the hurt he was creating."

"So that aspect of him has been a disappointment for you?"

"Yes."

Isabel's story reminded me that no one is without flaws, not even the man who taught her everything she knows about loyalty, honesty, and fairness. The guy who worked his tail off on the job could also spend endless hours sitting on it at home, mesmerized by a video display and lacking the wherewithal to change his ways despite his daughter's pleas. Yet he could still inspire her, motivate her, and make her feel as if she could do anything. Isabel said both of her parents had high expectations for their daughters, but it was her father who voiced them, who was more of the driving force behind her need to succeed. While Isabel had said her mother would describe her as a daddy's girl, I found it ironic because she clearly was not what I would think of as a daddy's *little* girl; she was manifestly able to stand up to her dad and make her own decisions.

"He never had a son, so he treated me as the son he never had," Isabel said. "It didn't matter that you were a girl; you were going to do the exact same thing that any boy can do." I asked her how that attitude made her feel.

"I guess you could say prideful. I have pride knowing that my dad didn't treat me any different just because I was a girl. I could do anything that my boy cousins could do. He didn't say, 'She can't do that because girls don't do that.' He never gave certain roles to me or my sister because that's what girls are supposed to do. Girls are supposed to be in the house cooking, baking, looking pretty—he never did that. He'd say, 'Come outside and mow the lawn.' I mowed the lawn up until I left home. I pulled the weeds. My dad taught me how to change the oil in my car, how to drive a stick shift. He made sure that . . . I learned how to drive a stick shift, because no other female in our family other than my mother knew how to drive a stick shift. He prided himself on his girls being able to do anything that a boy can do.

"To this day, in my job, I have that confidence, because he's instilled that in me. Being in a male-dominated profession, I don't have any lesser expectations on me as far as what I can do. I'm expected to do the exact same things a male deputy can do. Sometimes I am placed in some leadership positions where I'm leading the guys, and sometimes I am leading gentlemen that are older than I am. I have no problem with it."

Perfect father? No. Perfect relationship? No again. But perfectly within the realm of something going right, I would say.

PART III

You and Your Father:

When You Want to Make Things Better

[CHAPTER 10]

Who Is This Man?
If You Think You Know
Your Dad, Think Harder

O f all the unexpected revelations that sprang from my
research, two seemed particularly significant.

The first was that every woman I spoke with acknowledged
her father's importance in her life, even when her relationship
with him had been difficult, or worse. "To this day, my sister and
I refer to him as Señor Shithead," said Wendy, a fifty-four-year-
old single mother by choice of three adopted brothers from Pan-
ama, now ages fourteen, thirteen, and eleven. "He was
emotionally abusive. Never once did my sister or I ever hear him
tell us that he loved us. Nor did he ever really touch us. He did
not have the capability, on many levels, to be a father. But guess
what? I am probably 90 percent of who I am today because of him
and my relationship with him. It's not the warm, fuzzy type when
you go look at the experiences, but I can have a warm, fuzzy feeling about it, because I love who I am. I am grateful. I'm now to a
point where I wouldn't be who I am without all of that." Wendy

allowed that spending some time in therapy had helped her arrive at her sanguine view of the relationship, but my wonder remained. She could easily have relegated her father's memory to the trash heap, but the importance of his presence in her life demanded that she find a way of giving it value. In so doing, she gave herself value as well.

Consider also the comments of Zoe, a nineteen-year-old college student whose parents were both women and whose father was a sperm donor whom, she said, she wants to meet. "I definitely want to soon," she said. "I don't expect anything from him. I don't even know if he's alive. But I want to know him, to know if I am similar to him, to make comparisons. And if a relationship develops, that might be nice, too, to have a male figure in my life, because I've never really had that. I think my parents did an excellent job of raising me in many ways, values and those things. But to just have a male around to show me . . . to have him around and be comfortable with him would have been nice. To show me men can be trusted. I've had a lot of experiences in my life to the contrary and I think it would have been nice to have a model. It'd save me a lot of trouble." It was instructive that Zoe said her wish to meet the man who had fathered her issued from two places: her need to know what aspects of him, if any, had found their way into her and her desire to become acquainted with the essential nature and reliability of men.

The second significant revelation was that so many women seemed not to have thought much at all about their relationships with their dads. I was surprised by the number of "You know, I never thought about that" responses I got during the interviews. I mentioned earlier that one of the women contacted me afterward to tell me how helpful her friend, whom I had also interviewed, had found the process. "Sometimes—many times—one of the first steps toward healing is to realize that you're hurt in the first place," she said.

These two revelations inspired this part of the book, in

which I offer some suggestions for new ways daughters might want to think about their fathers that may improve the quality of their interactions with the first men in their lives. Even the most harmonious father-daughter connection features the occasional discordant note, as Fran, the physicist, revealed when expressing her frustration with her father's increasingly conservative views. Likewise, even the most troubled, overwrought, baggage-laden relationship is not without hope—if not of reconciliation, then at least of the daughter finding a new way of seeing her father that might help her make sense of the forces and motivations that shaped him and his actions. If nothing else, the daughter might come to understand that the discomfort or pain she feels in the presence of her father or his memory can be eased and perhaps even healed if only she first realizes that she has been hurt.

Part III begins with a questionnaire[1] to get you thinking about how well you really know your dad. The rest of the chapter is divided into a series of what-if relationship scenarios accompanied by discussion of some possible incarnations and suggestions for what I hope are novel ways of thinking about and practical techniques for dealing with their deleterious effects. I have not attempted to present anything akin to "Ten Foolproof Steps to Healing Your Relationship" because I believe there is no such thing. To suggest that there could exist a regimen of actions, behaviors, and attitudes that would work for every person is simply preposterous. Every daughter is different from every other daughter, just as every father is from every other father and every relationship is from every other relationship. And, in fact, every encounter is different from every other encounter. A daughter's amiable visit with a normally quarrelsome father might be followed a week hence by a more typical one, complete with fireworks (his) and premature leave-taking (hers). For the daughter to have thought that their troubles were over would have been naïve, and discovering that they were not over would have been discouraging (to say the least). It is to dismantle the cycle of disappointment and discouragement that I offer the following suggestions, questions, and insights, which are designed to gently poke confusion and complacency in the ribs and prod you to delve into parts of yourself you may not have visited lately. When you read through the what-if scenarios, see if any look familiar to you; likewise, when you read the interview quotes, listen to hear if any sound like you. If so, mull over the list of questions, suggestions, and insights. Allow yourself to look at yourself and your dad from an informed distance and be open to what you see and feel.

I offer the suggestions in Part III in response to the women who were so forthright in sharing their stories with me. Many of them said that the interview process made them think in ways they had not before; others said that answering my questions provoked far-flung fragments of memory and emotion to fly together like iron filings to a magnet, coalescing into a shape that they could recognize and think about. As you encounter the scenarios in the pages to come, think of them as magnets for your own fragmented thoughts and feelings. If you find them flying together, perhaps you will see something in them that speaks of you and your dad.

How Well Do You Really Know Your Dad?

T H E following questions are geared toward helping you think about the kind of connection you share with your dad. You don't have to write down any answers, just think about the questions. Most of the questions are about him; some are about you.

Feel free to share this questionnaire with your father. If you don't know the answer to a particular question, ask him. When you do know an answer, ask him to expand on it so you can learn more. For instance, even if you know where he was born, you might not know what it was like to live there when he lived there. Ask him about it. These sorts of questions can ignite conversations, and those conversations can take you to some exotic and unexpected places.

Understand that this might take some work: You are working with patterns of communication between daughters and dads that have been scripted by the dominant culture and circumscribed

200 OUR FATHERS, OURSELVES

by propriety over hundreds of years of history. Armed with these questions, take the initiative and sally forth. You never know.

QUESTIONNAIRE:
HOW WELL DO YOU KNOW YOUR DAD?

* Where was your father born?

* Where has he lived?

* Where did he go to elementary, middle, and high school? College? Graduate school?

* What was it like to live in those places?

* What were his parents like?

* What was his relationship with them like?

* How close was and is he to his brothers, sisters, and other family members?

* What has been his favorite job?

* Does he like the job he currently has?

* If he could do anything for a living, what would it be?

* What are his favorite books?

* What are his favorite movies?

* If he is a sports fan, which teams are his favorites?

* What were his dreams for himself when he was your age?

* Of all the gifts you've given him, which are his favorites?

* What is his fondest memory of you?

* What is your fondest memory of him?

* What is his least favorite memory of you?

* What is your least favorite of him?

* Have you ever talked about any of those four memories?

* What is the funniest thing you ever saw or did together?

* What is the saddest? The most poignant?

* How are you alike?

* How are you different?

* What have your similarities and differences meant to each of you?

* What did he mean to you as you were growing up?

* What does he mean to you now?

* Have you ever told him either of those things?

* What do you think about him that might surprise him?

* When was the last time you talked for at least an hour, just the two of you, either in person or on the phone?

* What would he say if you proposed that the two of you go for a walk?

* What would he say if you asked him to tell you something he's never told you about himself?

* What would you say if he asked you the same question?

* What could he mean to you that he doesn't now?

* How would you change that if you could?

* What aspects of a mate would you like to resemble those of your father? What aspects would you like to be different?

* What kind of mate does he want for you?

* If you already have a mate, how does he feel about him or her?

* What do you do if he makes a remark that you utterly disagree with—especially when it is about you or an aspect of your life?

* What happens when that situation is reversed?

* If he makes you angry, do you tell him?

* When he makes you happy, do you tell him?

WHEN YOU WANT TO MAKE THINGS BETTER

Sometimes you want to improve a relationship but don't have a clue as to how to begin. Maybe you've tried to express what you want and need from him, but the conversation always turns into an argument. Or perhaps you've tried to improve the way you interact with your dad, but it doesn't seem to change the way he responds to you. As I said earlier, I don't believe that any one set of instructions can be applied to every relationship and yield satisfactory results. But I do believe that thinking about a relationship in a new way introduces the possibility of changing it. You can't change people, after all, you can only change yourself. And your self is 50 percent of every relationship you're involved in.

Think about the relationship you share with your dad. Do

you regard it as a partnership for which you both share responsibility or as a hierarchical arrangement that he controls? Do you see the relationship as an organic outgrowth of your interacting personalities or as a static entity set in the stone of your interwoven histories? I believe that although most father-daughter relationships are anchored in the bedrock of family traditions and dynamics, they also ebb and flow with the emotional tides of the father and daughter in question. They are living, breathing connections, as welcoming of or resistant to change as the people who inhabit them. Even if you cannot imagine your father seeing your side of the story or changing his ways, you can still make it a point to see *his* side and change *your* ways. In so doing, you may not end up with the perfect relationship (as if such a thing even existed), but rather a more honest one in which you feel freer to be your authentic self.

In the pages that follow, I offer what I hope are some novel ways of reconsidering your relationship with your dad with an eye toward instigating change down the road My intention is to shake up your point of view and create a new picture, just like when you rotate a kaleidoscope and the shaken-up crystals form a fresh creation. The same glassy fragments somehow look different when the light shines through the new arrangement. So it is with relationships: When you shake up your perspective, you sometimes see things in a fresh, new light that illuminates the possibility of change.

WHAT IF YOUR DAD ISN'T AVAILABLE?

The unavailable father takes various forms. Perhaps the most familiar is the dad who works all the time, citing the exigencies of his job as the reason for his inattention. He doesn't mean to ignore his loved ones; rather, he understands his primary role to be that of breadwinner, making the money that will shelter, feed, and clothe the very people who want to hang out and have fun with him. Many of these dads try to be both providers and companions, like Nina's father, who brought paperwork to her soccer games and was poked by the mother sitting next to him whenever the ball came near Nina. Other dads use their jobs to escape from the demands of family interactions, focusing obsessively on their cell phones and computers. It's hard to lure someone away from a phone call, text message, or Web page that needs to be urgently attended to, so you stand around watching your dad watching his electronics. It's not that he doesn't want to be with you, it's just that he's always too busy or distracted to engage with you.

Then there's the father who is physically unavailable, who seldom hugs or even touches you. You may not even be aware that he is physically distant until after you're grown, when your boy-friend's dad gives you a great bear hug as if it's the most natural thing in the world. Suddenly, you realize that your own father has never held you in this way and that you've been missing something.

Finally, there's the father who has made himself unavailable to you for all practical purposes. Perhaps he abdicated his respon-sibilities after a divorce, imagining he was getting back at his ex-wife by refusing to pay child support or participate regularly in his children's lives. Or maybe he abandoned the relationship alto-gether, as one woman's father did, cutting off all communication with his children: "For a number of years, he just stopped speak-ing to us. That was the first of three times he did that. After a year, my sisters went back to the village where he was living and recon-nected with him, and then I did. But I changed my last name and took my mom's second married name. I did that as a 'screw you'— if you're going to kick us out, I'm going to change my name. I did that because I knew it was really important to him." This act of defiance felt good at the time, but when Gemma told me the story, it was twenty years later and she said she regretted it because of

the pain it caused her father and the damage it did to their already
battered relationship.

*If your dad isn't available, here are some things to do and
think about*

- * Your relationship with your father is like a dance whose
  steps you both know by heart and seldom alter. Now,
  think about how you might take the lead and change the
  steps, improvising a new way of moving together in a
  different direction.

- * How would you describe whatever intimacy there is
  between you and your father?

- * How much intimacy is enough for you? How much is too
  little? How much is too much?

- * Who makes the most effort to be close, you or your dad?
  Why is that?

- * If you make an effort to be close, what do you expect in
  return? Are you getting it? If not, what do you think you
  might do in response?

- * How much time and physical and emotional energy are
  you willing to invest in finding and maintaining a balance? How would your life be different if your father
  were more present in it?

- * If your father is absent, it does not mean that others can't
  provide the missing piece, even sometime later in life.

- * If your dad is not there to be a mentor, find another one.
  Nichelle, the budding investment banker whose father

could neither read nor write, found a mentor in an entrepreneur who told her, "I want to help you unleash what I
think is a star within you" and proceeded to underwrite
her new business. The world is full of accomplished,
successful professionals—both men and women—who
are eager to share their expertise with young people
starting out in their careers. It's up to you to find such a
person and cultivate a relationship with him or her.

* If your father chronically lets you down, can you write
  him off as a stroke of bad luck and move on, or do you
  feel a need to stay connected to him?

* Sometimes the father you want is never going to be there
  for you. As hard as it is, it's better to acknowledge this
  fact and adjust your expectations accordingly.

WHAT IF YOUR DAD DOESN'T LISTEN?

Like many women I interviewed, Rebecca, the marine biology
graduate student, wished her dad were a better listener: "Sometimes I get frustrated when I want to talk about something that I
am upset about, because he is always trying to fix it. . . . Sometimes I just want to explain why I am upset without anyone telling me how to fix it." Like Rebecca's father, most dads who don't
listen don't mean to ignore their daughters. To the contrary, many
of these dads urgently want to solve their daughters' problems
because they can't bear to see their little girls unhappy, confused,
or struggling. As soon as they've heard enough to grasp the gist of
the issue, they're offering their insights and telling them what to
do. That's what men do when confronted with conflict or stress:
They take action, and to a man, listening is not the same thing as
acting. Women are different; to us, listening is an act of comforting and companionship. But to men—and your dad is a man, after

all—listening feels passive. He's got to *do* something, so he tells you how to handle things, which may bear little resemblance to how you were thinking of handling it. You're left feeling frustrated and irritated because he just doesn't understand what you want from him. Later, you may feel a twinge of guilt for not showing how much you appreciated his help, however unhelpful it may have been.

The other sort of nonlistening dad is the one who thinks he knows what you're going to say and thinks he knows all the answers. He pontificates, lectures you, and tells you what to do without stopping to consider your point of view. He differs from the first sort of nonlistening dad in that he needs to establish his dominance over the situation. Bonnie, a jewelry designer in her thirties, said she has this issue with her father. "When I go to see him, I start to say something about myself and he interrupts with an expert opinion. I'll say, 'Hey, I read this book,' and he'll stop me with 'Oh, I know the CEO of the company that book is about,' or 'Yeah, I did a project with the guy who wrote it.' He's always trying to be the only person talking. It's not cruel. It's not cold. It's kind of ignoring the other people in the room." If your father behaves like Bonnie's, you may feel not only frustrated and irritated, but also invisible. They may not realize it, but by hijacking these conversations and shifting the focus toward themselves, these dads routinely supplant their daughters' needs with their own, making their daughters feel neither seen nor heard.

If your dad doesn't listen, here are some things to do and think about

* Many women who have strong relationships with their fathers also have a hard time finding their own voices. Do you have a strong relationship with your father? If

so, do you hear his voice inside your head more than your own?

* There's a fine line between unconditional support and overwhelming direction. Your father may want the best for you, but it's up to you to define what "best" really means.

* Is your father guiding you or dominating you?

* Is your father prodding you to reach your potential, or is he making it hard for you to trust your own judgment, learn from your mistakes, and think for yourself?

* Even if your father refrains from bombarding you with criticism, you may still find that his guidance, advice, or mentoring inhibits your ability to make the decisions you want to make and live the way you want to live.

* If you have a history of being dominated by your father, do you also find yourself adopting a submissive attitude at work and in other relationships? If the answer is yes, are you satisfied with the way that makes you feel?

WHAT IF YOUR DAD DOESN'T SEEM TO SEE YOU OR KNOW WHO YOU REALLY ARE?

It is common for a father's image of his daughter to be somewhat incongruent with reality; most of the women I spoke to, for example, said they never talked to their dads about their sex lives. Keeping this subject off-limits worked for all parties involved and represented a mutual forbearance: The daughters preserved their privacy and the fathers avoided getting too much information.

But a father may be unable to see his daughter as the grown woman she's become. He may be unable to comprehend that the girl who started out as a premed student now lives at an ashram and meditates for four hours a day, or that his once delicate girly girl now sports a nose ring and multiple tattoos. Perhaps he was seldom home when you were growing up and never got a chance to know you; now that you're grown and out of the house, it's almost as if you're strangers. Or maybe he just sees you as a generic female, as Margo's father saw her: "He was always taking my brother on vacations and trips—scuba diving, surfing, skiing. I know how to do all those things. He even took my husband on vacation, like a boys' trip thing. He always thought I wouldn't have any fun because I'd have no girls to go shopping with, which is not me at all." It's not that Margo's father didn't love her; he just didn't make the effort to see who was really there.

Then there's the father who simply seems unwilling to acknowledge who his daughter really is. He doesn't know what your goals and aspirations are, or what is important to you, or how you feel about things. It's not that he's never thought about it; it's that he refuses to think about it. Amanda, the kindergarten teacher whose father glazed over whenever she talked about her job, experienced his apathy even before she worked with kids. "Before I [taught]," she told me, "I worked in an art gallery. It was my first job out of college, and it was a big deal for me. He's not interested in the art world, which is fine, but I don't get any sense that he wants to learn about it. Sometimes it seems like he is in a box. We can talk about the things in the box. He's not able to process things outside of the box. It limits our relationship." This is even more painful than having a dad who's clueless, because an uninterested father seems to be making a choice to remain that way and, therefore, to be willfully distancing himself from you.

If your dad doesn't seem to see you or know you, here are some things to do and think about

   * You want your father to see you as you are. Do you see him as he is, or as you want him to be?

* Don't assume you know the man behind the title. Just because he reared you doesn't mean you know him. If you're like most women, you probably don't know as much about your father as you think you do.

* Bonds are built on trust, trust is built on understanding, and understanding takes work. Don't be afraid to blow up the old assumptions about what you mean to your father and what he means to you. Relationships run in two directions, not one. If you want him to be more tuned in to your life, you need to be more tuned in to his.

* The way to building a deeper relationship with your father may lie in evincing an interest in something that interests him, and for many dads, athletics is a good place to start. Deborah, a thirty-four-year-old press agent, said that her father worked all the time but she forged a lasting connection with him through his passion for sports. "I could tell you anything about any team. I watched ESPN in my spare time. I spent a lot of time with my father at sporting events growing up. I knew if I wanted to go, I would be able to be with him, and that's what would endear me to him." Now, Deborah turns to her dad when she needs advice on work-related issues, as does her husband, and she traces the durability of her adult relationship with her father to her childhood investment in his love of sports. Not all dads are into sports, of course, but most dads are into something. Yours may be a jazz aficionado or an opera buff; he may love to cook or know everything there is to know about the Civil War. What he cares about is not as important as your willingness to learn enough about it to start a conversation and open a channel of communication with him.

* Do you find it harder to accept your father's flaws than those of your friends? Do you find it easier?

* Don't expect more from your father than you do from your friends.

WHAT IF YOUR DAD IS UNCOMFORTABLE WITH OR UNSKILLED AT DEALING WITH FEELINGS, WHETHER HIS OR YOURS?

It's a rare dad who doesn't fall into this category at least some of the time. I heard a lot of stories about dads who shied away from all things emotional, whether out of discomfort, anxiety, or a disconnection with their own emotions. Maybe your dad shares these qualities and presents himself as a highly rational being who is unaffected by the vagaries of emotional engagement. When you tell him that he seems down, he assures you, scowling, that he's just as cheery as ever; if you ask him why he's angry or irritated, he denies that anything is wrong. You know better, of course; it's not that he doesn't have feelings, it's that, like many men, he was taught as a child that he should control and in some cases ignore his feelings as manifestations of vulnerability. He is also likely loath to admit to you, his daughter, that he sometimes has struggles of his own, because he has no doubt tried to appear big and strong since the day you were born. Burdening you with his problems is probably the last thing he wants to do because, in his mind, he's supposed to support and protect you, not the other way around. He thinks it's better to maintain a stoic façade than to have you worrying about him.

Another form of emotional detachment is when a father is unable to empathize with his daughter's feelings. One woman described having a devastating breakup with her first boyfriend when she was a teenager. "At one point, my dad said, 'When are you just going to get over this?' He yelled it, of course. That drew a line for me. My feelings were not considered. I was walking around crying and heartbroken for a long time, but it was still a pretty a-hole thing to say. I don't think I introduced him to a boyfriend in college." As heartless as this father's outburst sounds, my guess is that it resulted from his pain at seeing his daughter so distraught. Still, he wounded her, and she protected herself by not introducing him to any of her male companions for many years.

Insensitive dads don't have a monopoly on hurtful remarks, by the way; sometimes a loving dad thinks he's being funny and the joke backfires. Fran, the physicist with a strong relationship with her dad, remembered him teasing her about a boy she liked in first grade. "I was just mortified. I made a little vow in my six-year-old heart that I would never speak to my father about boys. When I was a senior in high school, I realized that I'd held on to that. I felt like I could talk to my dad about a lot of things, but not about boys." It's worth noting that when these daughters felt misunderstood by their dads, it had long-term effects, with both of them refusing to confide in their fathers about romance for many years. If this sounds familiar, you may want to reconsider the strategy because it deprives both daughter and father of opportunities for closeness long after the initial hurt has faded.

Finally, there's the frustration of wanting and needing your father's empathy, only to have him donate it to someone else. That's a tough one, because you can't accuse him of being out of touch with his feelings, he's just out of touch with yours. You may rationally accept that as an adult and competent human being, he has the right to decide for himself how he feels about things. But as his daughter, you might feel hurt and emotionally abandoned, as did Elyse, a music agent in her thirties: "The thing that upsets him the most is when I tell him there are things I'm not happy about with my husband. He just says, 'You have to make it work.' He gets very sad and withdraws. I have to justify why I am angry.

Then my dad will get angry with me, saying, 'You were too hard on him.' I'll say, 'You don't know the background. You don't know what's going on.' I try to explain it to him, but in those situations, I wish that he would be on my side." As a woman, I don't blame her, but as a psychologist, I understand him, too. As a man, this father may have found it easier to empathize with his son-in-law's take on things than with his daughter's, and perhaps he was trying to quell their marital discord by getting her to understand where her husband was coming from. I believe his intentions were good, but it didn't feel that way to his daughter. The solution? As is often the case, the best thing might be for her to tell her father how his response made her feel: "Dad, I'm grateful that you care about my husband and that you want our marriage to succeed. But I've got to tell you, when you take his side, I feel as if you're allied with him against me. I know you don't mean it that way, but that's how it feels."

If your father is awkward or unskilled at dealing with feelings, here are some things to do and think about

* Comedian Garry Shandling once said, "My friends tell me I have an intimacy problem, but they don't really know me." So it is with fathers and daughters. Sometimes the most significant elements of the relationship are visible to everyone except the father and daughter themselves. Could this be the case with you and your dad?

* Whose responsibility do you think it is to nurture a closer relationship between you and your father?

* Some women claim that they yearn for more closeness with their fathers but are unaware that they have trouble letting people get close to them. Might this be the case with you?

* Women who say they hunger for greater connection and closeness with their fathers often have a hard time defining what that means. What kind of closeness do you wish you had with your father? How little is not enough, and how much is too much?

* If your father has trouble dealing with emotions, set an example by managing yours. If he has a pattern of hurting or angering you, break the cycle by taking a deep breath, resisting the urge to lash out, and calmly telling him how his behavior makes you feel.

* Older people are often reluctant and sometimes unable to talk about their feelings because they were taught to keep them to themselves. Is it possible that your father was brought up this way?

* Your dad may have trouble opening up to anyone, let alone you, his daughter. If the relationship is slow to develop, it is important to give it the time and commitment it needs.

* If he does open up to you, pay attention to your response. How does it feel? Are you comfortable with the intimacy, or does it feel as if you're getting too much information?

WHAT IF YOU CAN'T GET THROUGH TO YOUR DAD?

This sort of dad is a hybrid, comprising elements of the dad who won't listen and the one who doesn't see or know you. He is set in his ways and convinced that the world would be a better place if everyone adopted his point of view. He comes off as rigid, inflexible, and convinced of the righteousness of his views. Trying to get him to consider an alternative is an exercise in futility. Some of these dads are tyrants, demanding that their wives and children live by the rules they have chosen for themselves; others are benign dictators, cloaking their rigidity in an ostensible show of concern for others' well-being.

Such was the case with a dad whose daughter lamented his critical clobbering: "My sister struggles with her weight. My dad says it's black-and-white: 'Why don't you just get on the treadmill? Let's get you a personal trainer.' It would be great if he said, 'It doesn't matter. Don't worry about it.' Instead, it's 'I don't understand. Just don't eat as much.'" I get why this woman, a thirty-year-old radio producer, wished her father would tell her sister that her weight didn't matter: We all want to be accepted and loved as we are, and we want this for our loved ones as well. But it's also possible that this father's criticism was founded on genuine concern for his daughter's health and he wasn't quite the cad he appeared to be. The real issue is that he viewed his daughter's weight problem in a facile way, reducing it to a simplistic equation of consuming too much food and doing too little exercise. Convinced that his logic was unassailable, he offered pronouncements on how to make things right, offending and infuriating the people around him and dismantling their hopes of mutual understanding and connection.

In some cases the stakes are higher, as they were for Asima, an American-born medical student whose immigrant parents were exerting significant pressure on her to conform to the tenets of their faith. "The big thing I'd want my father to understand is that I'm not religious and be okay with that. My parents want me to have an arranged marriage or they are trying to help me find a boy who is also Muslim and Pakistani, which I don't care for at all. My parents live in one house but they have separate bedrooms. And it makes me mad that they are trying to find someone for me. They can't even make their own relationship work; why should they try to make mine?" Now, *that* is unassailable logic. I salute Asima's ability to see the absurdity of her quarreling parents acting as matchmakers, not to mention that of expecting a woman who will one day be making life-and-death decisions to allow her parents to decide whom she will marry. For this woman, her father's intractability posed a far greater risk than enduring an onslaught of weight-loss advice. Still, for her and other daughters who can't get through to their dads, the frustration and longing for understanding are real.

If you can't get through to your dad, here are some things to do and think about

* When was the first time you realized that your father wasn't perfect and didn't know everything?

* Some people are inflexible not because they choose to be, but because they know no other way to be.

* Sometimes a person's rigidity is based in insecurity. Some people equate open-mindedness with weakness and tyranny with strength.

* Is there anything you believe in so strongly that you cannot imagine thinking differently about it? Do you perceive yourself as being rigid in this belief or loyal to it?

* Have you ever tried to challenge your father's pronouncements? If so, what tactics have you used?

* When were you angriest with your father? How did you handle it? How did it affect you? How did it affect him?

* Imagine what might happen if you went against your father's wishes. What is the worst that could happen?

* Now that you have imagined the worst, ask yourself if it is a reasonable scenario. If not, what might be a more likely outcome? If so, could you adapt to it and learn to live with it?

WHAT IF YOUR DAD EXPECTS YOU TO HONOR AND ACCOMMODATE HIS NEEDS, PRIORITIES, AND OPINIONS IN PLACE OF YOUR OWN?

Fathers who want their daughters to put their needs first take many forms. They range from the lonely divorced guy who just wants to spend more time with his daughter, as Kelly's father did when he invited her to regularly join him for drinks (she eventually told him she'd prefer he go with a friend instead), to the preening narcissist who is oblivious to everyone's needs but his own. Most fathers fall somewhere in between, pressuring their daughters to, say, come home every weekend for a family dinner and resenting it when they don't or admonishing them not to move in with their boyfriends and being disappointed in them when they do.

It can be hard to deal with this dynamic because the daughter feels responsible for nurturing her father's happiness and retaining his love. She might think, *What's so terrible about having dinner with the folks every Sunday? If it means that much to my dad, maybe it's worth it.* Well, maybe it is and maybe it isn't. The question is whether or not she is compromising her long-term happiness to assuage her father's short-term distress. Having dinner with your parents (or your dad, if he's on his own) every weekend may not be terrible at all if you enjoy one another's company and they understand that you'll sometimes be busy with other plans. But if family meals are nerve-racking affairs that send your blood pressure surging or if your father makes you feel that missing one will wreck his mood and ruin his weekend, it may be terrible after all.

This dynamic can do long-term damage, as was the case with Abigail, the biologist whose father so memorably doused the family's belongings with gasoline. Abigail was heavily involved in sports in middle school and high school, and that became a source of relentless strife between her and her dad after he moved to the Virgin Islands. When she needed to miss a waterskiing outing in the Islands to pitch a championship softball game on the mainland, he freely vented his anger and disappointment, pitting Abigail's love for him against her loyalty to her team. An emotionally healthy father would have tried to ease his disappointment at his daughter's absence by focusing on his pride in her commitment to her teammates. But Abigail's father, like some others, seemed utterly oblivious to his daughter's needs. "The summer he died," Abigail said, "I was going from eighth grade into high school. I really wanted to try out for the basketball team. It was hard to go so far away from friends every summer, so I had asked him if I could just come for half of the summer, so I could still try out for the team and meet the people I'd be going to high school with. He got really upset, mad, and hurt." In the end, Abigail did visit for half the summer and try out for the team. But her father's self-interest created sufficient emotional turmoil for Abigail that, sadly, she felt a measure of relief when he died—a feeling for which she still feels twinges of guilt.

Less damaging are the fathers who are not so much oblivious to their daughters' needs as unaware of their nuances. Paola, a software saleswoman in her late twenties, described the emotional complexities of trying to establish her own household: "At times, my father makes me feel guilty for not being so family centered. I want to buy an apartment. My father's like, 'Oh yeah, we can do that. We can live on the top floor. You can live on the bottom floor.' I try to express to him that I want to do it on my own, and he'll be okay with it, but he'll bring out little guilt trips here and there. Then I'll feel guilty. I will think, *I could be helping them; we could be together, it could be a family thing.* Then I think, *Why am I so independent?* Then I feel bad." I see this father's attitude as more presumptuous than selfish; his misstep was pushing the concept of "we" when his daughter was struggling to establish "I." Still, it created problems for Paola, who was trying to live as an autonomous adult. It sounded to me as if she had the moxie to enforce her boundaries and do it on her own, but it would have been better had she not been made to feel guilty about it.

If your father expects you to put his needs before your own, here are some things to do and think about

* Every young girl loves pleasing her dad—making him happy, making him laugh, making him proud. But once you're grown, it's normal and necessary to want to make your own decisions and your own mistakes. Some fathers—perhaps yours—respond to their daughters' moves toward independence by feeling alienated and hurt.

* The emotional terrain turns rocky when your father's interest in your life extends to trying to control it. The challenge is to balance intimacy with your father with independence for yourself.

* Many daughters are learning what sons have known for a long time: A father's expectations can be a heavy load to carry.

* You must build a relationship with your father that allows you to grow into having the life you want, not the one he wants for you.

* Let your father into your life, but don't let him control it.

* Your connection with your father is stronger than you think. You won't break it by marking your territory.

WHAT IF YOU NEVER FEEL YOUR DAD APPROVES OF YOU?

Many women lamented having this problem. Its manifestations ran the gamut from Justine's situation, in which her father prodded her to do more to enhance her career as a neurologist based on what had worked for him, to the frustrations faced by Giselle, an art gallery owner reared in Europe whose prosperous father had routinely disparaged her potential since she was a child. This anecdote tells it all: "I went to boarding school at the age of twelve. Right before I left, we were at this lunch with friends of my parents and their kids, who all went to the boarding school I was going to go to. I was young, intimidated. My father yells at me across the table—I guess because one of the sons was turning president of the school— 'You're never going to become president of the school.' Well, three years later I picked up the phone and said, 'Dad, I became president of the school.' He said, 'That's good.' It was a nonevent. When I came to America, he didn't want me to go anywhere that was like New York, so I ended up going to Wellesley [in Massachusetts]. Then I made him a deal that if I got into NYU, he would let me transfer. When I got in, he let me transfer there and I graduated summa cum laude, which was also a nonevent. He is extremely critical of my life now. He criticizes it all the time. It's consistent. He barges into it with almost insane ownership."

Giselle said it has taken her most of her adult life to learn to cope with her father's relentless belittlement, which smacks of competitiveness (you'll read more about that part of the story in the next section) and a need to assert ownership over his daughter's professional success. She still squanders precious emotional resources on resisting his attempts to quash her confidence, yet when he does occasionally acknowledge her achievements, she basks in the warmth of his praise.

Whereas both Giselle and Justine chafed under their fathers' comments, I believe Justine's burden was easier to bear because her dad's urgings were tempered by his acknowledgment that she was doing perfectly well without them. Giselle's father, on the other hand, seemed to derive a perverse satisfaction from undermining her self-confidence. Unlike Justine's father, he would not concede to her skill and good judgment. Exercising these capacities is, I believe, key to a daughter's developing the ability to successfully defuse the explosive effects of a father's disapproval (or a mother's, for that matter). As a daughter, you must be able to separate your father's perceptions of you from the truth of who you are. He may love you, but that doesn't mean he sees you clearly. Just as your perception of him is colored by how you viewed him as a child and who you wish he was now, so, too, is his perception of you shaded by the fantasies and dreams he's had of the woman you might one day become.

And then there's the dad who can't seem to approve of who you are personally, whether it's how you wear your hair, the style of your clothes, the friends you hang out with, or whom you choose to date or marry. Teenagers routinely test the limits of their parents' approval by trying out rude and obnoxious behaviors, seeing how far they can go before mom and dad withdraw their approbation. But such outrages seldom reflect the teenager's essential self; rather, they are attempts to see where the boundaries are so they can live as close to the edge as possible while retaining their parents' love.

Margo, the woman whose father didn't take her scuba diving or skiing because he thought she'd prefer to go shopping, recalled that even as an adolescent, she had wished her father understood her better: "Oh god, I wanted him to just accept me. I didn't know what to do. I was running in circles half the time trying to figure out how to get him to accept me or like me. My brother and I lived with my mom after my parents split up. I was running around with pink hair and purple hair and chains and everything, and I'd go to my dad's house and he was mortified. He'd throw me out of the house, ostensibly, a number of times, because I wouldn't change my hair color back to normal. I wanted him to understand me and get me. My mom did. She was fine with my pink hair. I didn't understand why one parent was and one parent wasn't."

Although her hair is no longer prismatically dyed, Margo is still waiting for her father to "get" her at the age of thirty-five. Which brings up yet again the big news that I found: No matter what age a woman was or how successful she had become, she never outgrew the need to know her dad approved of her. As Sondra, the health insurance executive, put it, "I definitely don't think my dad knows how seriously I take his opinion, and how much I value and seek his approval. I don't think he's ever thought about that." The answer, it seems to me, is for daughters to get their fathers to think about it. For some ways to approach this, read on.

If you feel your dad never approves of you, here are some things to do and think about

* Maybe your father has evolved into a new and improved modern dad. If he hasn't, he may be stuck in the traditional roles of provider, protector, and giver and enforcer of rules and standards, perhaps because that's what he saw at home when he was growing up. If this is the case, try to approach him with patience and compassion.

* Try to imagine circumstances under which a person might see it as his duty to correct other people, especially family members, as a means of helping them improve their lives. How do you think this might affect his parenting style?

* What do you imagine your father thinks he is accomplishing by criticizing you?

* When he criticizes you, is it helpful or hurtful?

* Do you take it, or do you fight back?

* Have you ever tried to tell him, calmly and with your feelings under control, that his methods aren't working? That he is hurting you? That he is damaging your relationship?

* Have you ever tried telling him how important it is for you to feel he approves of you?

* How much of a role did pleasing your father play in your choice of college? Career? Spouse or significant other?

* If pleasing him was a major factor, are you happy with your choice? If you wanted to go in a new direction, could you tell him?

* What does he want your life to be like?

* Can you feel good about yourself even when he lets you know that he doesn't feel all that good about you? If not, can you see that you are adopting his feelings about you and embracing them as the truth when they are merely his perceptions?

* Can you accept that your father's view of you may be colored by his own values, struggles, and biases, and may not be accurate?

WHAT IF YOU SENSE THAT YOUR DAD IS COMPETING WITH YOU, OR THAT YOU ARE COMPETING WITH HIM?

If you think about a father and son, it's easy to picture them competing: Just about every mother of an adolescent boy has watched him try to arm wrestle his dad into submission or stand back-to-back with him, straining to see who's taller. But a father compete with his daughter? Or she with him? What in the world is *that* about?

It's about the fact that, for the first time, many daughters are looking to their dads, not their moms, as role models and wondering how they measure up. And it's about time we looked at this dynamic more closely, because it's one that will become more commonplace as daughters increasingly occupy the place in the family formerly reserved for sons. Here's Giselle, the art gallery owner whose father had denigrated her competence since childhood: "I was the boy he never had. He drove me my whole life, to the point where I spent a few years thinking 'I'm a mess' because of it. Now I am learning how to deal with him. In a funny way, he wants my success more than he wants his success, but he wants my success to come from him, and he wants to be able to control my success. When I'm in a really good place, he's really tough with me and he brings me down. When I have a problem, he becomes the most incredible person in the world. If he can resolve my problem, he's amazing.

"When the market was bad in 2009, I had a really hard time with my business. He was there for me, but he was actually the most destructive person I've ever had. For literally seven months, he would tell me every day that I was an incapable loser." Giselle had her father's modus operandi nailed: When she was down, he was her savior, rescuing her from disaster and displaying his superior gifts. But when she succeeded, he undermined her confidence, intimating that success was hers only if he had something to do with it. The bottom line was that when it came to his daughter, it was all about him. If you have a similar dynamic with your father, mustering a solid sense of self is probably as hard for you as it was for Giselle.

Giselle's is an unusual example of father-daughter competition, but less dramatic varieties abound. Your dad may feel diminished because you are more successful in your career than he is or was in his, or you may feel guilty for the same reason. Joan, the veterinarian who rejected her husband's bid to buy a BMW, mentioned that her father was still working at retirement age—he had one child left to send through college—and that it bothered her. "Both my husband and I are financially better off than my parents," she said. "I try not to let them know what things cost or what we make. You feel kind of guilty when you've grown up and see how much you have taken from them. I feel bad for them a little bit. They probably could do nice things for themselves, but they don't. It makes me feel bad." Joan's struggle was twofold: Not only did she wish her father didn't have to work so hard, she also believed that if she had enough money to buy a European sports car, she ought to give the money to her parents instead. Simply put, she did not feel entitled to her own success.

Finally, you may be competing with your father if you feel you'll never be as successful in your career as he is or was in his. If you're following the same career path as your dad, your pride in perpetuating his legacy may be dimmed by fear that you won't be as competent as he was or make as much money as he did. You may worry about how to combine marriage and family with a high-powered career, or your career goals may be different from his, as was the case with Ginger, a medical student whose father was a physician.

"He is a lot more ambitious than I am," she told me. "His career has been extremely lucrative and he's been in a lot of different jobs and succeeded at a lot of different things. I think it would be impossible to keep up. But on the other hand, I recognize that that is not necessarily what I want for myself, because he's under a lot of pressure a lot of the time, and I'm a little bit more mellow. He's encouraged me to try my best, but also has encouraged me to be okay with myself when I don't do as well as I wanted to. I think that's been helpful. He's caused me to strive to do everything I can do and be able to let it go when it doesn't necessarily work out. On the other hand, I get frustrated with myself because I don't antici-pate having the degree of professional success that he has had. He is a very hard act to follow." From the sound of it, Ginger's dad gave her healthy doses of both motivation and reassurance. Still, she could not help but compare her potential success to her father's accomplishments. This was not a harbinger of doom by any means, but it was worth thinking about, which Ginger was doing. If you feel you may be competing with your dad, you might want to think about it, too.

If your dad competes with you or you do with him, here are some things to do and think about

* How does your father respond to your accomplishments? Are your triumphs his triumphs? Does he view your success as a manifestation of all he did to help you achieve it?

* Many women who outperform their dads say their dads respond with embarrassment and resentment and some-times insist upon giving advice about things they have never experienced or don't understand. Is this the case with you and your father?

* You are part of a generation of women who are in a position to outachieve their fathers. This is new, and it may take you and your dad a while to get used to it.

* Awkwardness can seep into your relationship with your dad because your life will probably turn out to be very different from his. If his life fell short of his expectations, he may feel embarrassment or shame.

* If your life is falling short of your father's expectations, you may feel embarrassed or ashamed.

* Embarrassment and shame can harden into resentment.

* If you're more successful than your dad, do you still value his advice? If you are less successful than you would like to be, are you able to take his advice?

* Are you comfortable with the differences between your standards of living?

* Can you see yourself buying him a car or helping with the mortgage? How would that make him feel? How would it make you feel?

WHAT IF YOUR RELATIONSHIP WITH YOUR DAD IS STRAINED OR FEELS DAMAGED BEYOND REPAIR?

You anticipate seeing him with anxiety and dread, and with good reason: No sooner do you walk in the door than he's in your face, making a remark guaranteed to set you off. Or you say something you see as innocuous and before you know it, he's jumping all over you. Both of you manage to get along well with other people but together, you're totally combustible and can't seem to be in the same room without arguing.

Julia, the organic farmer whose father had an explosive temper, put it this way: "It's a challenging relationship, because there's times when we're together and it couldn't be more frustrating. He'll be amped up and hard to be around. At the same time, you're always trying to prove yourself to him, prove that you are succeeding in your own life, you are doing well, and things are good." Julia was describing a daughter and father at cross-purposes, she eager to show her dad that she was doing well and perhaps garner some approval and he "amped up"—emotionally perturbed, I assume—and too shaken by his own agitation to connect with her in a satisfying way. If this happened only occasionally, it could be forgiven and forgotten; we all know what it's like to be short-tempered and snippy after a hellish day. But if your interactions with your dad are consistently contentious, the relationship could degenerate into a series of stressful, vexing encounters that deaden your feelings for him and exhaust your capacity to reach out.

That's what you have to fight against: emotional exhaustion that can set in and make you feel as if the relationship just isn't worth pursuing. Ariel, the woman whose father suffered an emotional breakdown when his own father died, said their relationship was so badly damaged by his unrelenting hostility that the only time she thinks to phone him is at Christmas, and then she's sick about it for days beforehand. It's not that she doesn't care about her father, it's that being around him means being bombarded with reproaches, rebukes, and slights that she no longer has the strength or will to endure.

Exhaustion can also result from living with resentment, as was the case with Mallory, the chiropractor who felt her father's emotional aloofness hobbled her ability to relate to men: "I have a lot of anger toward him because I don't have a good relationship with him, I don't have a close relationship with him, and I feel that, as the adult in the situation throughout my life, he should have been more involved and made more of an effort and been more loving toward me. It's definitely a strained relationship." Yes, he was the adult in the situation for many years, and he should have been more involved with his daughter. But given his history, he's not likely to change anytime soon, which means that if Mallory wants things to improve with her father, she may have to decide that she's going to be the adult, at least for a while.

Finally, there's the kind of strain that threatens to rip the connection between a father and daughter to shreds. When Elisabeth, a member of a well-established family and the publisher of an interior design magazine, told me this story, I was astonished not only by her father's obtuseness but also by the gutsiness of her response: "Now that my father thinks about his own mortality and looks at his will, I find myself suddenly in a role that is medieval, where I'm not really accounted for because he's thinking, *She's a girl and she got married and her husband is supposed to take care of her*—and my brothers are getting everything. I actually found myself in a situation where my father said to me, 'Elisabeth, it's going to be 33 percent for two of your brothers and 34 percent for the other.' I was like, 'You have four children; you realize that, right?' He was like, 'Yes, but you know, I mean . . .' He didn't really know what to say. So I said, 'Honestly, I even think that legally you don't have a right to cut me out. I'm not going to go searching for lawyers now, but I'm telling you, if you leave it this way, one day when you're gone I will go to that meeting with a lawyer in tow, because it's ridiculous. You can't cut me out. Why would you? I'm your only child who has actually created something. Why would you do that?' He was like, 'I thought it's for the boys and you are a girl.' He would actually say that.

"So anyway, he changed it because I said I was going on a campaign, and I rallied all the women—my aunts and everybody—and told them what was happening. The same thing happened to my aunt, my father's sister. I said, 'Can you believe this? I am being cut out. This is ridiculous.' They all called my father and asked what he was doing, and he said, 'Oh, no, it was a mistake.' He backpedaled and put me back in." Clearly, a logical argument would have been utterly useless against this man. But his daughter knew it, and she did him one better: She lobbied the women of the family to unleash their outrage on her father, and they bullied him into doing the right thing. I wouldn't recommend using this strategy in all situations, but in Elisabeth's, it worked.

If your relationship with your dad is strained or damaged beyond repair, here are some things to do and think about

* Many women take their relationships with their fathers for granted: It is what it is, and there's nothing to be done about it. Others may be desperate to change it, but don't know where to start. What about you? Do you think your relationship with your dad could be changed? Do you have an idea for how to make that happen?

* The first step toward building a better relationship with your dad is to connect with the man behind the hurt and resentment you associate with him.

* It is the time you spend alone with your father that helps you get closer to who he really is.

* That means thinking about the relationship you have compared to the one you want, and the one you never thought was possible.

* It means accepting that, contrary to the way they play out on sitcoms, life's episodes do not always end with a hug.

* One place to start is to ask yourself if you are able to

forgive him. If the answer is yes, how will you go about doing it? If the answer is no, can you imagine forgiving him at some point in the future?

* Sometimes our childhood selves are still dictating how we should feel to our adult selves, without us even realizing it. One woman, a thirty-eight-year-old children's book illustrator, spoke of being embarrassed by her father, who was a born-again Christian and minister and led church services that included speaking in tongues and the laying on of hands. "When I was younger, it was a little bit weird with all these people. You'd have a guy who wanders around preaching on the street with a giant cross and hands out tracts. He's invited to come stay at your house for a week because he's in town. So it's a lot of houseguests with people you're not really sure about. But as an adult, I've put it in its place. I wouldn't be embarrassed now because I see it as a personal choice that people make. What might be embarrassing to me—my father being religious—well, at least he wasn't drinking too much and at least he got along with his wife and wasn't living in a separate bedroom. When I looked around, I figured out that everyone is flawed." This woman's childhood feelings of embarrassment were put in perspective by her adult self, who was able to see the good in her father's ways and accept it along with the aspects she wasn't as crazy about. Can you temper your childhood self's feelings with your adult self's wisdom? Can you accept the less attractive aspects of your father without losing sight of the good in him?

* All relationships are works in progress, and the progress often depends on the quality of the work. Inadequate fathers and damaged relationships can be made whole with effort and patience. Can you bring yourself to

accept—no, to embrace—the chance to build a relationship with the first man in your life?

* Sometimes fantasy is all there is. Idealizing your father
can fill an aching and frightening void if he is hurtful or
unreachable.

* Women sometimes invent fantasy fathers: strong, depend-
able men who can be—in their minds, if not in reality—
what they are not. Have you ever imagined a fantasy
father?

* If you have, what was he like? Has that fantasy been
helpful to you? Has it been hurtful?

Afterword

I HAVE finally reached the end of my book. So why do I feel as if I'm just beginning?

Because in a way, I am. I am beginning to see fathers and daughters from a new, expansive vantage point, enriched by the wealth of stories I have heard and the father-daughter story I've been a part of for nearly twenty years.

When I began working on this book my daughter had just applied to college; now, as I finish it, she is happily ensconced there, far from the home she used to share with her father and me. She is on her own. And so are we, with both of our children now safely launched.

After depositing her at her dorm room, my husband and I were shooed off to occupy ourselves while she established her décor. We sat on a campus bench and talked, unspooling a high-lights reel of the events that had led us there. We had plenty to reminisce about: Married since college, we were in the midst of a journey whose countless exultant highs and occasional perplexing lows have taught us that we will never really know where it is leading. We had shared the challenges and gratifications of rearing a son and a daughter over a span of thirty years, and soon we found ourselves reliving some of the past year's most memorable moments.

Like many incipient high school graduates, our daughter had spent her senior year preparing her parents for her departure. She had spent less and less time at home, become vague about her evening and weekend plans, been less inclined to spend time with us, and become increasingly impatient with what she perceived as our shortcomings. My husband, who treasured his close connection with our daughter, was smarting from her forays into independence. Aware that she needed her space, he was both committed to respecting her boundaries and aching at the distance they imposed. "I feel obsolete," he said one evening. "I'm proud that she's able to do so much on her own, but I feel as if I've outlived my usefulness. She doesn't need me anymore, and I'm afraid I'm losing her."

My husband was grieving the departure of his little girl for womanhood, a destination for which she had been bound since the day she was born. He and I knew this was a natural and necessary phase of her development, and we comforted ourselves with the knowledge that our daughter's high spirits and competence were cause for celebration, not woe. Still, he felt as if he'd been cut adrift from the moorings of her need for him, and it hurt. I ached for him, because I knew the keen edge of loss so well myself. Whereas my husband's loss was expected and gradual, mine was stealthy and sudden. My father died before I could form lasting memories of him, so to keep him alive, I had spent a good part of my life thinking, imagining, and wondering about who he was and who I might have been had I known him. Because there were hardly any snapshots of my father and none of the two of us, it fell to me to create an image of him as well as of what shape my life might have assumed had it not been for his incomprehensible absence in it. For many years, the void of his absence seemed, to me, the essence of loss.

But then I started working on this book and a new, essential truth began to form.

As I conducted the interviews, I became aware of a less dramatic yet poignant loss that many of the women were feeling. Even when their fathers were alive and well, many women were grieving for the awe and admiration they had felt for their dads when they were girls. They ached for the safety they used to feel in their fathers' embraces, or mourned the comfort they'd never received. Many women cited their lack of closeness with their fathers as the source of their unease with men. Women spoke of how bereft they felt when their fathers could neither see them as they were nor appreciate the people they had become. And many women lamented the scant praise they received from their fathers, saying that whenever something good happened at work, their first instinct was still to call their dads.

For so many years I had believed that if only I'd had a father, my life would have been happy, perfect, whole. I had idealized the idea of having a father without examining, from up close, exactly what that might have meant.

Now I see things differently. In talking to these women, I participated with them in their process of self-discovery. I discovered that while it wasn't great growing up without a dad, it wasn't so great growing up with some of the dads I heard about, either. I learned that every daughter and father have their share of struggles, no matter how beloved they are to each other. I learned that the relationship between a father and daughter is an organic connection, pulsing with all the love and delight, generosity and need, mystery and darkness, simplicity and complexity that inform all human relations. It is an evolving bond that persists as long as daughter and father live, and often after one of them has died.

And I learned something else: My husband was wrong, he was not losing our daughter. Thanks to the women who spoke with me, I now know that a daughter never outgrows her need for her father, even when she has children of her own. I know that daughters are drawn to their dads even when the dads are otherwise engaged or distracted. I know that a daughter will pursue her father and try to provoke him into connecting with her and that, if he does, she will tend, nurture, and treasure the connection because she wants it and needs it. I know these things because every woman I interviewed spoke of her fundamental yearning for her father's love, guidance, and approval. And now that I know these things, I can share them with my husband.

And with you. Whether you are a daughter or the father of one, you are part of an ancient dynamic of primal, profound significance. And if the dynamic is less than you wish it were, you can choose to either perpetuate the disappointment or foment a solution. A relationship need not be idyllic to be worthwhile and deeply fulfilling: As a long-married woman, I feel amply qualified to speak on this point. If relentless sweetness and light are what you're after, you won't find it in a real relationship—not with anyone. Including your father (or your daughter, as the case may be).

The question is, how much do you want to be closer, more engaged with, more connected to your dad? How much darkness are you willing to venture into before you emerge into the light of deeper understanding? Because, like it or not, there are unknown, dark places in all of us and in all relationships, and you have to feel your way through them before you can make things better.

One wise woman put it thusly: "You need to face what you feel and walk through your tunnels and come out of your dark spaces into some light. Everybody needs to do that. Some people have got a short tunnel. Some of us have medium-sized tunnels. Some people's tunnels are so long and scary that they really feel if they enter them they'll never come out, so they choose whatever the semidarkness is that they live in, rather than risk the possibility that there is never a light."[1]

And so I encourage you to enter, explore, and find your way through your tunnels, however long, short, or dark they may be. A closer bond with your dad may await you at the end, or he may remain elusive and hard to reach. In either case, you will have the satisfaction of knowing that you embarked upon the journey toward a greater appreciation and understanding of your father, and also of your self.

My Process of Discovery

T o get to know the daughters whose stories you've read in this book, I interviewed seventy-five women, either in my New York office or over the telephone, between 2006 and 2010. The interviews, all of which I audiotaped and then had transcribed, were intense, sometimes spanning several hours and requiring follow-up e-mails and phone conversations to expand upon and clarify aspects of the subjects' responses. Two women elected to exclude their interviews from consideration for the book, one because she felt she was being disloyal to her father by discussing him with me and the other for reasons she chose not to articulate. Because I conducted the interviews over a four-year period, many facts of the women's lives will no doubt have changed by now; some who were single have probably found partners, others who were married may have divorced, and still others who were childless will have no doubt acquired an offspring or two.

This was not a process based on impersonal science in that I was not comparing disparate groups of daughters—middle class compared to upper or lower class, college educated compared to high school educated—to one another using statistical analyses to extract facts and figures and draw conclusions based on numbers. Rather, I believed that by engaging with women in conversation, I would begin to gain an understanding of how successful women perceived their fathers' contributions to their lives.

I developed a list of questions I planned to ask but decided that, should a question elicit an intriguing response, I would be free to abandon the prepared queries in favor of spontaneous new ones that would enable me to pursue the emerging conversation, wherever it led. And lead it did, sometimes to a well of unexplored deep feeling, other times to a pleasant but unremarkable dead end. Always, I found my way back to my prepared questions so everyone I interviewed would be invited to explore the same territory.

The women who came to my New York office were all living in the city at the time of their interviews, and I was able to document their physical appearance firsthand. Many of the women I interviewed over the phone, both New York residents and others, provided physical descriptions of themselves. Most were self-effacing ("Oh, I'm pretty average, about five foot five, brown hair, brown eyes, you know, kind of typical"); only one described herself in flattering terms, as others might see her ("I'm a pretty attractive woman, so I get a lot of attention from men"), but in her next breath, she said she didn't know how to handle the attention and usually averted her eyes rather than connecting with possible admirers. One woman spoke poignantly of her father walking her down the aisle at her wedding; later, she uploaded photographs of this and other moments from the ceremony to give me a visual sense of who her father was and what he meant to her.

The meetings in my office made up the minority of the interviews, and of the New York residents I spoke with, only seven had grown up there; the rest were from other parts of the country or the world. I conducted most of the interviews over the phone, which connected me with women living in communities across the United States. Because the study was limited almost exclusively to younger women, some of whom were college and graduate students living far from their permanent homes, in the book I sometimes defined where the interviewees were from as being where they grew up rather than where they were living at the time of their interviews, especially when they were barely out of adolescence. For example, I spoke with a nineteen-year-old Marylander at college in St. Louis whom I believe I'd have mis-represented by describing her as hailing from Missouri when she had lived more than 90 percent of her life in Maryland.

In terms of religion, it was a diverse group. Although none of the women described themselves as religious, several said they were practicing Christians. Others said that although they did not attend services regularly, they identified with the religion in which they had been raised, and of these, a few mentioned having bap-tized their children despite their lack of regular attendance at church. When I asked about their political affiliations, a few women described themselves as conservative; the majority said they were Democrats, somewhat fewer said they were liberals or Independents, and several said they had no political leanings to speak of. Interestingly, more made a point of mentioning that their fathers were either conservative or Republican than those who described their fathers as liberals or Democrats.

With two exceptions, all of the women held degrees from four-year colleges (of those who didn't, one had an associate's degree and the other had earned a year-and-a-half's worth of col-lege credits) and many were attending or had graduated from professional schools. Their careers ran the gamut, ranging from yoga instructor to urban planner and including everything in between. Apropos of this, it is important to acknowledge that the participants were not a random assortment, but rather a self-selecting group of women who were at least willing and in many cases eager to talk candidly about their relationships with their fathers. In selecting participants, I made no attempt to cover the extremes of the socioeconomic spectrum because it was not my intent to compare women living at the far ends of the grid. Instead, I wanted to focus on women who were gainfully employed and making their own ways in the world.

The quality of their responses varied widely, sometimes within a single interview: I often found myself receiving terse, controlled answers early on and more descriptive, revealing ones later, after the woman had become more comfortable with the process. Not surprisingly, the quality of the responses also varied widely from woman to woman, as some were far more self-aware and contemplative than others. It was common for an interviewee to respond to a question with "Gee, I never thought about that" and then proceed to wend her way through a thicket of feelings and memories she claimed never to have entered before. But the opposite phenomenon also occurred, as evidenced by the number of opaque responses that started and stopped with "I guess," "not really," or "no."

Finally, I want to emphasize that the fathers and daughters who enliven these pages represent neither pinnacles of perfection nor nadirs of disaster. The women and men who appear in these chapters were chosen not because their relationships were either exemplary or wretched, but because there was something in their connection, either good or bad (and sometimes a little of both), that I thought merited contemplation and exploration.

The women who populate this book were not handpicked to assemble a collection of heartwarming, gut-wrenching tales to inspire laughter, tears, and a movie-of-the-week catharsis; in fact, I deliberately chose not to interview anyone I knew well, sacrificing some whopping good stories along the way. Instead, I approached as many women as I could and asked if they'd be willing to participate in a research project about daughters and dads. When they said yes, I leapt at the chance to learn more about what goes on between fathers and daughters, now and in memory, encompassing everyday, ordinary occurrences and cataclysmic, once-in-a-lifetime events. Not all of the women I interviewed found their way into these pages, but they remain ensconced in my heart and mind, vivid in all their warmth, edginess, and scintillating variety.

Notes

INTRODUCTION

1. Peggy Drexler, *Raising Boys Without Men*. Emmaus, PA: Rodale, 2005.
2. C. Helmeke, K. Seidel, G. Poeggel, T. W. Bredy, A. Abraham, and K. Braun, "Paternal Deprivation During Infancy Results in Dendrite- and Time-Specific Changes of Dendritic Development and Spine Formation in the Orbitofrontal Cortex of the Biparental Rodent *Octodon degus*," *Neuroscience* 163 no. 3 (October 20, 2009): 790–798, as reported by Shirley S. Wang, "This Is Your Brain Without Dad," *Wall Street Journal*, October 27, 2009.
3. R. Jia, F. Tai, S. An, X. Zhang, and H. Broders, "Effects of Neonatal Paternal Deprivation or Early Deprivation on Anxiety and Social Behaviors of the Adults in Mandarin Voles," *Behavioural Processes* 82 no. 3 (November 2009): 271–278, as reported by Wang, "Brain Without Dad."

PART I

1. Barbara Holland, *When All the World Was Young: A Memoir*. New York: Bloomsbury, 2005.

CHAPTER I

1. Association of American Medical Colleges, "Applicants and Matriculants Data: Table 7: Applicants, First-Time Applicants, Acceptees, and Matriculants to U.S. Medical Schools by Sex, 1999-2010," Association of American Medical Colleges, October 19, 2010. https://www.aamc.org/data/facts/85908/applicantmatriculant.
2. Kathleen S. Turner and Thomas Griffin, "Distribution of Women in U.S. Medical Schools, 1970-71 and 1980-81," *Journal of Medical Education* 57 no. 8 (August 1982): 651–652.
3. Association of American Medical Colleges, "Applicants and Matriculants Data."
4. Deborah Prussel, "Women in Law," *Women's Village News*, IMDiversity.com, n.d. http://www.imdiversity.com/villages/woman/careers_workplace_employment/women_in_law.asp.
5. Law School Admission Council, *Thinking About Law School?* Newtown, PA: Law School Admission Council, n.d. http://www.lsac.org/LSACResources/Publications/PDFs/ThinkAboutLawSchool.pdf.
6. James Dao, "First Woman Ascends to Top Drill Sergeant Spot," *New York Times*, September 21, 2009. http://www.nytimes.com/2009/09/22/us/22sergeant.html.

7. Hugh Lessig, "First Woman Takes Helm of U.S. Carrier Strike Group,"
    DailyPress.com, July 29, 2010.

8. Daphne Merkin, "Daddy's Forgotten Girl," *New York Times*, June 18, 2006.
    http://www.nytimes.com/2006/06/18/magazine/18wwln_lede.html.

9. Victoria Secunda, *Women and Their Fathers*. New York: Delacorte Press,
    1992.

10. Secunda, *Women and Their Fathers*.

11. Deborah Tannen, *You're Wearing* That? *Understanding Mothers and
    Daughters in Conversation*. New York: Random House, 2006.

12. Kyle Pruett, "Girls and the Hard Sciences," LeapFrog.ca, n.d. http://www.
    leapfrog.ca/en/leapfrog_parents/preschool/science/article__girls_and.
    html.

13. Kyle Pruett, *Fatherneed: Why Father Care Is as Essential as Mother Care for
    Your Child*. New York: Broadway Books, 2001.

14. Calculated from 2005 American Community Survey data at US Census
    Bureau, "Table S0201. Selected Population Profile in the United States;
    Population Group: Asian Indian Alone or in Any Combination," Factfinder.
    census.gov, n.d.

15. Calculated from Jessica S. Barnes and Claudette E. Bennett, *The Asian
    Population: 2000*. Washington, DC: US Census Bureau, February 2002.

16. First appeared in Peggy Drexler, "Bondage: Can the New Ties Between
    Father and Daughter Go Too Far?" *Huffington Post*, May 31, 2007. http://
    www.huffingtonpost.com/peggy-drexler/bondage-can-the-new-
    ties-_b_50138.html.

17. An epigram by Jean-Baptiste Alphonse Karr (1808–1890) published in his
    journal *Les Guêpes* (*The Wasps*) in January 1849. http://en.wiktionary.org/
    wiki/plus_%C3%A7a_change,_plus_c%27est_la_m%C3%AAme_chose.

18. Untitled video clip, "Welcome to the 2010 Purity Ball! Host Your Own
    Purity Ball," Christian Center, n.d. http://www.purityball.com.

CHAPTER 2

1. Deborah Tannen, *You Just Don't Understand: Women and Men in
    Conversation*. New York: Morrow, 1990.

2. *An Education*, directed by Lone Scherfig and scripted by Nick Hornby, premiered
    at the 2009 Sundance Film Festival. Based on a memoir by Lynn Barber, it starred
    Carey Mulligan, Peter Sarsgaard, Alfred Molina, and Cara Seymour.

3. Mary McDonagh Murphy, *Scout, Atticus, and Boo: A Celebration of Fifty
    Years of* To Kill a Mockingbird. New York: HarperCollins, 2010.

4. Harper Lee, *To Kill A Mockingbird*. Philadelphia: Lippincott, 1960. The
    Pulitzer Prize–winning novel is usually identified as focusing on racism in the
    American South, but its Library of Congress Cataloging-in-Publication
    Data's main category as listed on the copyright page is fathers and daughters.

5. Michael E. Lamb, editor, *The Role of the Father in Child Development*. New York: Wiley, 1997.
6. In *You're Wearing That? Understanding Mothers and Daughters in Conversation* (New York: Random House, 2006), Tannen cites the work of Phyllis Bronstein, PhD, and Carolyn Pape Cowan, whose survey review focused on fathers, children, and play.

PART II

1. Phyllis McGinley, "Girl's-Eye View of Relatives: First Lesson," in *Times Three: Selected Verse from Three Decades, with Seventy New Poems* (New York: Viking, 1960), as cited in Robert Andrews, *The Columbia Dictionary of Quotations*. New York: Columbia University Press, 1993.
2. Anne Sexton, "A Small Journal," in *The Poet's Story*, edited by Howard Moss (New York: Macmillan, 1973), as cited in Andrews, *Columbia Dictionary*.

CHAPTER 3

1. Bruce Feiler, *The Council of Dads: My Daughters, My Illness, and the Men Who Could Be Me*. New York: William Morrow, 2010.
2. Tara Parker-Pope, "Now, Dad Feels as Stressed as Mom," *New York Times*, June 19, 2010.
3. Parker-Pope, "Now, Dad Feels as Stressed."
4. Brad Harrington, Fred Van Deusen, and Jamie Ladge, *The New Dad: Exploring Fatherhood within a Career Context*. Chestnut Hill, MA: Boston College Center for Work and Family, 2010. http://www.bc.edu/centers/cwf/meta-elements/pdf/BCCWF_Fatherhood_Study_The_New_Dad.pdf.
5. Laurie Tarkan, "Fathers Gain Respect from Experts (and Mothers)," *New York Times*, November 2, 2009, describing findings in Marsha Kline Pruett, Carolyn Pape Cowan, Philip A. Cowan, and Kyle Pruett, "Lessons Learned from the Supporting Father Involvement Study: A Cross-Cultural Preventive Intervention for Low-Income Families with Young Children," *Journal of Social Service Research* 35 no. 2 (2009): 163–179.
6. Tarkan, "Fathers Gain Respect."
7. According to a 2009 report from the Georgetown University Law Center, as cited by Parker-Pope, "Now, Dad Feels as Stressed."
8. According to the National Survey of Families and Households from the University of Wisconsin, as cited by Parker-Pope, "Now, Dad Feels as Stressed."
9. Parker-Pope, "Now, Dad Feels as Stressed."

CHAPTER 4

1. This actually happened to a son of someone I know. The identity of the school remains shrouded in secrecy.

2. In order to accurately convey the nature of Fran's (not her real name) professional activities, they are presented here as she described them to me, with her permission. There was no way I could disguise them and do justice to them and to her.

CHAPTER 6

1. Russ and Daughters, "Our History," n.d., http://www.russanddaughters.com/our_history.php.

CHAPTER 7

1. Title IX of the Education Amendments of 1972, Title 20, Section 1681 of the *US Code*. http://www.dol.gov/oasam/regs/statutes/titleix.htm.
2. Nikki Wedgwood, "Kicking Like a Boy: Schoolgirl Australian Rules Football and Bi-Gendered Female Embodiment," *Sociology of Sport Journal* 21 no. 2 (June 2004): 140–162.
3. Nicole Willms, "Fathers and Daughters: Negotiating Gendered Relationships in Sport," in Tess Kay, editor, *Fathering Through Sport and Leisure*. London: Routledge, 2009. pp. 124–144.

CHAPTER 8

1. Anahad O'Connor and Tim Stelloh, "Boy, 8, Dies in Brooklyn Fire," *New York Times*, September 30, 2010; and WABC-TV/DT, "Child Dead, 5 Kids Hospitalized in Brooklyn Fire," September 30, 2010, http://abclocal.go.com/wabc/story?section=news/local&id=7697398.
2. Kyle Pruett, *Fatherneed: Why Father Care Is as Essential as Mother Care for Your Child*. New York: Broadway Books, 2001.

PART III

CHAPTER 10

1. Peggy Drexler, "Fathers: An Instruction Manual—Who Is This Man? If You Think You Know Dad, Think Harder." *Huffington Post*, October 12, 2009. http://www.huffingtonpost.com/peggy-drexler/fathers-an-instruction-ma_b_317255.html

AFTERWORD

1. I never forgot these words, which were spoken by Mimi Halper Silbert, PhD, president and CEO of the Delancey Street Foundation (a renowned self-help residential rehabilitation center) when I interviewed her several years ago.

Acknowledgments

I WROTE this book about the special world of fathers and daughters because it is a place I could only visit and observe. I wanted to explore that world through the voices of real women, with the real joys and painful issues that populate one of nature's most powerful bonds. In their stories, I found perspective, advice, and inspiration.

My thanks to those who made it possible: Robin Cantor-Cooke, for the ability to bring all the pieces together in personal and powerful prose. The amazing and steady Gail Ross, agent, advisor, and friend. Rodale's Karen Rinaldi, Julie Will, Yelena Nesbit, and former CEO Steve Murphy for their belief in me and the story and for all their support in bringing it to life. Carla Rinaldi, for her valued assistance, her unwavering patience, and her otherworldly grace under pressure. My family, who allowed me to bring their lives into the work.

My special thanks to all of the extraordinary women who gave me their time, their thoughtful honesty, and a part of their lives.

And finally, my thanks to Myron Fischman, a father taken far too soon, but whose loving memory inspired me to take on this project, and guided me every step of the way.

Index